Survival

GLOBAL POLITICS AND STRATEGY

Volume 60 Number 2 | April–May 2018

T0333849

'African elites have found ways of enlisting intervention for their own purposes, in the process replacing liberal notions of order creation with stabilisation. This altered interpretation has aligned African governments with the three most important geopolitical actors on the continent: the United States, the European Union (and its member states), and the People's Republic of China.'

Ricardo Soares de Oliveira and Harry Verhoeven, Taming Intervention: Sovereignty, Statehood and Political Order in Africa, p. 19.

'In an age of ethical investing, banks and investment funds care about their reputation. Once nuclear weapons are declared illegal, many financial institutions will think twice before funding or investing in firms that are doing business in the nuclear-weapons sector.'

Paul Meyer and Tom Sauer, The Nuclear Ban Treaty: A Sign of Global Impatience, p. 67.

'Research into the digital vulnerabilities of smart cities remains in its infancy, with the field mostly limited to a small cadre of cyber-security researchers and professionals … The corporate sector, meanwhile, has continued to portray the smart city as a transformational innovation.'

Yu-Min Joo and Teck-Boon Tan, Smart Cities: A New Age of Digital Insecurity, p. 93.

Survival
GLOBAL POLITICS AND STRATEGY
Volume 60 Number 2 | April–May 2018

Contents

Cover: Albert Gonzalez Farran/AFP/Getty Images

On the cover
A member of peacekeeping troops from Ethiopia deployed as part of the United Nations (UN) Interim Security Force for Abyei (UNISFA) patrols at night on 14 December 2016.

On the web
Visit www.iiss.org/publications/survival for brief notices on new books on the United States, Politics and International Relations, and the Middle East.

Survival **editors' blog**
For ideas and commentary from *Survival* editors and contributors, visit www.iiss.org/politicsandstrategy.

Review Essay

Book Reviews

Closing Argument

Survival

GLOBAL POLITICS AND STRATEGY

The International Institute for Strategic Studies

2121 K Street, NW | Suite 801 | Washington DC 20037 | USA
Tel +1 202 659 1490   Fax +1 202 659 1499   E-mail survival@iiss.org   Web www.iiss.org

Arundel House | 6 Temple Place | London | WC2R 2PG | UK
Tel +44 (0)20 7379 7676   Fax +44 (0)20 7836 3108   E-mail iiss@iiss.org

14th Floor, GBCorp Tower | Bahrain Financial Harbour | Manama | Kingdom of Bahrain
Tel +973 1718 1155   Fax +973 1710 0155   E-mail iiss-middleeast@iiss.org

9 Raffles Place | #51-01 Republic Plaza | Singapore 048619
Tel +65 6499 0055   Fax +65 6499 0059   E-mail iiss-asia@iiss.org

Survival Online www.tandfonline.com/survival and www.iiss.org/publications/survival

Aims and Scope *Survival* is one of the world's leading forums for analysis and debate of international and strategic affairs. Shaped by its editors to be both timely and forward thinking, the journal encourages writers to challenge conventional wisdom and bring fresh, often controversial, perspectives to bear on the strategic issues of the moment. With a diverse range of authors, *Survival* aims to be scholarly in depth while vivid, well written and policy-relevant in approach. Through commentary, analytical articles, case studies, forums, review essays, reviews and letters to the editor, the journal promotes lively, critical debate on issues of international politics and strategy.

Editor **Dana Allin**
Managing Editor **Matthew Harries**
Associate Editor **Carolyn West**
Editorial **Jessica Watson**
Production and Cartography **John Buck, Kelly Verity**

Contributing Editors

Gilles Andréani	Bill Emmott	Jeffrey Lewis	Teresita C. Schaffer	David C. Unger
Ian Bremmer	John A. Gans, Jr	Hanns W. Maull	Steven Simon	Ruth Wedgwood
David P. Calleo	John L. Harper	Jeffrey Mazo	Angela Stent	Lanxin Xiang
Russell Crandall	Pierre Hassner	'Funmi Olonisakin	Jonathan Stevenson	
Toby Dodge	Erik Jones	Thomas Rid	Ray Takeyh	

Published for the IISS by
Routledge Journals, an imprint of Taylor & Francis, an Informa business.

SUBMISSIONS

To submit an article, authors are advised to follow these guidelines:

- *Survival* articles are around 4,000–10,000 words long including endnotes. A word count should be included with a draft. Length is a consideration in the review process and shorter articles have an advantage.
- All text, including endnotes, should be double-spaced with wide margins.
- Any tables or artwork should be supplied in separate files, ideally not embedded in the document or linked to text around it.
- All *Survival* articles are expected to include endnote references. These should be complete and include first and last names of authors, titles of articles (even from newspapers), place of publication, publisher, exact publication dates, volume and issue number (if from a journal) and page numbers. Web sources should include complete URLs and DOIs if available.
- A summary of up to 150 words should be included with the article. The summary should state the main argument clearly and concisely, not simply say what the article is about.

- A short author's biography of one or two lines should also be included. This information will appear at the foot of the first page of the article.
- *Survival* has a strict policy of listing multiple authors in alphabetical order.

Submissions should be made by email, in Microsoft Word format, to the Managing Editor, Matthew Harries, survival@iiss.org. Alternatively, hard copies may be sent to *Survival*, IISS–US, 2121 K Street NW, Suite 801, Washington, DC 20037, USA. Please direct any queries to Matthew Harries.

The editorial review process can take up to three months. *Survival*'s acceptance rate for unsolicited manuscripts is less than 20%. *Survival* does not normally provide referees' comments in the event of rejection. Authors are permitted to submit simultaneously elsewhere so long as this is consistent with the policy of the other publication and the Editors of *Survival* are informed of the dual submission.

Readers are encouraged to comment on articles from the previous issue. Letters should be concise, no longer than 750 words and relate directly to the argument or points made in the original article.

ADVERTISING AND PERMISSIONS

For advertising rates and schedules

USA/Canada: The Advertising Manager, Taylor & Francis Inc., 530 Walnut Street, Suite 850, Philadelphia, PA 19106, USA Tel +1 (800) 354 1420 Fax +1 (215) 207 0050.

UK/Europe/Rest of World: The Advertising Manager, Routledge Journals, Taylor & Francis, 4 Park Square, Milton Park, Abingdon, Oxfordshire OX14 4RN, UK Tel +44 (0) 207 017 6000 Fax +44 (0) 207 017 6336.

SUBSCRIPTIONS

Survival is published bi-monthly in February, April, June, August, October and December by Routledge Journals, an imprint of Taylor & Francis, an Informa Business.

Annual Subscription 2018

Institution	£505	$885	€742
Individual	£144	$243	€196
Online only	£442	$774	€649

Taylor & Francis has a flexible approach to subscriptions, enabling us to match individual libraries' requirements. This journal is available via a traditional institutional subscription (either print with online access, or online only at a discount) or as part of our libraries, subject collections or archives. For more information on our sales packages please visit http://www.tandfonline.com/page/librarians.

All current institutional subscriptions include online access for any number of concurrent users across a local area network to the currently available backfile and articles posted online ahead of publication.

Subscriptions purchased at the personal rate are strictly for personal, non-commercial use only. The reselling of personal subscriptions is prohibited. Personal subscriptions must be purchased with a personal cheque or credit card. Proof of personal status may be requested.

Dollar rates apply to all subscribers outside Europe. Euro rates apply to all subscribers in Europe, except the UK and the Republic of Ireland where the pound sterling rate applies. If you are unsure which rate applies to you please contact Customer Services in the UK. All subscriptions are payable in advance and all rates include postage. Journals are sent by air to the USA, Canada, Mexico, India, Japan and Australasia. Subscriptions are entered on an annual basis, i.e. January to December. Payment may be made by sterling cheque, dollar cheque, euro cheque, international money order, National Giro or credit cards (Amex, Visa and Mastercard).

Survival (USPS 013095) is published bimonthly (in Feb, Apr, Jun, Aug, Oct and Dec) by Routledge Journals, Taylor & Francis, 4 Park Square, Milton Park, Abingdon, OX14 4RN, United Kingdom.

The US annual subscription price is $842. Airfreight and mailing in the USA by agent named Air Business Ltd, c/o Worldnet Shipping Inc., 156-15, 146th Avenue, 2nd Floor, Jamaica, NY 11434, USA. Periodicals postage paid at Jamaica NY 11431.

US Postmaster: Send address changes to Survival, C/O Air Business Ltd / 156-15 146th Avenue, Jamaica, New York, NY11434.

Subscription records are maintained at Taylor & Francis Group, 4 Park Square, Milton Park, Abingdon, OX14 4RN, United Kingdom.

ORDERING INFORMATION

Please contact your local Customer Service Department to take out a subscription to the Journal: **USA, Canada:** Taylor & Francis, Inc., 530 Walnut Street, Suite 850, Philadelphia, PA 19106, USA. Tel: +1 800 354 1420; Fax: +1 215 207 0050. **UK/Europe/Rest of World:** T&F Customer Services, Informa UK Ltd, Sheepen Place, Colchester, Essex, CO3 3LP, United Kingdom. Tel: +44 (0) 20 7017 5544; Fax: +44 (0) 20 7017 5198; Email: subscriptions@tandf.co.uk.

Back issues: Taylor & Francis retains a two-year back issue stock of journals. Older volumes are held by our official stockists: Periodicals Service Company, 351 Fairview Ave., Suite 300, Hudson, New York 12534, USA to whom all orders and enquiries should be addressed. *Tel* +1 518 537 4700 *Fax* +1 518 537 5899 *e-mail* psc@periodicals.com *web* http://www.periodicals.com/tandf.html.

The International Institute for Strategic Studies (IISS) and our publisher Taylor & Francis make every effort to ensure the accuracy of all the information (the "Content") contained in our publications. However, the IISS and our publisher Taylor & Francis, our agents, and our licensors make no representations or warranties whatsoever as to the accuracy, completeness, or suitability for any purpose of the Content. Any opinions and views expressed in this publication are the opinions and views of the authors, and are not the views of or endorsed by the IISS and our publisher Taylor & Francis. The accuracy of the Content should not be relied upon and should be independently verified with primary sources of information. The IISS and our publisher Taylor & Francis shall not be liable for any losses, actions, claims, proceedings, demands, costs, expenses, damages, and other liabilities whatsoever or howsoever caused arising directly or indirectly in connection with, in relation to or arising out of the use of the Content. Terms & Conditions of access and use can be found at http://www.tandfonline.com/page/terms-and-conditions.

The issue date is April–May 2018.

The print edition of this journal is printed on ANSI conforming acid free paper.

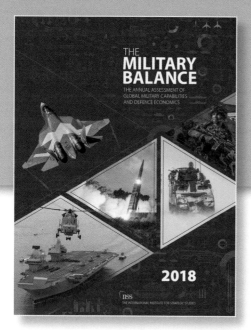

THE MILITARY BALANCE 2018

The annual assessment of global military capabilities and defence economics

The Military Balance is the annual IISS assessment of the military capabilities and defence economics of 171 countries. It is an indispensable handbook for anyone conducting serious analysis of security policy and military affairs.

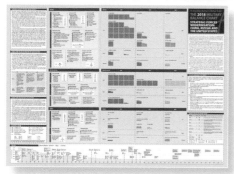

NEW FEATURES

- Complementing its regional military analysis, the book carries detailed assessments of defence developments in China, Russia and the United States, as well as France and the United Kingdom. There are also features on Norway, Qatar, Sudan, Taiwan, Uganda and Venezuela, among others.

- New thematic texts analysing Chinese and Russian air-launched weapons; big data, artificial intelligence and defence; and Russia's strategic-force modernisation.

- A new *Military Balance* wall chart, focused on strategic-forces modernisation in China, Russia and the US.

- New regional arms orders and deliveries sections, outlining significant defence-procurement events in 2017.

- Updated comparative defence-statistics section, with graphics showing key data relating to defence economics and major land, sea and air capabilities, including global UAV sales and Chinese and Asia-Pacific regional naval shipbuilding since 2000.

- Updated summaries of national military capability, at the start of each country entry.

- New maps comparing selected military training exercises in Europe and Russia and Eurasia in 2016–17.

- Updated entries relating to national cyber capabilities.

LAUNCHED/PUBLISHED

14 February 2018

 THE INTERNATIONAL INSTITUTE FOR STRATEGIC STUDIES

 Routledge
Taylor & Francis Group

Taming Intervention: Sovereignty, Statehood and Political Order in Africa

Ricardo Soares de Oliveira and Harry Verhoeven

Military intervention in weak states by their more powerful peers is one of the great constants in the history of international relations, and is closely related to the question of state survival. In an anarchical international system characterised by a scarcity of resources, how do feeble polities manage threats to their sovereignty? African states in particular have been subject to continual interventions by outside forces, whether those of multilateral organisations such as NATO and the EU, or of individual great powers. This trend has only increased in the last two decades, owing, inter alia, to the 'war on terror', deepening worries over a nexus between security and migration, and the seemingly growing fragmentation of authority in numerous African states. The continent is the subject of two-thirds of UN Security Council discussions on armed conflict and the theatre of more ongoing UN peacekeeping operations than the remaining world regions combined. Yet it is striking that African states have not only maintained independent statehood and resisted regime change, but in recent years have both clamoured for extra-regional intervention and become avid inter-regional interveners themselves. A continent that might once have been described as the world's most sovereigntist has thus, intriguingly, become highly tolerant, and even encouraging, of military intervention. Why?

Ricardo Soares de Oliveira is an Associate Professor at the Department of Politics and International Relations, University of Oxford. **Harry Verhoeven** is an Assistant Professor of Government at the School of Foreign Service, Georgetown University in Qatar.

Survival | vol. 60 no. 2 | April–May 2018 | pp. 7–32   DOI 10.1080/00396338.2018.1448558

We argue that what Christopher Clapham called 'the politics of state survival' continues to underpin African engagement with the international system.[1] But whereas intervention – by which we mean military intervention – has historically been considered an existential threat to weak governments and even to statehood itself, the logic of defending sovereignty has been flipped on its head. Intervention, in the last decade and a half, has been enlisted to buttress regime authority. By working with – and not against – powerful external interests in redefining intervention as 'stabilisation', African elites have been taming intervention: they have adopted interventionist tropes and practices so as to put them at the service of the (re-) enforcement of political order and to detach them from their earlier association with regime change and Western-style democracy-promotion. What was once seen as a dangerously revisionist practice is now perceived by African decision-makers as a way to enhance sovereignty.

Evidence of this shift can be found in the codification of interventionism in instruments such as the African Union's Constitutive Act (intervention in theory), and in the increase of (sanctioned and non-sanctioned) military forays by African states – as well as by extra-continental actors – across the continent (intervention in practice). From Mali to the Democratic Republic of the Congo to the Gulf of Aden, the use of intervention to provide security is proving largely uncontroversial, at least at the elite level. A clear majority of interventions by the United Nations, the African Union and the European Union are no longer normatively contested, but debated strictly in terms of their functional details: length, partnerships, mandate and so on.

Intervention has remained a constant throughout post-independence history, but its purposes and rules have altered. One crucial reason for this is that weak African states have displayed remarkable agency in turning their fragility into a discursive and material resource in an evolving transnational context. Intervention reinterpreted as stabilisation dovetails with a shift in global attention away from the threat of rogue regimes to state failure. As an agenda of coercively consolidating political authority without simultaneously pursuing societal transformation, stabilisation (as opposed to 'regime change', 'liberal democracy' or 'the Responsibility to Protect') aligns the interests of African regimes with those of a wide range of external actors. For weak African states, no less than for a post-neoconservative West and the Chinese Communist Party, intervention now mostly constitutes a means to neutralise threats to incumbents, and as such to strengthen the existing political order.

Intervention in the early post-colonial period

Intervention is more than the naked imposition of force by the mighty against the frail. Rather, power is a social attribute, situated at the intersection between cold material dynamics on the one hand and the realm of ideas and perceptions of authority on the other.[2] Who intervenes how, where and when, with whom and against whom, is as much a matter of continuously negotiated shared understandings of the character and methods of legitimate intervention as it is of military muscle. As Hedley Bull has argued, the historical conditions and constellations of power in which norms around interventionism emerge and then go on to influence inter-state relations underscore that violence exerted by states and international organisations, whether consensual or non-consensual, is 'an inherently normative phenomenon'.[3]

Put differently, intervention is a constant in international relations, but its purposes, pretexts and rules vary, not just because of transformations in the structure of the international system but also on account of ideational shifts. As Martha Finnemore wrote:

> What made 1815 a concert and 1950 a cold war was not the material distribution of capabilities but the shared meanings and interpretations imposed on those capabilities … Changes do not come about for material reasons, that is, they did not emerge because they became materially or technologically possible. Rather, they came about for social reasons: states understand different goals to be important and different actions to be effective or legitimate at different times.[4]

While changes in identities and beliefs among powerful states are more likely to bring about system-wide transformations than those in their weaker counterparts, the latter's practices and ideas are also relevant to, and occasionally transformative of, global politics.[5]

Seen through this prism, changes in African conceptions of sovereignty and political order in the post-colonial era reveal not just the hard edges of power but also shifts in the ideas governing the use of force, as co-produced by strong and peripheral states alike. For decades, the behaviour of African states in the international system has been characterised by a vociferous defence of sovereignty and a struggle to limit and mediate intervention by more powerful outside actors. This stance goes back to the genesis of African states, which are, almost without exception, the product of imperialist occupation. In their colonial form, African states were little more than a set of externally oriented, coercive and extractive institutions possessing narrow political economies centred on a handful of agricultural and mining activities.[6] Furthermore, African borders were entirely artificial, the result of negotiations among Europeans at the 1885 Berlin Conference and the tug-of-war of 'effective occupation'.

The result was a high casualty rate

Independence for most countries occurred at the height of the Cold War and was immediately followed by the attempted secessions of Katanga (1960, from Congo) and Biafra (1967, from Nigeria), which from the outset highlighted the importance of protecting post-colonial states' sovereign prerogatives. The fact that these separatist movements received outside support suggested an existential challenge to autonomous African states, which feared that the old colonial powers would continue to divide and rule Africa, reproducing patterns of exploitation.

Three interrelated developments were, however, to afford the newly independent African states greater leeway within the international system than expected. The first was a normative change that gave colonies the right to internationally recognised statehood merely by virtue of having been colonised. In previous eras, statehood had been premised on a state being able to fend for itself in the international system.[7] The result was a high casualty rate, as states were annexed by more powerful polities. The post-colonial age, by contrast, upheld an approach to sovereignty whereby states were accepted as such simply on the basis of recognition by others.[8] Thus, newly independent African states emerged at a time when the international standing of weak polities was being nurtured and affirmed.

The second development was the formation of the Organisation of African Unity (OAU) in 1963, which marked the triumph of a sovereigntist paradigm of post-colonial international relations over the Pan-Africanist vision of a supranational, continent-spanning authority.[9] Conscious of internal fractures and Africa's marginal position in the international system, the OAU adopted a consensus around juridical sovereignty and non-interference in internal affairs as the basis for African statehood. Shunning both the continental-unification model of the Pan-Africanists and proposals to redesign states along ethno-regional lines, African incumbents accepted colonial boundaries as the framework for their new states and crafted a strenuous non-interventionist rulebook to govern the relations between them, as well as their interactions with the international system.[10] The integrity of states would be respected on account of their international recognition and OAU membership. Solidarity between African states was seen as essential to preserve independence.

The third development was the overlapping of the first decades of African statehood with the Cold War. Neither superpower was normatively or practically wedded to juridical sovereignty, which empowers weak states and places barriers to the actions of stronger states. But the centrality of sovereignty in the international system – as seen in settings such as the UN General Assembly – and the OAU's rigid adherence to it meant that the superpowers and former colonial powers were more likely to support African states through the provision of aid, military assistance and external legitimacy than to seek to undermine them.

A robust consensus around non-intervention persisted through the 1960s, 1970s and 1980s, supported by a highly sovereigntist legal regime that prioritised the post-colonial status quo and condemned almost every form of interference, with the exception of the struggle against white-minority rule in Southern Africa. Inter-state conflict was strikingly rare on the African scene and, with the exception of the UN operation in Congo (1960–64), external multilateral missions were non-existent until the end of the Cold War.

What intervention did occur in practice was related to the extraversion agendas of African power-holders.[11] The weakness of African states inevitably resulted in a high degree of external influence. But far from seeking to fend off foreign involvement, incumbents often sought it out. To compensate for a dearth of domestic resources, they worked to pull extra-regional actors into the fray, often through the deployment of ideological tropes that appealed to outside sponsors – an approach that allowed African regimes to mostly mediate intervention through their own interests.[12] In retrospect, the Cold War stands out as an era during which, despite the suffering caused by foreign involvement on the continent, Africa's weak states enjoyed a remarkable degree of protection.[13]

This protective atmosphere started to dissipate in the 1980s. This was in part because being propped up primarily from the outside generated grave contradictions inside African states. The fact that their survival depended mainly on the external recognition of their juridical statehood and on externalised military assistance, financial aid or mineral rents meant that African states possessed little incentive to consolidate empirical statehood in a more conventional manner.[14] The difficult, protracted task of developing institutions such as an administrative grid across the country and a robust tax base was not a priority. When added to skewed patterns of clientelistic distribution, this led marginalised political actors to revolt against the status quo.[15]

A second factor was the global economic turbulence of the 1970s, which affected the continent disproportionately, sending it down a tragic three-decade-long spiral.[16] Cowed by debt, African states were forced to accept the conditionalities of the international financial institutions (IFIs), which represented an unprecedented degree of foreign intrusion in the post-colonial era. Even before 1989, therefore, Western clout was increasing.

The end of the superpower conflict was nonetheless a watershed in Africa's experience with foreign involvement. Socialist states could no longer provide Africans with the opportunity to triangulate Western demands. Western states and Western-controlled IFIs, meanwhile, now achieved a near monopoly over Africa's external relations, leading to signal shifts in Western approaches to sovereignty. The previous non-interventionist emphasis on juridical sovereignty was elbowed out in favour of a conditional approach that implicitly ranked states according to their performance, and countenanced forms of external involvement that had earlier been beyond the pale.[17] Enhanced conditionality went beyond the economic realm and was increasingly designed to promote democracy. In view of the precipitous decline of African states in the 1990s, which saw a continuation of the economic crisis and a proliferation of conflicts, the potential for extra-regional meddling seemed endless.[18]

The end of non-interference

While the end of Cold War bipolarity initially spurred enthusiasm for UN Security Council action to tackle African conflicts, Western hegemony was not the catalyst for increased intervention that the proponents of UN secretary-general Boutros Boutros-Ghali's *An Agenda for Peace* had hoped for.[19] The debacle of the US-led *Operation Restore Hope* in Somalia was followed by the Rwandan genocide, at the start of which ten Belgian peacekeepers were murdered, emasculating the United Nations Assistance Mission for Rwanda. In May 1994, the Clinton administration issued Presidential Decision Directive 25, which all but ruled out an American role in state-building and peacekeeping in Africa. In OAU circles, speculation had been rife about how unipolarity might curtail African sovereignty,[20] but the Somali and Rwandan fiascos appeared to cause the new-found appetite for interventionism to evaporate.

The UN and EU responded to conflicts and humanitarian emergencies in Europe and Asia with a robust interventionism that led to the de facto sharing of sovereignty[21] – neo-trusteeships were established in Afghanistan, Bosnia, East Timor and Kosovo[22] – but Africa remained untouched by the most radical suspensions of state authority. Western actors maintained their emphasis on structural adjustment and democratisation as solutions for the problems of state fragility and war then plaguing many African countries, while proving reluctant to deploy proconsuls and troops to Africa as they did to the Balkans and Asia. It was as if Africa seemed too unruly for the foundations of political order to take root via direct external intervention.[23]

The disconnect between, on the one hand, the professed ambitions of Washington Consensus-style conditionality and, on the other hand, declining Western interest in Africa – embassies and news agencies laying off staff, shrinking aid flows, a refusal to send Western peacekeepers to African arenas – reassured sovereigntists.[24] But major changes in terms of how

African leaders themselves perceived intervention were afoot, even in the absence of Western attention. Three main factors, internal to African politics and pushed by Africans themselves, catalysed this shift.

The first was a major change in state practice in the wake of the emergence of numerous (neo-)liberation regimes.[25] Dominated by former insurgents inspired by Marxism–Leninism and Pan-Africanism, these regimes seized power by overthrowing their predecessors.[26] While the newcomers were careful about pushing global revisionist agendas in the face of Western hegemony, they all contested the status quo in Africa's international relations.[27] For both strategic and ideological reasons, the Eritrean People's Liberation Front (EPLF), the Ethiopian People's Revolutionary Democratic Front (EPRDF), Uganda's National Resistance Army/Movement (NRA/M) and the Rwandan Patriotic Front (RPF) pursued regime change outside their borders throughout the 1990s – most significantly in Zaire/Democratic Republic of the Congo, where Mobutu Sese Seko was toppled in 1997, and in Sudan, where they sought to overthrow the military-Islamist Al-Ingaz regime. For these movements, the OAU's emphasis on absolute sovereignty and non-interference had greatly contributed to Africa's international marginalisation 30 years after independence.[28] Their fighters crossed borders without UN or OAU mandates, and their leaders explored new forms of regional integration, denouncing the 'neo-colonial structures' in vogue since 1963. They saw their own regional interventions as at once ideological (aimed at the export of their model of governance) and strategic (necessary for the survival of domestic revolutions). Their recurrent interventionism and use of subregional organisations such as East Africa's Intergovernmental Authority on Development to lend legal legitimacy to their forays helped transform intervention both in practice and in theory.

Leaders explored new forms of regional integration

These new regimes also contributed to a second shift, namely a growing tendency to contest the OAU's sacrosanct colonial-era frontiers. Africa's sovereigntist regime had supported the freezing of Africa's borders, the principle of non-interference and the recognition of the inalienable right of the former European colonies to exercise authority over their territories.[29] But East Africa's liberation movements emphasised the idea of regional integration, the virtues of porous borders – a 'Greater Horn of Africa'[30] – and the principle of self-determination. In 1993, Eritrea achieved independence from Ethiopia after the twin struggles of the EPLF and EPRDF, with the latter conceding to the Eritrean people the right to determine their own destiny. Similarly, the EPLF, EPRDF, NRM and RPF also acknowledged South Sudan's right to self-determination, calling for its secession to be internationally recognised in 2011. This marked a sharp disjuncture with Africa's historical 'secessionist deficit': the continent's near-total absence of breakaway states prior to the 1990s, the result of an OAU incentive structure that imposed prohibitively high material penalties for unrecognised statehood.[31] The creation of two new African countries in the last 25 years, Eritrea and South Sudan, is indicative of the growing erosion of the principles of non-interference, border integrity and sovereignty that have structured Africa's international relations since 1963.

The third important spur for the alteration of the sovereigntist regime was the rise of politicians embracing Pan-Africanist themes to positions of influence, including UN secretary-general Kofi Annan, South African presidents Nelson Mandela and Thabo Mbeki, Nigerian president Olusegun Obasanjo and African Union commission chairman Alpha Oumar Konaré. These men combined a belief in the necessity of African self-reliance – Somalia and Rwanda were seen as proof that Africa could not rely on outsiders to protect its people and interests – with an acceptance of interventionism, including the use of force.[32] From this viewpoint, Africa's conflicts, underdevelopment and poor governance were interlinked, and could not be solved so long as the straitjacket of judicial sovereignty and non-interference allowed incumbents to get away with mass murder.[33] This new cohort of leaders pushed for the OAU to be transformed in 2001–02 into the African Union (AU), which adopted a liberal doctrine of humanitarian intervention – the union has a mandate to respond by all means necessary to genocide, crimes against humanity and gross human-rights violations – and outlawed unconstitutional changes of power (with AU sanctions overriding domestic decision-makers). The AU also inaugurated a Peace and Security Council to operationalise the shift from non-interference to non-indifference.[34] The Pan-Africanists' rise transformed the legal status of intervention in Africa, ensuring that it had powerful backers.

Intervention as stabilisation

The ascendancy of Kofi Annan, a high-profile advocate of non-indifference, coincided with the gradual subordination of the UN's Department of Political Affairs to its Department for Peacekeeping Operations, with significant consequences for the African security landscape.[35] Between 1990 and 2009, more than 60 peace operations – ranging from monitoring assignments to forces capable of deploying lethal firepower against belligerents – were undertaken on the African continent by numerous actors, including the UN, the European Union, the OAU/AU and Africa's subregional organisations.[36] From Liberia and Côte d'Ivoire to Darfur and South Sudan, tens of thousands of UN blue helmets were deployed (and have remained in the field for a decade or more), as were thousands of AU troops to Burundi and Somalia – a development that was hardly imaginable as recently as 2000, when mustering even 500 peacekeepers seemed a stretch and puny observer missions were the rule.[37] Recently, the number of interventions has increased further, in the Abyei region contested by Sudan and South Sudan (UNISFA from 2011), in Mali (MINUSMA from 2013) and in Central African Republic (MISCA/MINUSCA from 2013), which, combined, field more than 32,000 participants.

It is not just the material fact of intervention that has become significantly more prominent, but its content has changed too. While the discourse of traditional 'peacekeeping' persists, it has in many cases been superseded by the practice of coercive 'stabilisation',[38] a trend emphasised by adding that term (the 'S' in UNISFA, MINUSMA and MINUSCA) to mission names. The UN Security Council and the AU Peace and Security Council are granting their missions greater leeway to use force to (re-)establish governmental and international authority.[39] Increased reference to 'spoilers' – or, to use Stephen Stedman's words, 'leaders and parties who believe that peace emerging from negotiations threatens their power, worldview, and interests, and use violence to undermine attempts to achieve it'[40] – and 'negative forces' (a term favoured by UN operations[41]) represent an attempt to delegitimise political challenges to existing power structures.[42] Such language allows the intervener to exclude certain belligerents and their grievances from any 'reasonable' peace settlement and to prioritise others – almost unfailingly the incumbent government.

Intervention as stabilisation, then, is about state enhancement by external actors who provide support of various kinds to the formal holders of state power, with military assistance being the most crucial. The Force Intervention Brigade in the Democratic Republic of the Congo, for example, was created in 2013 as part of the Mission de l'Organisation des Nations Unies pour la Stabilisation en RD Congo (MONUSCO) with the sole objective of neutralising those *forces négatives* that were seen as threatening the authority of the Congolese state and the security of civilians.[43] Underlining the Africanisation of stabilisation is the fact that Tanzanian and South African troops constitute the majority of the brigade. UN Security Council Resolution 2098, which in March 2013 authorised the brigade for a maximum of 12 months, stressed that it was exceptional in nature and would not create a precedent. However, the actual conduct of the mission belies such soothing language. Not only is the Intervention Brigade now in its fifth year of operation, but it has inspired initiatives elsewhere. In August 2016, for example, the Security Council approved a regional protection force within the United Nations Mission in South Sudan (UNMISS) with an enhanced mandate to impose order and protect civilians.[44] Today, the neutralisation of armed non-state actors by the UN in the Democratic Republic of the Congo, Mali and Central African Republic, and by the African Union Mission in Somalia (AMISOM), appears uncontroversial. Most of the troops taking part in these UN and AU operations are African, debunking the conventional wisdom pitting Western interventionists against African sovereigntists.[45]

Growth in the number and size of stabilisation operations, along with their increasingly robust mandates to use force, form part of the broader militarisation of responses, by Africans and non-Africans alike, to perceived security hazards emanating from the continent. International terrorism, organised crime, migration, piracy and 'fragile states' have been framed as major threats warranting an urgent security response.[46] (This represents a significant change from the 1990s, when Western actors mostly perceived African conflicts as tragic but containable.) Jihadism, geopolitical competition with Asia and a perceived relationship between unemployment, crime and African migration to Europe have all contributed to the view that Africa is crucial to Western security.[47] As such, Western forces have deployed multiple combat missions to the continent. For example, EU and American warships have targeted Somali pirates in the Indian Ocean since 2008.[48] In Libya, NATO aircraft and special forces enforced the no-fly zone and were essential to the 2011 ousting of Muammar Gadhafi. In Côte d'Ivoire (2011), Mali (2013) and Central African Republic (2013–14), decisive French interventions swung the politico-military balance in favour of actors recognised by the UN Security Council and the AU as the countries' legitimate power-holders.[49] Between 2010 and 2017, US drones and 'advisers' hunted the Ugandan rebels of the Lord's Resistance Army throughout equatorial Africa. US forces have also proved vital in beating back the Boko Haram threat in Northern Nigeria, Cameroon and Chad, as well as holding the jihadists of the Islamic State in Libya and of al-Shabaab in Somalia at bay, having carried out assassinations of the groups' senior leaders. Western military personnel are stationed on bases across the continent, from Djibouti to Senegal, in greater numbers than at any point since independence.

It is striking how uncontroversial this sharpened appetite for intra- and extra-regional interventionism on African soil has proven to be. A clear majority of African states, as expressed through the AU Peace and Security Council, votes in the UN Security Council and diplomatic statements, fully supported intervention in the Central African Republic, Côte d'Ivoire, Mali, Nigeria, Somalia, Sudan, South Sudan and more. Despite subsequent criticism of Western bungling of the post-conflict situation in Libya, the operation to stop the large-scale killing of civilians there enjoyed considerable African support: all African Council members voted in favour of UN Security Council Resolution 1973.[50] Many African incumbents were privately delighted to see Gadhafi, notorious for fuelling conflicts in the Sahel and West Africa, ousted.[51] Similarly, while avoiding the language of regime change, the Economic Community of Central African States (known by its French acronym CEEAC) worked in close cooperation with Paris to reverse the takeover of the government in the Central African Republic by the Seleka alliance of militias. Seleka leader Michel Djotodia was obliged by CEEAC to resign from the presidency and disband the militias in January 2014 as parallel French and AU missions got under way.[52] Previously, Paris and the Economic Community of West African States had collaborated to have Alassane Ouattara recognised as Côte d'Ivoire's legitimate president after disputed elections, in the process helping to coercively defeat Laurent Gbagbo.[53] In June 2017, France and five African states also persuaded the Security Council to adopt a resolution authorising a 5,000-strong multilateral force comprising African soldiers – backed by French intelligence and *légionnaires* carrying out search-and-destroy missions across West Africa as part of *Opération Barkhane* (2014–) – to target networks of terrorists, drug smugglers and human traffickers in the Sahel.[54]

A new consensus

Growing convergence between African and external actors around a reworked 'intervention as stabilisation' regime should not be taken to mean that African elites are endorsing a liberal agenda still strongly associated with Europe and North America. Disagreements over the International Criminal Court (ICC) are rife; Washington Consensus-style market reforms and Western-style democracy promotion remain controversial; and many Africans blame the West for the calamitous aftermath of the Libya intervention. Furthermore, the Responsibility to Protect continues to be viewed with suspicion by those who discern in it a neo-colonial agenda of regime change. Still, African incumbents have clearly accepted intervention, whether by Africans or non-Africans, as a mainstream instrument in the international relations of the continent.

The chief reason for this is that African elites have found ways of enlisting intervention for their own purposes, in the process replacing liberal notions of order creation with stabilisation. This altered interpretation has aligned African governments with the three most important geopolitical actors on the continent: the United States, the European Union (and its member states), and the People's Republic of China. This convergence is striking given the pervasive pessimism in the literature following the Darfur crisis, which warned that new norms of protection risked being stillborn owing to global and regional antagonisms.[55]

Why did this unusual set of partners, with ideological views and global interests that frequently diverge, develop an interventionist consensus? The answer lies in the framing of intervention not as a project of remaking Africans or undertaking costly external peacebuilding through trusteeship, but as a way of restoring order. As an influential paper posited in 2004:

> Even before September 11, the world was changing in such a way that the main security threats and problems now emerge not from great power security competition – Russia and China, for example – but from the consequences of political disorder, misrule, and humiliation in the third world.[56]

African constituencies for intervention have found common ground with Western policy audiences and the Chinese Communist Party concerning political order: all concur that the principal problem is not rogue regimes, as liberals and neo-conservatives believed in the 1990s and early 2000s, but rather weak states.

Pragmatic African elites have long seen intervention as something that is best engaged with and, to the extent possible, taken advantage of. However, the goal in the early twenty-first century goes well beyond the aim of past African governments to lower the costs to their legitimacy (and, on occasion, their survival) of interventions that were unmediated by African states and regional institutions. Properly conceived of and co-managed by African incumbents, intervention is now seen as a major resource in regime consolidation, and is increasingly being carried out by Africans themselves.

Reframed as stabilisation, intervention is no longer the hard tool of a liberal critique of African regimes. Quite the contrary: intervention has become a way of strengthening incumbents. This support can take the form of aid flows, bilateral and multilateral political backing, the provision of armaments, training and, last but not least, the occasional wholesale substitution of local forces by international troops that can conquer and hold contested territories.[57] Thus, intervention as stabilisation can strengthen the territorial coverage of regimes that previously had only a loose hold over their peripheries. A pro-incumbent approach tends to quarantine rebel gains and provides the rationale for intensified anti-insurgency efforts spearheaded by external forces, as in Mali and Somalia.[58] African states that are significant promoters of intervention and major troop contributors, such as Rwanda and Uganda, have also been able to obtain considerable international tolerance for their domestic illiberal practices.

Such manoeuvring is unambiguous extraversion, whereby African states that lack certain resources (legitimacy, material and coercive assets) actively tap into the international wellsprings of these resources and redeploy them domestically to the benefit of power-holders. But the omnipresence of interventionism is not merely a function of transnational rent-seeking[59] or a way for authoritarians to insulate themselves from liberal criticisms of their human-rights records.[60] More importantly, stabilisation is a response to the enduring challenge of managing state fragility. In earlier decades, Africans defended African sovereignty by largely shunning intervention, at least in principle (Cold War practice was a more ambivalent matter). In the early twenty-first century, African sovereignty is defended – internally as well as externally – by taming and mainstreaming intervention.

Stating this does not eliminate a role for alternative explanations, including those citing the emergence of a liberal sensibility and a push to achieve the 'Africanisation of security'.[61] Concerns for the suffering of fellow Africans, especially in the aftermath of atrocities, have been articulated by those in favour of African-led solutions, including public intellectuals, politicians and members of international organisations.[62] However, such strands of opinion do not explain why a majority of African states, some of which have authoritarian regimes and their own history of atrocities, enthusiastically sign up to the practice of both extra-regional and intra-regional intervention. The African consensus in favour of an interventionism mediated by incumbents is remarkably broad-based.

This does not imply that all African states embrace in equal measure the growing acceptance of interventionism both from without and within. The language of non-interference and anti-imperialism still resonates in some quarters – Algeria, for instance, remains famously sovereigntist in its official positions.[63] Still, outright opposition to intervention is difficult to sustain, especially given how many other African elites benefit from the reworked approach. More common are the worries shared by several African incumbents about peers who are perceived to be seizing on the mantra of order-creation to pursue aspirations of regional hegemony (such as Ethiopia, South Africa and Uganda).[64] These states take part in stabilisation missions not just to consolidate their authority internally and to insulate themselves from external criticism, but also to project power abroad. Their interventions are, invariably, framed at both the African and global levels as maintaining regional security and, owing to these states' judicious alignment with the permanent members of the UN Security Council, they are almost never condemned in multilateral forums, let alone blocked. This combination of enthusiasm for interventionism on the part of globally well-positioned African states and external tolerance (and sometimes even encouragement) of intra-regional interventionism is crucial to the mainstreaming of intervention in Africa's international relations.

African attempts to tame intervention – and downplay liberal norms – would not have been possible without a marked convergence with global actors. Western motivations for intervention in Africa have altered considerably over the last decade. Even at the height of the Western self-confidence that spawned liberal state-building projects in Kosovo, Bosnia, East Timor and elsewhere, Africa saw only parsimonious efforts of this kind. More recently, the pursuit by outsiders of agendas with such transformative aspirations has become inconceivable. This is not always apparent, because Western interventionism remains couched in the language of grand liberal goals, at least before audiences for whom such language still carries weight.[65] Nevertheless, Western interventions now centre on the legitimation of the (existing) state, at the expense of the alternative, transformative goals of peacebuilding.[66] Such reduced ambitions and pro-incumbent preferences mitigate the dilemma of previous interventions that needed to find a way to stabilise their targets without undermining their sovereignty.[67]

Several factors account for the West's reorientation towards stabilisation. Firstly, across much of Africa – and especially in the Sahelian 'arc of crisis' – Western policymakers are principally concerned with jihadist groups such as Boko Haram, al-Qaeda and al-Shabaab. As a result, their policies are aimed at destroying these groups, ending the training and arming of supportive local actors, and providing funding and political support to regimes advancing counter-terrorist agendas. Because the nurturing of states that are capable allies is of paramount importance to these efforts,[68] the character of their domestic politics and the cultivation of liberal governance within them are secondary concerns.[69] Secondly, stabilisation missions featuring extensive African 'ownership' and troop contributions have enabled Western decision-makers to sustain the liberal rhetoric of global governance and the protection of civilians – which remain important to certain constituencies in Europe and North America – while in actual fact scaling back their ambitions in these areas.[70] The promotion of 'African solutions to African problems' is intended to lend legitimacy to intervention efforts while reducing the financial and political pressures on Western militaries. The requisite degree of African

African buy-in is now available

buy-in and associated mutual legitimation that global (UN) and regional (AU) partnerships bring[71] had been difficult to achieve under a liberal banner, but is now available. Without this, the new interventionism would have neither the legitimacy nor the personnel needed to get off the ground.

An additional contributor to this process has been China. A decade ago, Beijing was still asserting a classic sovereigntist approach in post-Cold War Africa. Indeed, its sceptical take on intervention (and other forms of external involvement in the domestic politics of African states) was an essential part of its effort to distinguish itself from the Western presence on the continent.[72] However, China too has since welcomed the new regime, and has increasingly abandoned its once ironclad commitment to the principle of non-interference. This is because of China's deepening material interests in Africa.[73] Today, rather than being able to singularly approach Africa as a source of economic opportunity, China is increasingly forced to navigate a more complex landscape of risk and liability. Greater exposure means greater vulnerability and anxiety as material interests become entrenched and the costs of insecurity more salient.[74] Chinese diplomats have become increasingly involved in African conflicts – meeting rebel leaders and negotiating peace deals in South Sudan, for example, and urging a hardline stance against al-Shabaab in Somalia. Beijing contributes more personnel to UN peacekeeping missions than any other veto-holding member of the Security Council, and has sent thousands of military and police officers to Africa, including combat troops to confront jihadists (Mali) and protect Chinese oil interests and civilians (South Sudan). China's naval forces began participating in anti-piracy operations off the Somali coast nearly a decade ago, and successfully evacuated more than 35,000 Chinese nationals from Libya in 2011. In 2015, China opened its first naval base outside its borders in the strategically located Djibouti. Beijing also tolerated (indeed, tacitly supported) intervention in Central African Republic, Côte d'Ivoire and Libya, even if this entailed the use of force to tilt the political balance against sitting (but internationally discredited) leaders.[75] The Chinese Communist Party continues to reject (non-consensual) interference, but maintains that it does not oppose intervention with state consent.

Several reasons undergird Beijing's support for the new interventionist regime. Firstly, China is aware of changing African perceptions of intervention, and its stance has evolved in tandem with its growing acceptability on the continent. The fact that the Communist Party still rhetorically distinguishes its interventionism from interference in domestic affairs resonates with the state-centric preferences of African elites. Secondly, China's armed forces desire expeditionary experience commensurate with the country's great-power ambitions, and are therefore increasingly in favour of intervention, as long as there is a UN or AU mandate.[76] Thirdly, China's considerable presence in Africa has led to concerns about chaotic conditions in areas where the writ of sovereign states does not reach. Beijing has concluded that some coercion may be necessary to ensure that Chinese investors can operate safely.[77] Finally, China – no less than authoritarian African incumbents such as Ethiopia and Chad – has been encouraged by shifts in the discourse and practice of intervention away from liberal governance towards stabilisation. This toning down of the normative dimension, combined with the upholding of the practice of seeking host-country consent for operations,[78] makes it much easier for China to accept intervention, to the extent that it has come up with its own quasi-doctrine for such missions.[79]

The apparent malleability of the discourse of intervention has allowed it to be used by a range of actors to underpin agendas that differed strongly from the early post-Cold War blueprint advanced by Western states and Western-dominated international organisations. A case in point is the conceptual takeover by Russia of the Responsibility to Protect during the 2008 Georgia War, which subverted liberal interpretations.[80] Of course, norms and institutions are not endlessly adaptable, and in some circumstances, rejection rather than taming is the outcome. The trajectory of the ICC provides a cautionary counterpoint here. In the early 2000s, a large number of African states signed up to the Rome Statute, to some extent on account of Western pressure, but also in the expectation that it might be a politically useful tool. The Democratic Republic of the Congo and Uganda were early users, for example. However, it soon became clear that the ICC would not be easily manipulated, and might indeed turn against its signatories, many of which have since sought to obstruct it or threatened to leave it altogether.[81] Intervention, however, is an altogether fuzzier proposition that has proven more amenable to taming – and hence of more use to weaker states.

*   *   *

How and why have weak African states morphed from defenders of a strenuous anti-interventionist regime into vocal advocates for external intervention on the continent, both by other African states and extra-regional actors? The very weakness of African states ensured that intervention has been central to their politics since 1960, but the specific role it has played has changed dramatically over time. Contrary to neoliberal and neorealist accounts focused on inter-state competition, 'organized hypocrisy'[82] and often futile opposition by weak states to outside meddling, African states have found ways of turning their fragility, and the interventionist tendencies that both contribute to it and result from it, into a resource for regime survival. They have successfully engaged in the management of dependence and harnessed changing systemic conditions to pursue 'subaltern Realism'[83]: with domestic and international order so intertwined, the securing of one's internal authority is at the very heart of both foreign policy and state-making.

While in the first decades after independence this meant selectively inviting external involvement but maintaining a rigid anti-interventionist norm, Western hegemony from the 1980s onwards put African sovereignty on the defensive. Yet in the last 10–15 years, an apparently counter-intuitive shift towards embracing intervention not only in practice but also in theory (a qualitatively new development) has been accomplished by African elites. The emergent regime is not predominantly a function of the putative adoption of liberal norms,[84] but rather of African agency that shrewdly helps to subvert earlier understandings of intervention. Today, the domestic and external drivers of intervention are mutually reinforcing: African elites and outside actors have both championed the new interventionism, each for their own reasons, but nevertheless in tandem. The reason why Africans increasingly intervene across national borders, and why outsiders increasingly intervene in Africa, is that intervention has been reinterpreted as stabilisation.

Taming intervention has proven to be an effective strategy in confronting the domestic challenge of state fragility and the external threat of regime change in the 1990s and early 2000s. Rather than relying on international law to defend their fledgling sovereignty, African states have turned to a revised concept of intervention, correctly sensing that external actors' main concern on the continent is with possible security threats emanating from weak statehood and a lack of political order rather than with creating liberal-democratic societies. Working with outsiders to reinterpret intervention as stabilisation has allowed them, for the most part, to turn the potentially dangerous trend of sovereignty infringement into a project of regime consolidation.

The alignment of African governments, European progressives, North American conservatives and the Chinese Communist Party around a 'stabilising' interventionist regime in Africa brings together a group of actors that is otherwise characterised by major differences in terms of ideological affinities and material capabilities. The indistinct character of intervention has gone a long way toward reconciling these, but this does not mean that the concept has become totally vacuous. To the contrary, the specific interpretation of intervention as order-creation responds to global concerns with fragile African statehood, and to the needs of African elites to deal with a new generation of insurgent challengers. Sceptics might well point to the tenuous and under-specified nature of the 'order' that the interventionist consensus is seeking to build, given that the various interventionist constituencies hold widely diverging interpretations of what durable, legitimate authority should look like in the long run. But such considerations appear to matter little, at least at this politico-historical juncture, for either the theory or the practice of intervention on the continent.

Notes

1   Christopher Clapham, *Africa and the International System: The Politics of State Survival* (Cambridge: Cambridge University Press, 1996).

2   Andrew Hurrell, *On Global Order: Power, Values, and the Constitution of International Society* (Oxford: Oxford University Press, 2006).

3   Hedley Bull, 'Recapturing the Just War for Political Theory', *World Politics*, vol. 31, no. 4, 1979, p. 595.

4   Martha Finnemore, *The Purpose of Intervention: Changing Beliefs about the Use of Force* (Ithaca, NY: Cornell University Press, 2003), pp. 94–5.

5   Rey Koslowski and Friedrich V. Kratochwil, 'Understanding Change in International Politics: The Soviet Empire's Demise and the International System', *International Organization*, vol. 48, no. 2, 1994, pp. 215–47.

6   Frederick Cooper, *Africa Since 1940: The Past of the Present* (Cambridge: Cambridge University Press, 2002).

7   James Mayall, *Nationalism and International Society* (Cambridge: Cambridge University Press, 1990).

8   Pierre Englebert, *Africa: Unity, Sovereignty, and Sorrow* (Boulder, CO: Lynne Rienner Publishers, 2009), p. 204.

9   Sabelo J. Ndlovu-Gatsheni, 'Pan-Africanism and the International System', in Tim Murithi (ed.), *Handbook of Africa's International Relations* (London: Routledge, 2014), pp. 21–9.

10 The principle of *uti possidetis*, whereby territory remains under the control of whoever possesses it at the end of a conflict, was imported from nineteenth-century South America and became an accepted norm in international law, including in Africa. See James Mayall, 'Humanitarian Intervention and International Society: Lessons from Africa', in Jennifer M. Welsh (ed.), *Humanitarian Intervention and International Relations* (Oxford: Oxford University Press, 2004), pp. 120–41.

11 Jean-François Bayart, 'Africa in the World: A History of Extraversion', *African Affairs*, vol. 99, no. 395, 2000, pp. 217–67.

12 Arne Odd Westad, *The Global Cold War: Third World Interventions and the Making of our Times* (Cambridge: Cambridge University Press, 2005).

13 Robert H. Jackson and Carl G. Rosberg, 'Why Africa's Weak States Persist: The Empirical and the Juridical in Statehood', *World Politics*,

vol. 35, no. 1, 1982, pp. 1–24.

14 Robert H. Jackson, *Quasi-states: International Relations, Sovereignty and the Third World* (Cambridge: Cambridge University Press, 1990).

15 Christopher Cramer, *Civil War Is Not a Stupid Thing: Accounting for Violence in Developing Countries* (London: C. Hurst & Co., 2006).

16 See Giovanni Arrighi, 'The African Crisis', *New Left Review*, vol. 15, no. 5, 2002, pp. 5–36; and Nicolas Van de Walle, *African Economies and the Politics of Permanent Crisis, 1979–1999* (Cambridge: Cambridge University Press, 2001).

17 For a discussion of the problems with Westphalian and juridical sovereignty and a plea for re-conceptualising it as limited, multidimensional and performance-based, see Robert O. Keohane, 'Political Authority after Intervention: Gradations in Sovereignty', in Jeff L. Holzgrefe and Robert Keohane (eds), *Humanitarian Intervention: Ethical, Legal, and Political Dilemmas* (New York: Cambridge University Press, 2003), pp. 275–98.

18 Pierre Englebert and Denis M. Tull, 'Postconflict Reconstruction in Africa: Flawed Ideas About Failed States', *International Security*, vol. 32, no. 4, 2008, pp. 106–39.

19 Walter S. Clarke and Jeffrey Herbst (eds), *Learning from Somalia: The Lessons of Armed Humanitarian Intervention* (Boulder, CO: Westview, 1997).

20 For a discussion of the US, Africa and the multilateral system, see Boutros Boutros-Ghali, *Unvanquished: A U.S.–U.N. Saga* (London: I.B. Tauris, 1999), pp. 53–60 and 92–125.

21 Stephen D. Krasner, 'Building Democracy after Conflict: The Case for Shared Sovereignty', *Journal of Democracy*, vol. 16, no. 1, 2005, pp. 69–83.

22 Richard Caplan, *International Governance of War-torn Territories: Rule and Reconstruction* (Oxford: Oxford University Press, 2005).

23 Robert Kaplan, 'The Coming Anarchy', *Atlantic*, vol. 273, no. 1, 1994, pp. 44–76. For reflections on 'African exceptionalism' in international-relations theory, and on how perceptions of an African 'other' as a counterpoint to Western modernity have shaped international relations, see Kevin C. Dunn and Timothy M. Shaw (eds), *Africa's Challenge to International Relations Theory* (Basingstoke: Palgrave, 2001).

24 Christopher Clapham, 'Africa and Trusteeship in the Modern Global Order', in James Mayall and Ricardo Soares de Oliveira (eds), *The New Protectorates: International Tutelage and the Making of Liberal States* (London: C. Hurst & Co., 2011), pp. 67–82.

25 Philip Roessler and Harry Verhoeven, *Why Comrades Go to War: Liberation Politics and the Outbreak of Africa's Deadliest Conflict* (London: Hurst and Oxford University Press, 2016), chapters 2 and 3.

26 Christopher Clapham, 'Introduction: Analysing African Insurgencies', in Christopher Clapham (ed.), *African Guerrillas* (Oxford: James Currey, 1998), pp. 1–18.

27 William Reno, *Warfare in Independent Africa* (New York: Cambridge University Press, 2011), pp. 119–62. Although he frames it differently,

John F. Clark makes a similar argument in 'A Constructivist Account of the Congo Wars', *African Security*, vol. 4, no. 3, 2011, pp. 147–70.

28 In his maiden speech at the May 1993 OAU summit in Cairo, Eritrean President Issayas Afewerki – then not the internationally isolated figure he is today, but a towering regional leader – declared: 'the sad fact remains that the OAU has become a nominal organization that had failed to deliver on its pronounced objectives and commitments'.

29 Jeffrey Herbst, 'The Creation and Maintenance of National Boundaries in Africa', *International Organization*, vol. 43, no. 4, 1989, pp. 673–92.

30 Roessler and Verhoeven, *Why Comrades Go To War*, pp. 412–13.

31 Pierre Englebert and Rebecca Hummel, 'Let's Stick Together: Understanding Africa's Secessionist Deficit', *African Affairs*, vol. 104, no. 416, 2005, pp. 399–427.

32 Chris Landsberg, 'South Africa and the Making of the African Union and NEPAD: Mbeki's "Progressive African Agenda"', in Adekeye Adebajo, Adebayo Adedeji and Chris Landsberg (eds), *South Africa in Africa* (Scottsville: University of KwaZulu-Natal Press, 2007), pp. 195–212.

33 See Kofi Annan, *In Larger Freedom: Towards Development, Security and Human Rights for All* (New York: United Nations Publications, 2005); and Francis M. Deng et al. (eds), *Sovereignty as Responsibility: Conflict Management in Africa* (Washington DC: Brookings Institution Press, 1996).

34 See Omar A. Touray, 'The Common African Defence and Security Policy', *African Affairs*, vol. 104, no. 417, 2005, pp. 635–56; and Paul D. Williams, 'From Non-intervention to Non-indifference: The Origins and Development of the African Union's Security Culture', *African Affairs*, vol. 106, no. 423, 2007, pp. 253–79.

35 For a discussion of the rise of the Department for Peacekeeping Operations and Kofi Annan's vision as the department's head and as UN secretary-general, see James Traub, *The Best Intentions: Kofi Annan and the UN in the Era of American World Power* (New York: Macmillan, 2006).

36 Paul D. Williams, *War and Conflict in Africa* (Cambridge: Polity Press, 2011), p. 184.

37 Eric Berman and Katie E. Sams, 'The Peacekeeping Potential of African Regional Organizations', in Jane Boulden (ed.), *Dealing with Conflict in Africa: The United Nations and Regional Organisations* (New York: Palgrave, 2003), pp. 35–77.

38 Devon Curtis, 'The Contested Politics of Peacebuilding in Africa', in Devon Curtis and Gwinyazi A. Dzinesa (eds), *Peacebuilding, Power, and Politics in Africa* (Athens, OH: Ohio University Press, 2012), pp. 11–13.

39 John Karlsrud, 'The UN at War: Examining the Consequences of Peace-enforcement Mandates for the UN Peacekeeping Operations in the CAR, the DRC and Mali', *Third World Quarterly*, vol. 36, no. 1, 2015, pp. 40–54.

40 Stephen John Stedman, 'Spoiler Problems in Peace Processes', *International Security*, vol. 22, no. 2, 1997, pp. 5–53.

41 Security Council communiqués

of in-depth briefings on ongoing efforts to stabilise places such as the Democratic Republic of the Congo, for example, often carry titles such as 'At Security Council Debate on Preventing Conflicts in Great Lakes Region, Secretary-General Calls for Efforts to Neutralize Negative Forces' (SG/SM/17619-SC/12295-AFR/3350, 21 March 2016) and 'Special Envoy, in Security Council, Stresses Need for Concerted Efforts to Secure Gains Made against Great Lakes Region's "Negative Forces"' (SC/12573, 2 November 2016).

42 Sharath Srinivasan, *When Peace Kills Politics: International Intervention and Unending Wars in the Sudans* (London: C. Hurst & Co., forthcoming).

43 UN Security Council Resolution 2098, UN Doc. S/RES/2098, 28 March 2013.

44 UN Security Council Resolution 2304, UN Doc. S/RES/2304, 12 August 2006.

45 On 31 August 2016, 8,156 out of 11,883 personnel serving under MINUSMA came from African countries. For MINUSCA, this was 8,934 out of 12,152. For MONUSCO, African contributions were less impressive as a proportion of the total (6,477 out of 18,620), but the Force Intervention Brigade – its key coercive instrument – consists solely of African troops. See http://www.un.org/en/peacekeeping/contributors. As an AU mission, AMISOM is, by definition, entirely African in composition.

46 See, for example, Robert Rotberg (ed.), *When States Fail* (Princeton, NJ: Princeton University Press, 2004); and Robert Frith and John Glenn, 'Fragile States and the Evolution of Risk Governance: Intervention, Prevention and Extension', *Third World Quarterly*, vol. 36, no. 10, 2015, pp. 1,787–1,808.

47 See Rita Abrahamsen, 'A Breeding Ground for Terrorists? Africa and Britain's "War on Terrorism"', *Review of African Political Economy*, vol. 31, no. 102, 2004, pp. 677–84; and Sabelo Ndlovu-Gatsheni and Victor Ojakorotu, 'Surveillance Over a Zone of Conflict: Africom and the Politics of Securitisation of Africa', *Journal of Pan African Studies*, vol. 3, no. 6, 2010, pp. 94–110.

48 Marianne Riddervold, 'Finally Flexing its Muscles? Atalanta – The European Union's Naval Military Operation Against Piracy', *European Security*, vol. 20, no. 3, 2011, pp. 385–404.

49 Roland Marchal, 'Military (Mis) Adventures in Mali', *African Affairs*, vol. 112, no. 448, 2013, pp. 486–97.

50 On the importance of regional (Arab and African) players in enabling the NATO intervention, see Luke Glanville, 'Intervention in Libya: from Sovereign Consent to Regional Consent', *International Studies Perspectives*, vol. 14, no. 3, 2013, pp. 325–42.

51 On Gadhafi's relationship with other African strongmen, see Alex de Waal, 'African Roles in the Libyan Conflict of 2011', *International Affairs*, vol. 89, no. 2, 2013, pp. 365–7.

52 Martin Welz, 'Briefing: Crisis in the Central African Republic and the International Response', *African Affairs*, vol. 113, no. 453, 2014, pp. 601–10.

53 Giulia Piccolino, 'David Against Goliath in Côte d'Ivoire? Laurent Gbagbo's War against Global Governance', *African Affairs*, vol. 111,

no. 442, 2012, pp. 1–23.

54   UN Security Council Resolution 2359, UN Doc. S/RES/2359, 21 June 2017.

55   Harry Verhoeven, Jagannath Madhan Mohan and Ricardo Soares de Oliveira, 'To Intervene in Darfur, or Not: Re-examining the R2P Debate and its Impact', *Global Society*, vol. 30, no. 1, 2016, pp. 21–37.

56   James Fearon and David Laitin, 'Neotrusteeship and the Problem of Weak States', *International Security*, vol. 28, no. 4, 2004, p. 6.

57   For an early example of this, see Paul Omach, 'The African Crisis Response Initiative: Domestic Politics and Convergence of National Interests', *African Affairs*, vol. 99, no. 394, 2000, pp. 73–95.

58   See, for example, Jonathan Fisher, 'Framing Kony: Uganda's War, Obama's Advisers and the Nature of "Influence" in Western Foreign Policy Making', *Third World Quarterly*, vol. 35, no. 4, 2014, pp. 686–704.

59   Alex de Waal, *The Real Politics of the Horn of Africa* (Cambridge: Polity Press, 2015), pp. 182–93.

60   Jonathan Fisher and David M. Anderson, 'Authoritarianism and the Securitization of Development in Africa', *International Affairs*, vol. 91, no. 1, 2015, pp. 131–51.

61   Benedikt Franke, *Security Cooperation in Africa: A Reappraisal* (Boulder, CO: First Forum Press, 2009).

62   Paul D. Williams, 'Keeping the Peace in Africa: Why "African" Solutions Are Not Enough', *Ethics and International Affairs*, vol. 22, no. 3, 2009, pp. 309–29.

63   Jean-François Daguzan, 'La politique étrangère de l'Algérie: le temps de l'aventure?', *Politique étrangère*, vol. 46,

no. 3, 2015, pp. 31–42.

64   See Rene Lemarchand, 'Foreign Policy Making in the Great Lakes Region', in Gilbert Khadiagala and Terrence Lyons (eds), *African Foreign Policies: Power and Process* (Boulder, CO: Lynne Rienner, 2001), pp. 87–106; and Abdi Ismail Samatar, 'Ethiopian Invasion of Somalia, US Warlordism and AU Shame', *Review of African Political Economy*, vol. 34, no. 111, 2007, pp. 155–65.

65   Michael W. Doyle, *The Question of Intervention* (New Haven, CT: Yale University Press, 2015). On the scaling down of state-building ambitions while formally maintaining a liberal discourse, see Paul D. Miller, *Armed State Building: Confronting State Failure, 1898–2012* (Ithaca, NY: Cornell University Press, 2013).

66   Dominik Zaum, 'Statebuilding and Governance: the Conundrums of Legitimacy and Local Ownership', in Devon Curtis and Gwinyazi A. Dzinesa (eds), *Peacebuilding, Power, and Politics in Africa* (Athens, OH: Ohio University Press, 2012), pp. 47–62.

67   Nina Wilén, *Justifying Interventions in Africa: (De)stabilizing Sovereignty in Liberia, Burundi and the Congo* (Basingstoke: Palgrave Macmillan, 2016), p. 1.

68   Jan Bachmann, 'Policing Africa: The US Military and Visions of Crafting "Good Order"', *Security Dialogue*, vol. 45, no. 2, 2014, pp. 119–36.

69   Amitai Etzioni, *Security First: For a Muscular, Moral Foreign Policy* (New Haven, CT: Yale University Press, 2008).

70   Cf. David Chandler, *Empire in Denial: The Politics of State-building* (London:

Pluto Press, 2006).

71 Linnea Gelot, *Legitimacy, Peace Operations and Global–Regional Security: The African Union–United Nations Partnership in Darfur* (London: Routledge, 2012).

72 Chris Alden, Abiodun Alao, Zhang Chun and Laura Barber (eds), *China and Africa: Building Peace and Security Cooperation on the Continent* (Basingstoke: Palgrave Macmillan, 2017).

73 Harry Verhoeven, 'Is Beijing's Non-Interference Policy History? How Africa Changed China', *Washington Quarterly*, vol. 37, no. 2, 2014, pp. 55–70.

74 Devon Curtis, 'China and the Insecurity of Development in the Democratic Republic of the Congo (DRC)', *International Peacekeeping*, vol. 20, no. 5, 2013, pp. 551–69.

75 This does not preclude Chinese scholars from sounding warnings about the dangerous 'slippery slope' that these interventions represent. See, for example, Liu Tiewa and Zhang Haibin, 'Debates in China about the Responsibility to Protect as a Developing International Norm: A General Assessment', *Conflict, Security and Development*, vol. 14, no. 4, 2014, pp. 403–27.

76 Michael S. Chase et al., *China's Incomplete Military Transformation: Assessing the Weaknesses of the People's Liberation Army* (Santa Monica, CA: Rand Corporation, 2015).

77 Pak K. Lee and Lai-Ha Chan, 'China's and India's Perspectives on Military Intervention: Why Africa but not Syria?', *Australian Journal of International Affairs*, vol. 70, no. 2, 2016, pp. 179–214.

78 Ian Johnstone, 'Managing Consent in Contemporary Peacekeeping Operations', *International Peacekeeping*, vol. 18, no. 2, 2011, pp. 168–82.

79 On China as a norm entrepreneur, see Chris Alden and Daniel Large, 'On Becoming a Norms Maker: Chinese Foreign Policy, Norms Evolution and the Challenges of Security in Africa', *China Quarterly*, vol. 221, no. 1, 2015, pp. 123–42.

80 Xymena Kurowska, 'Multipolarity as Resistance to Liberal Norms: Russia's Position on Responsibility to Protect', *Conflict, Security and Development*, vol. 14, no. 4, 2014, pp. 489–508.

81 Adam Branch, 'Dominic Ongwen on Trial: The ICC's African Dilemmas', *International Journal of Transitional Justice*, vol. 11, no. 1, 2017, pp. 33–7.

82 Stephen D. Krasner, *Sovereignty: Organized Hypocrisy* (Princeton, NJ: Princeton University Press, 1999).

83 Mohammed Ayoob, 'Subaltern Realism: International Relations Theory Meets the Third World', in Stephanie G. Neumann (ed.), *International Relations Theory and the Third World* (New York: St Martin's Press, 1998), pp. 31–54.

84 Alex J. Bellamy, 'The Responsibility to Protect – Five Years On', *Ethics and International Affairs*, vol. 24, no. 2, 2010, pp. 143–69.

Russia's Nuclear Policy: Worrying for the Wrong Reasons

Bruno Tertrais

The dominant narrative about Russia's nuclear weapons in Western strategic literature since the beginning of the century has been something like this: Russia's doctrine of 'escalate to de-escalate', and its large-scale military exercises, show that Moscow is getting ready to use low-yield, theatre nuclear weapons to stop NATO from defeating Russia's forces, or to coerce the Atlantic Alliance and end a conflict on terms favourable to Russia.

Examples of this narrative abound in recent official and non-official statements and writings. In 2015, two senior US Department of Defense (DoD) officials testified to Congress that 'Russian military doctrine includes what some have called an "escalate to de-escalate" strategy – a strategy that purportedly seeks to deescalate a conventional conflict through coercive threats, including limited nuclear use'.[1] In 2016, Admiral Cecil Haney, then commander of US Strategic Command, said that Russia was 'declaring and recklessly demonstrating its willingness to escalate to deescalate if required'.[2] That same year, a NATO secretary-general report claimed that Russian large-scale 'exercises include simulated nuclear attacks on NATO Allies (e.g., ZAPAD)'.[3] A US expert declares that 'in the event of a major war with the North Atlantic Treaty Organization [Russian] plans call for "de-escalatory" nuclear strikes. That is, Vladimir Putin would order limited nuclear attacks early, so as to frighten the US into ending the conflict on terms favourable to Moscow.'[4] A towering figure of the US strategic community asserts that: 'The Russian military has devised a doctrine which envisions

Bruno Tertrais is Deputy Director of the Fondation pour la recherche stratégique.

Survival | vol. 60 no. 2 | April–May 2018 | pp. 33–44   DOI 10.1080/00396338.2018.1448560

using a small number of very low-yield nuclear weapons to attack NATO forces defending Alliance territory'.[5] A European analyst writes that during recent exercises, 'Russia rehearsed the use of limited low-yield nuclear strikes to intimidate the West into accepting Russian territorial gains'.[6] Breathless reporting in Western media often includes the same claims.

The 2018 US Nuclear Posture Review (NPR) exemplifies this narrative and paints a rather frightening picture of the Russian theatre-nuclear threat. To wit:

> Russia's belief that limited first use, potentially including low-yield weapons, can provide such an advantage is based, in part, on Moscow's perception that its great number and variety of non-strategic nuclear systems provide a coercive advantage in crises and at lower levels of conflict. Recent Russian statements on this evolving nuclear weapons doctrine appear to lower the threshold for Moscow's first-use of nuclear weapons. Russia demonstrates its perception of the advantage these systems provide through numerous exercise and statements.

> Russia may also rely on threats of limited nuclear first use, or actual first use, to coerce us, our allies, and partners into terminating a conflict on terms favorable to Russia …

> [Russia] mistakenly assesses that the threat of nuclear escalation or actual first use of nuclear weapons would serve to 'de-escalate' a conflict on terms favorable to Russia …

> [Russia] is also building a large, diverse, and modern set of non-strategic systems that are dual-capable (may be armed with nuclear or conventional weapons). These theater- and tactical-range systems are not accountable under the New START Treaty and Russia's non-strategic nuclear modernization is increasing the total number of such weapons in its arsenal, while significantly improving its delivery capabilities …

> Most concerning are Russia's national security policies, strategies, and doctrine that include an emphasis on the threat of limited nuclear

escalation, and its continuing development and fielding of increasingly diverse and expanding nuclear capabilities. Moscow threatens and exercises limited nuclear first use, suggesting a mistaken expectation that coercive nuclear threats or limited first use could paralyze the United States and NATO and thereby end a conflict on terms favorable to Russia. Some in the United States refer to this as Russia's 'escalate to de-escalate' doctrine. 'De-escalation' in this sense follows from Moscow's mistaken assumption of Western capitulation on terms favorable to Moscow.[7]

Most of the elements of this narrative, however, rely on weak evidence – and there is strong evidence to counter many of them. Russia is not building new dedicated theatre-nuclear systems, and there is little evidence of new 'low-yield' warheads; it does not have an 'escalate to de-escalate' doctrine; and it is not practising the use of nuclear weapons in large-scale military exercises. The Russian nuclear problem is real and serious – but it is political more than it is military.

Russia's arsenal

Almost all open sources, including the US 2018 NPR, refer to a Russian non-strategic nuclear weapons (NSNW) arsenal of about 2,000 warheads ('non-strategic' here referring to those weapons not designed to be carried by New START-constrained launchers). The same sources differ in their evaluation of the number of operationally available warheads (that is, those which are available for planning and are not held in reserve). The most detailed recent open-source study, published in 2012, suggests that out of 1,900, only about half of this arsenal is available, most of it being assigned to naval, air and air-defence forces in western Russia.[8] A total of 1,900 would amount, according to data provided by the author of the study, to less than 10% of the late Cold War Soviet NSNW arsenal. Such a 93% reduction, one should note, would not be vastly different from what NATO's own deployed NSNW arsenal has undergone since its 1970s peak (a 97% reduction).[9]

Rumours and Russian threats of new nuclear deployments in Kaliningrad started about two decades ago. These rumours and threats generally involved a degree of confusion, perhaps deliberate, between missiles capable of carrying nuclear warheads, on the one hand, and the warheads themselves, on the other. References were made first to the dual-capable short-range missiles SS-21 *Tochka*-U, and then, in the past ten years, to the more modern SS-26 *Iskander*-M, which is almost certainly dual-capable, although its nuclear capability has never been publicly acknowledged by Moscow.[10] After years of Russian threats to do so, the *Iskander*-M was deployed in the enclave in 2016, allegedly temporarily, as a supposed reprisal for the deployment of NATO ballistic-missile defences. Specific references to nuclear warheads, however, have been scant. It is possible that Kaliningrad, which hosts large military facilities, has been a depot of nuclear warheads for some time, notably for the Russian navy; but there is no evidence of nuclear-warhead deployments dedicated to the *Iskander*-M. It has been speculated that the nuclear warhead for this missile could be either the one designed for the SS-21 or the one designed for the SS-23 *Oka*.[11] Given the relatively short shelf life of Russian non-strategic warheads, it is at least equally possible that Russia adapted one of these designs.

Has Russia developed new types of warheads of the low-yield variety? It is possible that it reduced the yield of existing ones, as several nuclear powers have done in the past or are doing today, by reducing the amount of fissile or fusible material contained in the warhead. But evidence of new types of low-yield warheads is absent – and programmes to develop such warheads would be of dubious reliability in the absence of full-scale testing. The only available source is a nearly 20-year-old declassified (though heavily redacted) CIA Intelligence Memorandum, which seems to refer to Russian interest in, more than development of, a new, tailored, low-yield warhead.[12]

Ambiguity is at the core of Russian strategy. However, for our purposes here we should distinguish between ambiguity as a political strategy (intentionally projecting uncertainty about the nature of the threat) and ambiguity as a technical fact (the built-in dual capability of launchers). Dual capability applies to many bombers and missiles: it is in the genes of Russian strategic culture. It is also a product of the severe budgetary constraints of the 1990s and 2000s, as well as a practical matter, to simplify force management. Lest we forget, some Alliance assets are also dual-capable (the F-16, *Tornado* and *Rafale* bombers). Finally, as others have observed, retaining a large NSNW arsenal may also be a bargaining chip: 'Russia is quite simply loath to give up something it has a lot of without getting something else in return.'[13]

Yes, Russia is ramping up the development, deployment and use of theatre-range launchers and missiles – including the new SSC-8, a cruise missile that almost certainly violates the Intermediate-Range Nuclear Forces (INF) Treaty. But this does not mean a renewed emphasis on the *nuclear* capability of such systems.

Russia's doctrine

In 2010, Russia raised its stated nuclear threshold. Today, its doctrine no longer emphasises nuclear deterrence, but 'strategic deterrence' (nuclear and non-nuclear). As described in the 2014 military doctrine:

> The Russian Federation reserves the right to use nuclear weapons in response to the use of nuclear and other types of weapons of mass destruction against it and (or) its allies, as well as in the event of aggression against the Russian Federation with the use of conventional weapons when the very existence of the state is threatened.[14]

This wording – the same as in 2010 – suggests that NSNW are no longer weapons to compensate for military weakness or reverse the course of a battle, but rather instruments of war termination. That is, they would be used to re-establish deterrence more than they would be used to win the war in military terms. Russian officials have suggested that in 2010 a secret document accompanying the published doctrine was also adopted.[15] But, rather than being a 'secret nuclear doctrine' to contradict the official one, this is much more likely to have been a more detailed version of the official document, for the purposes of planning or programming.

This change is not surprising; indeed, it is consistent with what we know about the evolution of Russian conventional armed forces over the past decade. Moscow feels much more comfortable with its capabilities than it did ten years ago, at the time of the invasion of Georgia.

Does the expression 'escalate to de-escalate' aptly characterise Russian nuclear doctrine? Taken literally – as its original authors (three Russian military experts) suggested in 1999 – there is nothing shocking about this concept.[16] It suggests that, if Russia found itself in a losing situation, the limited use of nuclear weapons would aim at an early termination of the conflict by re-establishing deterrence. Isn't that how NATO and its nuclear powers have traditionally thought about limited use?

In any case, the expression has long since disappeared from official Russian writings. As a matter of fact – and although some Russian officials occasionally used it in public statements in the 2000s – the word 'de-escalation' seems to have appeared only *once* in a Russian official document, a Ministry of Defence report of 2003. That document described four missions for strategic deterrence: 'in peacetime – to prevent power politics and aggression against Russia or its allies; in wartime – de-escalation of aggression; termination of hostilities on conditions acceptable to Russia; impair the adversary's capability to a target level'. The report also included a box defining de-escalation as follows: 'De-escalation of aggression: forcing the enemy to halt military action by a threat to deliver or by actual delivery of strikes of varying intensity with reliance on conventional and (or) nuclear weapons.'[17] (Note, incidentally, that the de-escalatory threat was much broader than nuclear use.) As Olga Oliker, a noted expert on Russia, puts it, 'the evidence that Russia's nuclear strategy is one of "de-escalation", or that it has lowered its threshold for nuclear use, is far from convincing'.

It is thus baffling that the US NPR referred to this expression. At least its drafters were wise enough to be cautious in one of the two references: 'Some in the United States refer to this as Russia's "escalate to de-escalate" doctrine.'[18]

Of course, at the end of the day, it is likely, as a NATO analyst put it after a careful review of Russia's military thinking, that 'Russia's nuclear threshold in a crisis or conflict would be … subject to political decisions in the circumstances of the moment. The bottom line is that Russia's nuclear threshold would be wherever the president, as commander-in-chief, chooses.'[19] However, this last sentence, taken literally, is also true for France, the United Kingdom and the United States.[20]

As for Russian 'nuclear threats', these are generally made by mid-level officials and parliamentarians. By contrast, President Vladimir Putin's own statements on this question are rarely shocking. To give but one example,

Putin's much-discussed 2015 statement about the Crimean crisis was simply an *ex post* declaration stating that Putin had been 'ready' to put nuclear forces on alert if need be.[21] Hardly a threat.

Russia's exercises

Exercises are important for understanding Russia's nuclear posture, because, as the saying goes, Moscow trains as it fights and fights as it trains. So what do large-scale ones such as the *Zapad* (Western front) and *Vostok* (Eastern front) exercises tell us?

They tell us that the last time one of them indisputably included nuclear use was almost 20 years ago, in 1999 (Russia was explicit about it), and that no known theatre military exercise has included nuclear-weapons use for a decade. This is unsurprising: Russia now 'wins' – or at least 'resists' – without nuclear weapons.

It is often claimed that *Zapad* 2009 included a nuclear strike against Europe, but this claim comes from a single source, a report by the Polish magazine *Wprost*. A cable reporting on a NATO debriefing of the exercise shows how the frequent confusion between 'nuclear' and 'nuclear-capable' permits speculation to be reported as fact. The US ambassador to NATO described it as follows: 'The exercise included … missile launches, some of which may have simulated the use of tactical nuclear weapons.'[22] However, as quoted by a respectable expert, this became: 'A Wikileaks document suggests that recent military exercises in the Baltic region and the Russian Far East involved simulated nuclear launches.'[23]

Regarding *Zapad* 2013, an in-depth analysis of the exercise co-published by the Jamestown Foundation – hardly known as a hotbed of Russia appeasers – concludes that 'the limited use of nuclear weapons was not simulated during *Zapad-2013*'.[24] Same for *Zapad* 2017: a conservative US expert on Russian military issues concluded in a long analysis that 'Unlike the earlier *Zapad* exercises, there was no indication that Russia was in a desperate situation when they initiated simulated nuclear strikes. Indeed, they had won'.[25]

There *is* a nuclear dimension overshadowing large-scale exercises such as *Zapad*s. In 2017, for instance, RS-24 intercontinental ballistic missile (ICBM) tests bracketed or bookended *Zapad*: one (silo-based) test took place on 12 September, two days before the exercise; another (mobile) one happened on 20 September, its last day, although there was no indication that it was part of *Zapad*.[26] A ballistic missile was reportedly 'launched' from a Northern Fleet submarine during the defensive phase of *Zapad* 2017, but an official Ukrainian statement – another source not known for disparaging Russian military threats – refers to it as only an 'electronic' launch, or a simulation.[27]

Nuclear exercises may thus be connected with, yet separated from, recent *Zapad*s. (Autumn is generally the season of Russian strategic-nuclear-forces readiness exercises.) As an in-depth Swedish analysis of Russian exercises from 2011 to 2014 put it, 'nuclear forces often, but not always, trained in connection with annual strategic exercises or major surprise inspections'.[28] If so, this suggests an obvious conclusion: Russia would see any conflict with the West as a potentially nuclear one, and Moscow would engage in nuclear signalling during the conflict for the purpose of political coercion.

The psychological dimension of this issue is important. When Russia uses dual-capable bombers such as the *Tupolev*-22, observers often *choose* to see a nuclear strike even though nothing indicates that this is the case. They are subject to confirmation bias. A long-distance strike against Sweden was simulated by such bombers in late March 2013. Its claim to fame stems from the fact that this was – bizarrely – mentioned as a 'nuclear' strike in a NATO secretary-general public report.[29] But there is no evidence that this was the case. Sloppy drafting happens even in respectable organisations. Likewise, the dual-capable *Iskander*-M is often used in exercises – but short-range conventional ballistic missiles have been a fixture of Russian theatre operations from Afghanistan to Georgia and Syria, so there is no intrinsic reason to believe that this is a simulation of nuclear use.

For observers who genuinely think that Russia has a low nuclear threshold and regularly practises theatre-nuclear strikes, analysing its exercising can trigger cognitive dissonance: they can only reconcile the facts with their beliefs by choosing to see a nuclear strike even though nothing indicates that this is the case. This author remembers that in 2015, during a discussion with Western experts, an analyst confessed that having studied Russian large-scale exercises, he 'could not understand' why there seemed to be less and less emphasis on the nuclear dimension. Having unconsciously discarded the hypothesis according to which Russia was increasingly comfortable with its classical forces, he had forgotten the cardinal rule of research sometimes known as Ockham's razor: the simplest explanation is often the correct one. There might be an element of groupthink here.

* * *

Russia is once again proud of its conventional forces, and it wants to be perceived as an equal to the United States. Hence its emphasis on 'strategic deterrence' and the use of long-range conventional cruise missiles such as *Kalibr* in Syria. Moscow is deliberately ambiguous about the characteristics of its forces and the nature of the exercises it conducts: it does not say whether they are nuclear or conventional. This is probably a political strategy. Russia has seen that nuclear ambiguity makes us uncomfortable, and that it potentially complicates our thinking and our planning. So Russia plays with that fact. As Oliker has observed of the nuclear arming of *Iskander-M*, 'the Russians have realized that the prospect makes the United States and its NATO allies nervous'.[30]

To reiterate the point, it would not make sense for Russia to hide a renewed emphasis on nuclear weapons or a low nuclear threshold, because it knows that this is what scares us. Alternative explanations are unsatisfying: it is highly dubious, for instance, that the absence of a nuclear element in recent exercises reflects 'concern over the unfavourable publicity' that it would bring Moscow.[31]

To be clear, this has no direct implications for the Atlantic Alliance's nuclear posture. Irrespective of what Russia's nuclear policy is, NATO needs to have a solid deterrent that includes the possibility to selectively strike Russia to deter Moscow from – and, if needed, respond to – limited nuclear use. Thus, even if the US NPR's diagnosis of Russian nuclear policy is flawed, it does not necessarily follow that its decisions with regard to the improvement of deterrence in Europe are off the mark.

But the Russian nuclear-threat narrative needs to be deconstructed. There are enough good reasons to worry about Russia's behaviour – from its reckless and dangerous military provocations to its violations of arms-control and disarmament treaties, and its temptation to play the nuclear card as a tool of political coercion – to worry about its nuclear weapons for the wrong reasons. Kristen Ven Bruusgaard, a prominent European analyst of Russian military affairs, has it right: 'The fixation with the alleged "lowered nuclear threshold" is a symptom of a larger challenge the West has not had to face for some time: a nuclear-armed adversary with mature capabilities and concepts designed to take advantage of Western weaknesses.'[32]

Acknowledgements

The author would like to thank Isabelle Facon, Thomas Moore and Brad Roberts for their comments on an earlier draft of this article.

Notes

[1] 'Statement of Robert Work, Deputy Secretary of Defense, and Admiral James Winnefeld, Vice-Chairman of the Joint Chiefs of Staff, Before the House Committee on Armed Services', 25 June 2015, p. 4, http://docs.house.gov/meetings/AS/AS00/20150625/103669/HHRG-114-AS00-Wstate-WorkR-20150625.pdf.

[2] Admiral Cecil D. Haney, remarks to the Project on Nuclear Issues Capstone Conference, Offutt Air Force Base, Nebraska, 13 April 2016, http://www.stratcom.mil/Media/Speeches/Article/986478/project-on-nuclear-issues-capstone-conference/.

[3] Jens Stoltenberg, 'Secretary General's Annual Report 2015', NATO, 28 January 2016, p. 19, https://www.nato.int/nato_static_fl2014/assets/pdf/pdf_2016_01/20160128_SG_AnnualReport_2015_en.pdf.

[4] Matthew Kroenig, 'The Case for Tactical US Nukes', *Wall Street Journal*, 24 January 2018, https://www.wsj.com/articles/the-case-for-tactical-u-s-nukes-1516836395.

[5] Franklin C. Miller, 'The Nuclear Posture Review: Fiction and Fact', Real Clear Defense, https://www.realcleardefense.com/articles/2018/02/20/the_nuclear_posture_review__fiction_and_fact_113080.html.

[6] Gustav Gressel, 'The Draft US Nuclear Posture Review Is Not As Crazy As It Sounds', European Council on Foreign Relations, 19 January 2018, http://www.ecfr.eu/article/commentary_the_draft_us_nuclear_posture_review_is_not_as_crazy_as_it_sounds.

[7] US Department of Defense, 'Nuclear Posture Review 2018' [hereafter 2018 NPR], February 2018, pp. XI–XII, 7, 9 and 30, https://media.defense.gov/2018/Feb/02/2001872886/-1/-1/1/2018-NUCLEAR-POSTURE-REVIEW-FINAL-REPORT.PDF.

8   Igor Sutyagin, 'Atomic Accounting: A New Estimate of Russia's Non-Strategic Nuclear Forces', Royal United Services Institute, 2012, https://rusi.org/sites/default/files/201211_op_atomic_accounting.pdf.

9   US Department of Defense, 'Report of the Secretary of Defense Task Force on DoD Nuclear Weapons Management, Phase II: Review of the DoD Nuclear Mission', December 2008, p. 59, https://www.defense.gov/Portals/1/Documents/pubs/PhaseIIReportFinal.pdf.

10 For background, see Nikolai Sokov, 'A Second Sighting of Russian Tactical Nukes in Kaliningrad', James Martin Center for Nonproliferation Studies, Middlebury Institute of International Studies at Monterey, 15 February 2011, https://www.nonproliferation.org/a-second-sighting-of-russian-tactical-nukes-in-kaliningrad-2/.

11 Sutyagin, 'Atomic Accounting: A New Estimate of Russia's Non-Strategic Nuclear Forces'.

12 See Central Intelligence Agency, 'Evidence of Russian Development of New Subkiloton Nuclear Warheads', 30 August 2000, https://www.cia.gov/library/readingroom/docs/DOC_0001260463.pdf; and Jeffrey G. Lewis, 'Russian Tactical Nuclear Weapons', Arms Control Wonk, 3 December 2010, https://www.armscontrolwonk.com/archive/203309/russian-tactical-nuclear-weapons/.

13 Olga Oliker and Andrey Bakilitsky, 'The Nuclear Posture Review and Russian "De-Escalation": A Dangerous Solution to a Nonexistent Problem', War on the Rocks, 20 February 2018, https://warontherocks.com/2018/02/nuclear-posture-review-russian-de-escalation-dangerous-solution-nonexistent-problem/.

14 'Voennaya Doktrina Rossiiskoi Federatsii 2014' [The 2014 Military Doctrine of the Russian Federation], paragraph 27, http://Kremlin.ru/media/events/files/41d527556bec8deb3530.pdf.

15 See Mark B. Schneidet, 'Escalate to De-Escalate', *Proceedings*, vol. 143, no. 2, February 2017, https://www.usni.org/magazines/proceedings/2017-02/escalate-de-escalate.

16 Major General V.I. Levshin, Colonel A.V. Nedelin and Colonel M.E. Sosnovskii, 'O primenenii yadernogo oruzhiya dlya deeskalatsii voennykh deistvii' [On the use of nuclear weapons for the purposes of de-escalation of military confrontation], *Voennaya Mysl'* [Military Thought], Moscow, January 1999, http://dlib.eastview.com/browse/doc/2449543.

17 'Aktoual'nye zadatchi razvitiia vooroujennykh sil Rossiiskoï Federatsii' [Priority Tasks for the Development of the Russian Federation's Armed Forces], October 2003. For the English text, see p. 70 of http://red-stars.org/doctrine.pdf.

18 Olga Oliker, 'Russia's Nuclear Doctrine. What We Know, What We Don't, and What That Means', Center for Strategic and Security Studies, May 2016, p. 2, ttps://csis-prod.s3.amazonaws.com/s3fs-public/publication/160504_Oliker_RussiasNuclearDoctrine_Web.pdf.

19 Dave Johnson, 'Russia's Conventional Precision Strike Capabilities, Regional Crises, and Nuclear Thresholds',

Livermore Papers on Global Security, no. 3, February 2018, p. 69, https://cgsr.llnl.gov/content/assets/docs/Precision-Strike-Capabilities-report-v3-7.pdf.

20 Johnson rightly notes, in this regard, that the mention of 'the State' (*gosudarstvo*) should be understood as state institutions or the normal functioning of the central government. See David Johnson, 'Nuclear Weapons in Russia's Approach to Conflict', *Recherches & Documents*, no. 06/16, Fondation pour la Recherche Stratégique, November 2016, p. 61.

21 'Ukraine Conflict: Putin "Was Ready for Nuclear Alert"', BBC, 15 March 2015, http://www.bbc.com/news/world-europe-31899680.

22 'NATO–RUSSIA: NAC DISCUSSES RUSSIAN MILITARY EXERCISES', cable, 23 November 2009, available at https://www.aftenposten.no/norge/i/BlJ7l/23112009-NATO-RUSSIA-NAC-DISCUSSES-RUSSIAN-MILITARY-EXERCISES.

23 Sutyagin, 'Atomic Accounting', p. 54.

24 Liudas Zdanavičius and Matthew Czekaj (eds), 'Russia's Zapad 2013 Military Exercise: Lessons for Baltic Regional Security', Jamestown Foundation, December 2015, p. 6, https://jamestown.org/wp-content/uploads/2015/12/Zapad-2013-Full-online-final.pdf.

25 Mark B. Schneider, 'Zapad-2017: A Major Russian War Against NATO, Again', *Real Clear Defense*, 6 October 2017, https://www.realcleardefense.com/articles/2017/10/06/zapad-2017_a_major_russian_war_against_nato_again_112441.html.

26 *Ibid.*

27 See Johnson, 'Russia's Conventional Precision Strike Capabilities, Regional Crises, and Nuclear Thresholds', p. 88; and National Security and Defense Council of Ukraine, 'Olexandr Turchynov: Missile-Nuclear Finale of the "Zapad-2017"', http://www.rnbo.gov.ua/en/news/2887.html.

28 Johan Norberg, 'Training to Fight: Russia's Major Military Exercises 2011–2014', Totalförsvarets forskningsinstitut [Swedish Defense Research Agency], December 2015, p. 61, https://www.foi.se/reportsummary?reportNo=FOI-R--4128--SE.

29 Stoltenberg, 'Secretary General's Annual Report 2015', p. 19.

30 Oliker, 'Russia's Nuclear Doctrine', p. 11.

31 Zdanavičius and Czekaj (eds), 'Russia's Zapad 2013 Military Exercise', p. 9. A possible explanation would be fear of pre-emption; but nothing indicates that this is actually the case.

32 Kristin Ven Bruusgaard, 'The Myth of Russia's Lowered Nuclear Threshold', War On The Rocks, 22 September 2017, https://warontherocks.com/2017/09/the-myth-of-russias-lowered-nuclear-threshold/.

Strategic Stability, Uncertainty and the Future of Arms Control

Heather Williams

Reactions to the 2018 US Nuclear Posture Review (NPR) have ranged from highlighting its continuity with the views of the Obama administration,[1] on the one hand, to warning that it is 'hastening the rise of a more dangerous world' by increasing reliance on nuclear weapons, on the other.[2] One analyst, somewhere in between these two poles, acknowledges a continuity of doctrine in practical terms, but argues that the 'tone' and spirit of US nuclear policy has changed.[3]

The true picture is perhaps more subtle. It is not so much that the United States is changing the way it thinks about nuclear weapons themselves; instead, the divergence from previous policy reflects changes in how the US thinks about its broader strategic environment. In particular, the NPR shows the United States coming to terms with two developments: Russian provocations in Europe that cross strategic domains, and the implications of an era of rapid technological evolution.

One significant shift in the NPR is an adjustment to how the United States defines strategic stability, a Cold War concept typically associated with maintaining a survivable nuclear second-strike capability. This is not just an academic point; America's vision of what undermines or strengthens stability drives its force posture and is the underlying philosophy behind its approach to deterring adversaries and assuring allies.

Heather Williams is a Lecturer in the Defence Studies Department and the Centre for Science and Security Studies at King's College London.

Survival | vol. 60 no. 2 | April–May 2018 | pp. 45–54   DOI 10.1080/00396338.2018.1448561

With this NPR, the United States' approach to strategic stability now more closely resembles that of Russia. This includes non-nuclear capabilities such as advanced conventional weapons, and emerging technology, especially cyber capabilities, as factors affecting crisis stability and arms-race stability. This new concept of strategic stability is applied throughout the NPR to various aspects of US nuclear posture, including deterrence and assurance.

There is a clear gap, however, in thinking about what this means for arms control beyond existing agreements. To some extent this is understandable; the NPR begins from the premise that the strategic environment is defined by uncertainty and the need for flexibility. Nonetheless, this new vision of strategic stability suggests serious challenges for the future of arms control. The United States is implicitly acknowledging Russia's long-held argument that non-nuclear forces and the overall offence–defence balance are essential to strategic stability. It will be difficult for Washington to continue to avoid arms-control limitations on these capabilities. The challenge is to create an updated concept of arms control to incorporate new technologies, crossing domains. And among these technologies, perhaps the most important to future arms-control agreements, at least in the medium to long term, is missile defence.

An age of uncertainty

The NPR is one of a number of key strategy documents, alongside the National Security Strategy (NSS) and the Missile Defense Review, in which incoming administrations can describe their view of the geopolitical environment and define America's role in the world. The 2001 NPR, under the Bush administration, came on the heels of the 9/11 terrorist attacks and described an increasingly complex world defined by threats from non-state actors as well as from peer competitors. Nine years later, the 2010 Obama administration NPR came amid a 'reset' in US–Russia relations, when a conflict of the sort seen in Ukraine four years later seemed highly unlikely, and both Russia and the US considered arms control to be in their interests. In other words, these documents are in large part a product of their immediate context.

The 2018 NPR describes a world defined by strategic uncertainty deriving from changes in technology and geopolitics. Uncertainty, in turn, according to the NPR, necessitates flexibility, diversity and resilience in America's own strategic capabilities. This theme was present in the National Security Strategy, released in late 2017, which stated: 'We face simultaneous threats from different actors across multiple arenas – all accelerated by technology.'[4] The emphasis on geopolitical uncertainty is largely a response to Russian actions in eastern Ukraine and Crimea, which came as a strategic shock to the Obama administration; and, as an example of the problems posed by rapid innovation in technology with military application, the NPR spends a great deal of time on cyber threats to nuclear command, control and communication.[5]

Another theme common to the NPR and the NSS is that of an America which feels it has been taken advantage of. The NSS states that

> These competitions [with Russia and China] require the United States to rethink the policies of the past two decades – policies based on the assumption that engagement with rivals and their inclusion in international institutions and global commerce would turn them into benign actors and trustworthy partners. For the most part, this premise turned out to be false.[6]

The NPR applies this theme to arms control. 'Moscow', it says, 'must understand that the United States will not forever endure Russia's continuing non-compliance.'[7] Recent attempts at cooperation were instead perceived as weakness, so the United States must realign itself with a policy of 'peace through strength', which means diversifying US capabilities, responding to Russian aggression and modernisation, and maintaining scepticism about additional partnership.

This is not only due to a change in administration. The NPR is right to observe that the world has changed, and it is reasonable to argue that America's strategic forces must change with it. The NPR's authors believe that the United States should learn from what has happened since the last NPR – and the lesson is that America should be ready for strategic surprise.

An IISS analyst called this vision 'nervous';[8] the NPR calls it 'hedging'.[9] Whatever the right word, America is keeping its options open.

Much criticism of the NPR has focused on the relatively technical matter of whether a new low-yield warhead for submarine-launched ballistic missiles (SLBMs) and a new sea-launched cruise missile (SLCM) will be destabilising.[10] A broader and more fundamental debate, however, concerns whether the NPR is exaggerating the Russian threat. The Polish analyst Lukasz Kulesa argues, for example, that 'there is little to suggest that the Russian leadership would pursue a high-risk strategy of limited nuclear use just because there was a non-strategic weapons capability gap on the US/NATO side'.[11] But it is this circumspect and complex view of the world that shapes the NPR.

Strategic stability in the twenty-first century

Strategic stability is typically defined as encompassing crisis stability (that is, whether there is an incentive for one side to strike first) and arms-race stability (whether one side believes it can outsprint the other in technical terms). The concept has been subject to considerable challenge; many experts consider it outdated – a Cold War relic – or focused on technical matters at the expense of the political.[12] In a 2013 volume on the topic, for example, James Acton suggested that, in addition to its traditional definition, the term could also be used to describe the absence of conflict between nuclear powers or, even more broadly, a global order characterised by 'peaceful and harmonious relations'.[13] The NPR neither discards the concept of strategic stability nor embraces this ambitious meaning. Instead, it keeps the capability-focused framework and expands its scope.

In hindsight, this NPR might turn out to be remembered best not for its introduction of additional limited nuclear options, but as the moment when the United States finally changed its official definition of and approach towards strategic stability. For decades, the concept has been interpreted in US strategy to require survivable second-strike forces, such that the nuclear arsenal is sufficiently large and secure to ensure that a conflict will not escalate and that deterrence will hold due to the threat of American retaliation. The NPR is driven by a different logic: 'They [potential adversaries] must understand that there are no possible benefits from non-nuclear aggression or limited nuclear escalation. Correcting any such misperceptions is now critical to maintaining strategic stability in Europe and Asia.'[14] The thinking beyond this broader approach is that a more diverse set of factors affect whether crises can escalate, potentially to nuclear use, and whether states engage in arms races. This expands beyond a consideration for nuclear balance of forces to incorporate non-nuclear threats across domains, including the potential impact of defences.

In this regard, the United States is to some extent playing catch-up with Russia, which has for years attempted to incorporate the topic of defences into strategic-stability discussions with the United States. Moreover, Russian 'strategic deterrence', as aptly summarised by Kristin Ven Bruusgaard, includes nuclear, non-nuclear and non-military components, in stark contrast to America's stubborn insistence that it should only include offensive nuclear capabilities.[15]

The US shift is the culmination of a gradual trend rather than an aberration. Thomas Schelling's essay in the 2013 volume on strategic stability acknowledged the challenges of its application because, as he put it, 'the world is so much changed, so much more complicated, so multivariate, so unpredictable, involving so many nations and cultures and languages in nuclear relationships, many of them asymmetric'.[16] Prior to the NPR, and even during the Obama administration, there were indications of a changing US approach, signalling a broadening out to include defensive and non-nuclear capabilities. In 2014 congressional testimony, for example, deputy assistant secretary of defense Elaine Bunn stated: 'We would welcome the opportunity to take additional steps with Russia to enhance strategic stability, including exploring opportunities for missile defense cooperation and further nuclear reductions.'[17]

A broader approach to strategic stability has implications for the implementation of deterrence and assurance. The NPR fleshes this out in at least three ways. Firstly, the document's declaratory policy expands the role of nuclear deterrence to include 'significant non-nuclear strategic attacks', which include, 'but are not limited to, attacks on the U.S., allied, or partner civilian population or infrastructure, and attacks on U.S. or allied nuclear forces, their command and control, or warning and attack assessment capabilities'.[18] The 2010 NPR had roughly similar language and did not restrict nuclear weapons to the sole purpose of deterring nuclear use; however, the 2018 document is more ambiguous and does not tie negative security assurances to compliance with the Non-Proliferation Treaty, as stipulated in the 2010 NPR.

Secondly, the new concept of strategic stability leads to an emphasis on tailoring: 'Tailored deterrence strategies are designed to communicate the costs of aggression to potential adversaries, taking into consideration how they uniquely calculate costs and risks.'[19] This includes shaping capabilities and postures to different actors, situations and means of communication.[20] Similarly, assurance can also be tailored, to account for different threat perceptions among America's various allies.[21]

Thirdly, the NPR explores the intersection of nuclear weapons with emerging technology, such as cyber threats to America's nuclear command and control, and space-based assets. The idea that such attacks would merit a nuclear response is controversial; after all, if no, or very few, people are killed, is nuclear retaliation really credible?[22] But the issue is emphasised in the NPR because the threats to the United States considered strategic now cross domains, and non-nuclear threats have a potential impact on the capability and credibility of America's nuclear deterrence. Strategic stability is no longer a purely nuclear business.

If the new approach to strategic stability is defensible, however, it is worth noting that it has implications beyond deterrence. Now that the United States has shifted its definition closer to that of Russia, it will impact their relationship not only as peer competitors, but also in cooperative efforts.

The arms-control problem

While the NPR considers the implications of the new strategic stability on many aspects of America's nuclear posture, the same consideration is not given to arms control. To some extent, this is unsurprising: arms control is typically associated with *limiting* capabilities, while this NPR is about hedging. The NPR does not wholly ignore arms control, but rather argues that 'further progress is difficult to envision' because of a combination of alleged Russian violations of existing treaties and geopolitical uncertainty.

The NPR outlines the potential benefits of arms control: transparency, predictability, avoiding miscalculation, risk reduction, communication and sharing of best practices.[23] And it does commit the United States to future arms control with Russia to strengthen strategic stability. Yet it does so without apparent consideration for how arms control might actually help to reduce the uncertainty that the US fears, and increase the flexibility it seeks.

Differing definitions of strategic stability have historically complicated US–Russia arms control. The preamble to the 2010 New START Treaty offers a prime example:

> Recognizing the existence of the interrelationship between strategic offensive arms and strategic defensive arms, that this interrelationship will become more important as strategic nuclear arms are reduced, and that current strategic defensive arms do not undermine the viability and effectiveness of the strategic offensive arms of the Parties.[24]

Following the treaty's conclusion, the American negotiators and senior officials made it very clear in congressional ratification debates that in no way did this language limit America's missile-defence plans.[25] Meanwhile, Russia's ratification debate stressed that the language *did* limit US missile defences and reserved the right to withdraw from the treaty if these were expanded.[26] The next round of arms control will not be able to skirt around this difference.

And herein lies the arms-control problem inherent to the NPR. By expanding its definition of strategic stability to more closely align with that of Russia, it will be increasingly difficult for the United States to avoid incorporating missile defence and advanced conventional weapons into arms-control agreements – something the United States has rejected for decades.[27] This new strategic stability could subject the United States to playing by Russia's rules at the negotiating table.

So is arms control still a tool for promoting strategic stability? What type of arms control would contribute to the new, broader strategic stability? And, perhaps most challenging, where do American and Russian interests overlap on arms control in this age of uncertainty?

Arms control can contribute to cross-domain strategic stability if it, too, adapts and expands. This could include traditional bilateral strategic agreements between the United States and Russia, but it should also involve risk reduction and crisis communication. For the United States, arms control offers an opportunity to increase its own flexibility by restraining Russia. If the US is truly concerned about the expansion of Russia's offensive strategic and tactical weapons, and its anti-access/area-denial capabilities, then arms control may be the best option for imposing limitations. But Russia will only be convinced to give up some of its current capabilities if it is getting something in return.[28] Moreover, arms control can provide greater transparency into Russia's arsenal, again allowing the United States to better tailor its own capabilities and, potentially, save money.

The only remaining 'low-hanging' fruit in arms control is to extend the 2010 New START agreement. But there are at least three follow-on options for arms control that could serve US interests. Firstly, the United States and Russia could pursue a new arms-control agreement linking strategic offensive and strategic defensive systems, similar to the joint arrival of Strategic Arms Limitation Talks (SALT) and the 1972 Anti-Ballistic Missile (ABM) Treaty. While offensive and defensive systems may ultimately be regulated separately, discussions around the issue of the offense–defence balance can occur concurrently.

Secondly, the United States could make use of arms control as a means of hedging against threats from emerging technologies, particularly cyber capabilities. The United States, Russia and China could, for example, sign a joint declaration, similar to the 1990 US–Soviet declaration on future negotiations on nuclear and space weapons, stating they will not use cyber attacks against each other's nuclear command, control and communications. Such statements cannot be verified, of course, but they provide an opportunity for dialogue and trust-building, and could potentially reduce uncertainty and instability during a crisis.

Lastly, asymmetry across domains in the new strategic stability can be reflected in asymmetric arms control, an idea which can be defined as the management of current and future weapons across a range of domains. The SALT and ABM talks are one example of mixing capabilities in arms limitations. Another example, which I have suggested elsewhere,[29] is trading reductions in Russian tactical nuclear weapons for legally binding limits on American missile defence. A more short-term, and perhaps more likely, example is reciprocal inspections of systems that each side alleges are in violation of the Intermediate-Range Nuclear Forces (INF) Treaty. This would entail Russia visiting missile-defence sites in Europe to confirm interceptors are not nuclear-capable, and Americans inspecting Russian cruise missiles.[30]

This call to arms control comes with obvious challenges. Most notably, at present it is extremely hard to envisage further progress until disputes around compliance with the INF Treaty are resolved. Additionally, Russia can be expected to distrust any American overtures about returning to arms control, especially if it includes missile defence, given America's withdrawal from the ABM Treaty in 2002 and a prevailing sentiment in Moscow that arms control typically takes advantage of Russia. Any limitations on America's missile-defence capabilities, particularly if they require inspection, will be controversial among allies. And, on the American side, new initiatives on arms control might be a topic that has to wait for a new administration. That does not mean that thinking cannot begin now.

Notes

1   John R. Harvey, Franklin C. Miller, Keith B. Payne and Bradley H. Roberts, 'Continuity and Change in U.S. Nuclear Policy', *Real Clear Defense*, 7 February 2018.

2   Adam Mount, 'Trump's Troubling Nuclear Plan', *Foreign Affairs*, 2 February 2018.

3   Anna Peczeli, 'Continuity and Change in the Trump Administration's Nuclear Posture Review', *Bulletin of Atomic Scientists*, 20 February 2018.

4   White House, 'National Security Strategy of the United States of America' [hereafter NSS], December 2017, p. 26.

5   James Acton, 'Command and Control in the Nuclear Posture Review: Right Problem, Wrong Solution', War on the Rocks, 5 February 2018.

6   NSS, p. 4.

7   US Department of Defense, 'Nuclear Posture Review 2018' [hereafter NPR], February 2018, p. 74.

8   Matthew Harries, 'A Nervous Nuclear Posture Review', *Survival*, vol. 60, no. 2, April–May 2018.

9   NPR, p. 20.

10 Gustav Gressel, 'The Draft US Nuclear Posture Review Is Not As Crazy As It Sounds', European Council on Foreign Relations, 19 January 2018.

11 Lukasz Kulesa, 'The 2018 US Nuclear Posture Review: A Headache for

Europe', European Leadership Network, 6 February 2018.

12 See, for example, Nancy Gallagher, 'Re-thinking the Unthinkable: Arms Control in the Twenty-First Century', *Nonproliferation Review*, vol. 22, no. 3–4, 2015, pp. 469–98.

13 James Acton, 'Reclaiming Strategic Stability', in Elbridge A. Colby and Michael S. Gerson (eds), *Strategic Stability: Contending Interpretations* (Carlisle, PA: U.S. Army War College Press, 2013), p. 117.

14 NPR, p. vii.

15 Kristin Ven Bruusgaard, 'Russian Strategic Deterrence', *Survival*, vol. 58, no. 4, August–September 2016, pp. 7–26.

16 Thomas Schelling, 'Foreword', in Colby and Gerson (eds), *Strategic Stability*, p. vii.

17 M. Elaine Bunn, 'Statement before the House Committee on Arms Services Subcommittee on Strategic Forces', 8 April 2014.

18 NPR, p. 21.

19 *Ibid.*, p. 26.

20 See, for example, M. Elaine Bunn, 'Can Deterrence Be Tailored', *INSS Strategic Forum*, no. 225, January 2007.

21 Heather Williams, 'Tailoring Assurance: Geopolitical Uncertainty amidst NATO–Russia Competition', *IFRI Proliferation Paper*, forthcoming.

22 See, for example, Acton, 'Reclaiming Strategic Stability'.

23 NPR, p. xvi.

24 'Treaty Between the United States of America and the Russian Federation on Measures for the Further Reduction and Limitation of Strategic Offensive Arms', 2010.

25 See, for example, Robert M. Gates, 'Statement before the Senate Foreign Relations Committee Hearing on the New START Treaty', 18 May 2010. Gates said: 'First, the treaty will not constrain the United States from deploying the most effective missile defenses possible, nor impose additional costs or barriers on those defenses ... We made this clear to the Russians in a unilateral statement made in connection with the treaty.'

26 Anatoly Diakov, Eugene Miasnikov and Timur Kadyshev, 'Nuclear Reduction After New START: Obstacles and Opportunities', *Arms Control Today*, 3 May 2011.

27 An important exception to this was the New START Treaty, which would have covered strategic conventional weapons in delivery-vehicle counting rules, but America's Conventional Prompt Global Strike programme is not likely to be completed before New START expires. See, for example, James M. Acton and Lora Saalman, 'Conventional Prompt Global Strike and Strategic Stability', Carnegie Endowment for International Peace, 21 February 2012.

28 Olga Oliker and Andrey Baklitskiy, 'The Nuclear Posture Review and Russian "De-Escalation": A Dangerous Solution to a Nonexistent Problem', War on the Rocks, 20 February 2018.

29 See, for example, Heather Williams, 'From Reykjavik to Twitter: A Toolkit for Avoiding Instability in U.S.–Russia Relations', presentation to US–Russia Track 1.5 Dialogues, Moscow, 19 October 2017, http://www. nonproliferation.org/wp-content/ uploads/2017/11/us-russian-dialogue-on-strategic-stability__avoiding-insta-bility-heather-williams.pdf.

30 James M. Acton, 'A Strategy for (Modestly Increasing the Chance of) Saving the INF Treaty', *Russia Matters*, 11 May 2017.

A Nervous Nuclear Posture Review

Matthew Harries

The 2018 US Nuclear Posture Review (NPR), released on 2 February, contains troubling recommendations to broaden the role of nuclear weapons in American strategy, but omits more radical options that some observers had anticipated. Overall, it feels more swamp than Trump – that is, it gives the impression of having been written by informed professionals within the mainstream of US national-security thinking, albeit clearly at the hawkish end of that spectrum.

The NPR's most eye-catching feature is the call for the United States to develop new nuclear capabilities to deter limited nuclear use by others. The NPR calls for a low-yield warhead on the existing *Trident* D-5 submarine-launched ballistic missile as an interim measure, and a new sea-launched nuclear cruise missile for the longer term.

The idea behind these new weapons is to solve an apparent deterrence problem that for the last few years has been keeping Western defence planners up at night. The problem is this: what happens if an enemy country, having started a conflict in its near abroad, uses the threat of limited nuclear use to get the US and its allies to back down? Worse, what if that country actually carries out a small-scale nuclear strike and threatens more of the same if the US chooses to fight on?

The enemy country in this scenario is usually Russia, and the conflict is typically a small to medium-scale war in a Baltic state. What worries some

Matthew Harries is Managing Editor of *Survival*, and Senior Fellow for Transatlantic Affairs at the IISS. An earlier version of this commentary appeared on Politics and Strategy, the *Survival* editors' blog.

Survival | vol. 60 no. 2 | April–May 2018 | pp. 55–57   DOI 10.1080/00396338.2018.1448562

officials is the perception that the US cannot deter such threats because it lacks an equivalent capability to match Russia, which has clung on to many hundreds of short-range and low-yield nuclear weapons, and is busy developing and deploying short- and medium-range missiles capable of carrying conventional and nuclear warheads. US officials fear that they could be left with two bad options: either backing down and giving Russia the huge victory of a politically broken NATO, or escalating to mutually catastrophic strategic nuclear war.

The concern is not totally baseless. Russia has annexed a portion of a neighbouring country and continues to wage limited war against it. Russian President Vladimir Putin has repeatedly reminded the world of Russia's nuclear potential. And Russia has in the past envisaged, in official policy, the possibility of limited nuclear use along roughly these lines, although in public doctrine published since 2010 it has not done so. It is by no means clear that Russian leaders are actively considering nuclear use as a way of ending a limited conventional conflict – but it is not impossible to imagine a crisis in which the thought might cross their mind.

Wrong answer

If the NPR's diagnosis is understandable, however, the prescription is deeply misguided. For one thing, the military rationale for new limited nuclear options is dubious. The US already has low-yield nuclear warheads that can be delivered on gravity bombs (including those hosted by NATO countries) and air-launched cruise missiles. There might be some added theoretical value of a sea-launched nuclear option in terms of its ability to get through Russian air defences, but not enough to justify the political and monetary costs. Those costs will no doubt be on Congress's mind in deciding whether to green-light new nuclear capabilities – and whether or not anything gets built, American adversaries have been handed an easy talking point to justify their own nuclear upgrades.

More importantly, NATO's deterrence task is primarily conventional, not nuclear. The Baltic states border Russia, not the United States, and they are an awfully long way from the bulk of NATO ground troops. Preventing Russia from successfully pulling off a limited incursion, and reinforcing front-line forces in a developing crisis or war, are grave and ongoing challenges that new nuclear weapons do little to address.

In any event, the toughest problem the US and NATO face is political, and well beyond the scope of the NPR's mandate. Defence planners ultimately worry about the limited-war contingency because they fear that the West does not have the guts to risk a serious war with Russia in order to defend the eastern allies. This problem predates the Trump administration, but having a president who crudely derides US partners surely does not help. Proposing new nuclear weapons is perhaps a natural answer for nuclear-weapons specialists to offer – but it does not make for effective US strategy.

As a foreign observer, what I find most surprising about the call for new low-yield nuclear weapons is how nervous it shows the United States to be. If it is true that Russia's supposed strategy is concerning, it is also true that for Russia to actually execute this strategy would be a thoroughly stupid idea. Does Russia really want to become the first country to use nuclear weapons since 1945, all for the sake of capturing a slice of the Baltics? Securing Crimea and spoiling Ukraine's Western shift was one thing – but risking an honest-to-God war with the United States just to prove that NATO's Article V is shaky?

Russia has attacked the foundations of post-Cold War order in Europe, and has provided shelter and comfort to a chemical-weapons user in the Middle East. Getting tough is not necessarily a bad idea. But Russia is a threat that a confident United States – vastly more powerful in economic terms, and still superior in military terms, especially in the aggregate – should be able to handle without recourse to new nuclear hardware. This NPR, along with the debate over preventive war with North Korea, suggests that the United States is not sure it can still deter weaker adversaries. Here's hoping America holds its nerve.

Noteworthy

35
Number of countries that registered gains in political rights and civil liberties in 2017, according to Freedom House

71
Number of countries that experienced a net decline in political rights and civil liberties

62
Number of countries that have registered gains since 2006

113
Number of countries that have experienced a decline[1]

26
Percentage of British students who say they would vote to leave the European Union if a second Brexit referendum were held

64
Percentage of retired people who say so[2]

0.02%
Mortality rate for children under four in Venezuela in 2012

2%
Morality rate in 2015[3]

Bad neighbours

'Let us promote contact, travel, cooperation and exchange between the north and the south on a wide scale to remove mutual misunderstanding and distrust and make all the fellow countrymen fulfill their responsibility and role as the driving force of national reunification!'
North Korea releases an 'appeal to all Koreans' to work toward the reunification of the two Koreas in the run-up to the 2018 Winter Olympics in Pyeongchang, South Korea.[4]

'Young people seem to think of North Korea as strangers who barge into their party bringing with them nothing but empty spoons.'
Former South Korean foreign minister Kim Sung-hwan comments on resistance among South Koreans to the announcement that North and South Korea would send a joint women's hockey team to the Pyeongchang games.[5]

$225 million
Minimum net worth in 2017 dollars required to join the *Forbes* list of the 400 wealthiest Americans in 1982, the first year the list was published[6]

$2 billion
Minimum net worth required in 2017[7]

DOI 10.1080/00396338.2018.1448573

£350 million

Amount the pro-Brexit campaign claimed was being sent by the UK to the EU every week, and that could be saved if the country left the union

£350 million

Amount that the Brexit vote has cost the UK economy per week, according to research carried out by the *Financial Times*[8]

700 gigawatt hours

Quantity of energy consumed annually by homes in Iceland

840 gigawatt hours

Quantity of energy Iceland's Bitcoin-mining data centres are expected to consume annually[9]

19,628

Number of applications for asylum in Japan in 2017

20

Number of applications accepted by the Japanese government[10]

12

Number of aircraft in Qatar's air force

84

Number of aircraft Qatar has ordered from the US and Europe since June 2017[11]

A longer walk to freedom

'No life should be lost in my name. The ANC should never be divided in my name. I have therefore come to the decision to resign as president of the republic with immediate effect.'

Jacob Zuma resigns as president of South Africa on 14 February 2018 after facing accusations of corruption.[12]

'This is not yet *uhuru* (freedom).'

Cyril Ramaphosa takes over as president.[13]

4.4

Percentage of the global population accounted for by Americans

42

Percentage of global gun ownership accounted for by Americans[14]

Eyes only for the dollar

'My father sees one colour: green.'

Eric Trump, son of US President Donald Trump, denies his father is a racist after reports emerged that the president had used vulgar language to describe several Central American and African countries.[15]

Sources

1 Freedom House, 'Freedom in the World 2018: Democracy in Crisis', https://freedomhouse.org/report/freedom-world/freedom-world-2018#fiw-key-findings.

2 'How Britain's Views Have Changed – Full Brexit Poll Results', *Guardian*, 26 January 2018, https://www.theguardian.com/politics/ng-interactive/2018/jan/26/guardian-icm-brexit-poll-full-results.

3 Meridith Kohut and Isayen Herrera, 'Venezuela Children Starving', *New York Times*, 17 December 2017, https://www.nytimes.com/interactive/2017/12/17/world/americas/venezuela-children-starving.html?hp&action=click&pgtype=Homepage&clickSource=story-heading&module=photo-spot-region&region=top-news&WT.nav=top-news&_r=1.

4 'DPRK Joint Conference Calls for Making This Year Noteworthy in History of Nation', KCNA Watch, 25 January 2018, https://kcnawatch.co/newstream/1516833076-923326330/dprk-joint-conference-calls-for-making-this-year-noteworthy-in-history-of-nation/.

5 Choe Sang-Hun, 'Olympic Dreams of a United Korea? Many in the South Say, "No, Thanks"', *New York Times*, 28 January 2018, https://www.nytimes.com/2018/01/28/world/asia/koreas-olympics-reunification.html?hp&action=click&pgtype=Homepage&clickSource=story-heading&module=first-column-region&region=top-news&WT.nav=top-news.

6 Carl O'Donnell, 'What Does It Take to Make the Forbes 400? Increasing More and More', *Forbes*, 3 October 2014, https://www.forbes.com/sites/carlodonnell/2014/10/03/what-does-it-take-to-make-the-forbes-400-increasingly-more-and-more/#7dbba11dbbd4.

7 Luisa Kroll, 'Forbes 400 2017: Meet the Richest People in America', *Forbes*, 17 October 2017, https://www.forbes.com/sites/luisakroll/2017/10/17/forbes-400-2017-americas-richest-people-bill-gates-jeff-bezos-mark-zuckerberg-donald-trump/#26b35c635ed5.

8 Chris Giles, 'The Real Price of Brexit Begins to Emerge', *Financial Times*, 18 December 2017, https://www.ft.com/content/e3b29230-db5f-11e7-a039-c64b1c09b482?emailId=5a388bd46c4d3e0004e6d43b&segmentId=22011ee7-896a-8c4c-22a0-7603348b7f22.

9 Chris Baraniuk, 'Bitcoin Energy Use in Iceland Set to Overtake Homes, Says Local Firm', BBC News, 12 February 2018, http://www.bbc.co.uk/news/technology-43030677.

10 Justin McCurry, 'Japan Had 20,000 Applications for Asylum in 2017. It Accepted 20', *Guardian*, 16 February 2018, https://www.theguardian.com/world/2018/feb/16/japan-asylum-applications-2017-accepted-20.

11 Figures derived from IISS, *Military Balance Plus*. See also Declan Walsh, 'Tiny, Wealthy Qatar Goes Its Own Way, and Pays for It', *New York Times*, 22 January 2018, https://www.nytimes.com/2018/01/22/world/middleeast/qatar-saudi-emir-boycott.html?hp&action=click&pgtype=Homepage&clickSource=story-heading&module=photo-spot-region&region=top-news&WT.nav=top-news.

12 Jason Burke, 'Jacob Zuma Resigns as South Africa's President on Eve of No-Confidence Vote', *Guardian*, 14 February 2018, https://www.theguardian.com/world/2018/feb/14/jacob-zuma-resigns-south-africa-president.

13 Jason Burke, 'Ramaphosa Vows Anti-Corruption Drive as He Takes Over in South Africa', *Guardian*, 15 February 2018, https://www.theguardian.com/world/2018/feb/15/cyril-ramaphosa-to-be-elected-president-of-south-africa-jacob-zuma.

14 Max Fisher and Josh Keller, 'What Explains U.S. Mass Shootings? International Comparisons Suggest an Answer', *New York Times*, 7 November 2017, https://www.nytimes.com/2017/11/07/world/americas/mass-shootings-us-international.html?hp&action=click&pgtype=Homepage&clickSource=story-heading&module=b-lede-package-region&region=top-news&WT.nav=top-news.

15 Fox & Friends, interview with Eric Trump, via Twitter, https://twitter.com/foxandfriends/status/953643087305166858.

The Nuclear Ban Treaty: A Sign of Global Impatience

Paul Meyer and Tom Sauer

Future historians may record summer 2017 as the beginning of the end of the nuclear age. On 7 July 2017, 122 states adopted the text of a legally binding international treaty that provides for a comprehensive ban on nuclear weapons (or 'ban treaty').[1] The treaty was opened for signature on 20 September 2017, and at the time of writing, 56 states had signed and five had ratified.

The nine nuclear-weapons states and their allies are still in a state of denial, however.[2] They have consistently resisted the very idea of a treaty banning nuclear weapons, despite their obligation under the 1970 Nuclear Non-Proliferation Treaty (NPT) to pursue multilateral negotiations on the elimination of nuclear weapons. They have ridiculed the Humanitarian Initiative that was the driving force behind the ban treaty, convinced that it would fail just as previous disarmament efforts by NGOs and like-minded states had done. They regarded the states advocating for the treaty as 'unimportant', an expression used by a former high-level American arms-control expert in a Track Two workshop. In 2017, the nuclear-weapons states and the NATO member states (excepting the Netherlands) boycotted the multilateral negotiations that produced the ban treaty, something that had never been seen before with respect to a negotiation authorised by the UN General Assembly. (States have sometimes rejected outcomes from such negotia-

Paul Meyer is an Adjunct Professor of International Studies at Simon Fraser University, Vancouver, and a former Ambassador of Canada for Disarmament. **Tom Sauer** is an Associate Professor in International Politics at the Universiteit Antwerpen, Belgium.

Survival | vol. 60 no. 2 | April–May 2018 | pp. 61–72   DOI 10.1080/00396338.2018.1448574

tions, but to boycott an approved process en masse was unprecedented.) By doing so, they ignored the basic requirements of the NPT and responsible multilateralism, and missed the chance to shape the treaty in accordance with their own wishes.

Critics of the treaty point out that it is very unlikely that any of the nuclear-weapons states or their allies will be among the first group of signatories.[3] Yet treaty advocates knew this would be the case right from the beginning.[4] Just as slavery was not abolished through the efforts of slave owners, the abolition of nuclear weapons is not expected to be accomplished by the possessors of nuclear arms.

Scope and drivers of the treaty

The ban treaty will forbid the development, production, testing, acquisition, stockpiling, transfer, possession and stationing – as well as the use and threat of use – of nuclear weapons. Consequently, the decades-old doctrine of nuclear deterrence will become illegal for the signatory states, and in the eyes of the hundreds of millions of citizens around the world who support the treaty. Whether it will eventually gain the status of customary international law will depend on state practice in the future, but a major normative step has been taken towards that goal. At the very least, the 'taboo'[5] against the use – now extended to the possession – of nuclear weapons will be strengthened.

The treaty will enter into force once 50 states have ratified it, thus ensuring that it commands wide support while avoiding the pitfall of requiring ratification by specific states, which has prevented the Comprehensive Test-Ban Treaty (CTBT) from entering into force. Given that 122 states voted in favour of the adoption of the treaty, the agreement is likely to enter into force sooner rather than later (estimates have ranged from late 2018 to mid-2019), although this will require sustained political action and advocacy on the part of its supporters.

The nuclear-weapons states and their allies have two options under the treaty: they can either destroy their nuclear weapons and then join the treaty, or join the treaty and at the same time make specific plans to eliminate their nuclear weapons. For their nuclear-dependent allies, this will require disavowal of the doctrine of nuclear deterrence and its enabling systems, such as providing basing or aircraft for the delivery of nuclear weapons. Of course, the nuclear-weapons states may well persist in their rejection of the treaty, and proceed with their plans to retain and modernise their nuclear weapons at a cost of hundreds of billions of dollars. Such a stance would, however, guarantee a schism between non-nuclear-weapons and nuclear-weapons states, thus threatening the foundations of the nuclear non-proliferation regime established by the NPT.

Given that the mainstream media largely ignored the ban-treaty negotiations, some may be surprised to learn that a majority of NPT states have already agreed that nuclear weapons should be banned.[6] Indeed, a major challenge to the existing nuclear order has been in the making for some time.[7] The underlying driver of the ban treaty has been the frustration among the non-nuclear-weapons states with the unfulfilled promises of the nuclear-weapons states to pursue total nuclear disarmament. There are currently some 15,000 nuclear weapons on earth. Most of these weapons have a destructive capacity that is ten or even 100 times greater than the bomb that wiped out Hiroshima. The use of only a fraction of these weapons could render the planet uninhabitable. For anyone who is not absolutely sure that nuclear deterrence will always work, the risks associated with these weapons are unacceptably high.

For decades, the NPT was seen as the primary legal framework for managing the risks presented by nuclear weapons. This widely supported treaty, signed by 191 states, codified a 'grand bargain' in which the non-nuclear-weapons states promised never to obtain nuclear weapons, the five existing nuclear-weapons states committed to work towards the elimination of their nuclear arsenals, and all NPT signatories pledged to cooperate on the peaceful uses of nuclear energy.

Probably the greatest lacuna of the NPT is the absence of a deadline for realising nuclear disarmament as required by Article VI of the treaty. While the nuclear-weapons states point to the many thousands of nuclear weapons that have been removed from their operational arsenals, the non-nuclear-weapons states have always expected the complete elimination of such weapons. This is the only way of overcoming the discriminatory character of the NPT, which currently accepts a distinction between nuclear 'haves' and 'have-nots'.

Over the years, the frustration of the non-nuclear-weapons states over the limited progress toward nuclear disarmament has only grown. These frustrations were especially evident during the NPT Review Conferences convened every five years.[8] Indeed, the origins of the Humanitarian Initiative can be directly linked to the failure of the 2005 NPT Review Conference. Other contributing factors were the stagnation seen in multilateral arms control in the preceding decade (1995–2005), and the successful campaigns against landmines (1997) and cluster munitions (2008) that resulted in what became known as 'humanitarian disarmament' accords. These suc-cesses triggered ideas for launching a new campaign with the ambitious goal of eliminating nuclear weapons – the only weapon of mass destruc-tion not covered by a comprehensive prohibition agreement. NGOs such as International Physicians for the Prevention of Nuclear War (which received the Nobel Peace Prize in 1985) were at the forefront of establishing a new global movement that came to be known as the International Campaign to Abolish Nuclear Weapons (ICAN). Today encompassing more than 400 NGOs from over 100 states, ICAN was the recipient of the 2017 Nobel Peace Prize for its advocacy and lobbying efforts on behalf of the ban treaty.[9]

At the same time that ICAN was gathering momentum, the International Red Cross and Red Crescent movement put the abolition of nuclear weapons higher on its agenda. Together with Switzerland, they were able to include a reference to the 'catastrophic humanitarian consequences' of the use of nuclear weapons in the final document of the 2010 NPT Review Conference.[10] The language used was agreed by all member states, includ-ing the nuclear-weapons states. In all likelihood, they were not aware that these words would constitute the starting point of the journey towards the ban treaty.[11]

The main idea behind the Humanitarian Initiative was, and still is, to shift the nuclear narrative away from its focus on deterrence, which simul-taneously encompasses a strategic rationale for the non-use of nuclear weapons and a threat to employ them if deterrence fails, to a concern with the dangers attendant upon the actual use of these weapons. The former is an abstract theory that is used by defence intellectuals to legitimise the maintenance of nuclear arsenals. Its advocates believe that the existence of nuclear weapons has prevented the outbreak of a third world war. The fact that nuclear weapons have not been used since the end of the Second World War is also attributed to deterrence.[12] Critics have pointed out, however, that these claims are impossible to prove.[13] Other factors, such as the memory of the two world wars with their tens of millions of casualties, European integration and global economic interdependence could be cited as reasons why there has not been a global war since 1945. Moreover, nuclear deterrence has sometimes blatantly failed, as in the case of the Yom Kippur War (1973), the Gulf War (1991) – in which Israel's nuclear arsenal failed to deter Iraq from launching missile attacks against it – and Pakistan's Kargil incursion (1999). Nuclear abolitionists emphasise the dangers and high material costs of having nuclear weapons on high alert, ready to be launched on a moment's notice.

Nuclear deterrence has sometimes blatantly failed

While the debate between advocates and critics of nuclear weapons has been ongoing for some time, the Humanitarian Initiative has sought to draw attention to the potential consequences if nuclear weapons were actually used, something that has rarely been discussed. What would be the physical consequences in terms of heat, blast and radioactive fallout? Are societies ready to deal with so much as a single nuclear explosion, let alone a nuclear war? The hope is that a greater awareness of the dangers posed by nuclear weapons, and the limitations of any humanitarian response, would generate increased support for nuclear disarmament. Thus, the initiative has asked whether humanity is prepared for the immediate destruction and long-term effects such weapons can be expected to cause. It invited scientists to present updated studies on the phenomenon of 'nuclear winter', for example, a prospect that had been studied in the 1980s on the premise that a major nuclear exchange between the US and USSR would cause so much dust and smoke to enter the atmosphere that it would block the sun's rays. One updated study was based on a scenario of a 'limited' nuclear war between India and Pakistan involving the use of 100 nuclear weapons. The study found that even such a restricted nuclear exchange would directly kill 30 million people and imperil hundreds of millions more by lowering the earth's temperature and thereby contributing to crop failures.[14] Other experts demonstrated the virtual certainty of killing large numbers of civilians even in the case of a single nuclear weapon targeting a military installation.[15] This analysis reinforced the view that any conceivable use of nuclear weapons would contradict international humanitarian law, with its principles of proportionality, discrimination and precaution.

Future of the treaty

The ultimate goal of the Humanitarian Initiative was to demonstrate that any use of nuclear weapons would be unacceptably destructive, immoral and illegitimate, and therefore that these weapons should be made illegal, just as chemical and biological weapons, and even landmines and cluster munitions, have been. It determined that an international treaty prohibiting the possession and use of nuclear weapons would be one way of doing so. The negotiation of such a treaty was regarded as an achievable short-term goal that would constitute the first step towards the complete elimination of nuclear weapons.

The Humanitarian Initiative organised three international conferences in 2013–14 (in Norway, Mexico and Austria) that brought together increasing numbers of NGOs and government representatives, and which generated support for UN resolutions and statements at NPT meetings. In 2016, the UN General Assembly adopted a resolution authorising the convening of multilateral negotiations in 2017 to develop a legally binding agreement to prohibit nuclear weapons.[16] Importantly, the resolution specified that General Assembly rules of procedure would apply, meaning that decisions would be taken by majority vote instead of by consensus. Too often, the need to achieve consensus on previous disarmament-related initiatives had allowed the nuclear-armed states to stymie these efforts. This time, the non-nuclear-weapons states would be able to prevent such obstruction. Having been denied their usual method of blocking progress on disarmament, the nuclear-weapons states and their allies (with the notable exception of the Netherlands) opted to boycott the proceedings. The fact that, in the end, the

Netherlands decided to cast the sole negative vote against adoption of the treaty demonstrated the wisdom of circumventing the consensus trap.

The ban treaty, like any treaty, is not without its flaws, not least because it was negotiated in a very short time span. One of its flaws is that it represents a mixture of both a prohibition and an elimination treaty. While many had expected that it would be limited to a simple prohibition statement that would later be supplemented by a more extensive Nuclear Weapon Convention detailing the process of elimination, the actual treaty contains both elements, and is therefore best regarded as a framework agreement that will require subsequent supplementary arrangements to specify verification and other procedures. Far from being a major weakness of the treaty as some have suggested,[17] however, this pragmatic approach recognises that eventual adherence by nuclear-weapon-possessing states will require their input into how 'irreversible' elimination (admittedly a high standard, but one which all parties to the NPT have affirmed) would take place. The interests of non-nuclear-weapons states will be assured through the involvement of a 'competent international authority' and agreement on terms by a meeting of treaty signatories. This may be challenging, but is not infeasible.

Although the treaty's adoption at the close of negotiations by 122 states certainly represents a major diplomatic achievement, it is fair to ask what its impact on global nuclear affairs will ultimately be. Sceptics point out that the treaty is of mainly symbolic importance, and that the nuclear-weapons states and their allies, the treaty's main targets, will not change their policies as they continue to assert that nuclear deterrence is essential for their security. Nevertheless, the treaty's advocates, while harbouring no delusion that the nuclear-weapons states will radically change course in the short term, believe that it sets in motion two forces that may eventually serve to alter the behaviour of these states and their allies. The first of these is the way the treaty may encourage enhanced restraint by private-sector firms (especially banks and investment funds) with respect to their exposure to the nuclear-weapons industry.[18] In an age of ethical investing, banks and investment funds care about their reputation. Once nuclear weapons are declared illegal, many financial institutions will think twice before funding or investing in firms that are doing business in the nuclear-weapons sector.

Indeed, a large Norwegian pension fund changed its policy even before the treaty was agreed, and a Dutch pension fund followed suit shortly afterwards.[19] It is possible that many more banks will come under pressure to do likewise, which would in turn cause problems for nuclear-weapons-related businesses. This could have implications for state policy.

Secondly and more fundamentally, the treaty will demonstrably strengthen the global norm against nuclear weapons, thereby increasing the stigma for states that continue to possess them.[20] It is possible that as support for the treaty grows, new societal and political debates about the future of nuclear weapons will emerge within the nuclear-weapons and allied states themselves, especially the five basing states for NATO's nuclear forces in Europe.[21] Indeed, official policy in the Netherlands has already been influenced by civil-society activism. Pax, the main peace movement in that country, successfully collected 40,000 signatures on a 2016 petition against nuclear weapons. That achievement led automatically to a debate on the subject being held in the Dutch parliament on 28 April 2016. The four-hour debate was attended by the Dutch minister of foreign affairs, Bert Koenders, and resulted in motions calling upon the Dutch government to at least attend the ban-treaty negotiations. (These motions received the approval of both opposition and governmental parties.) Despite enormous pressure from the US, the UK and France, as well as other allies, Dutch diplomats did attend, and contribute to, the negotiations – though, as noted, the Netherlands was the only delegation to vote against the treaty. Meanwhile, eminent members of society in many non-nuclear NATO member states have spoken in favour of their governments adopting a positive stance towards the treaty. Once it enters into force, pressure will grow on at least some of these governments (to possibly include Belgium, Canada, Germany, the Netherlands and Norway) to sign the treaty or align their security policies with its goals.[22]

One nuclear-weapons state may feel the near-term effects

At least one nuclear-weapons state may also feel the near-term effects of the ban treaty. In the UK, the costly renewal of the *Trident* nuclear deterrent has already triggered a societal debate. Most Scottish politicians are against the retention of nuclear weapons, reflecting in part the fact that the only British nuclear base is less than 65 kilometres from Glasgow. Labour Party leader Jeremy Corbyn is a lifelong member of the Campaign for Nuclear Disarmament, and even attended the 2014 Vienna Conference on the Humanitarian Impact of Nuclear Weapons. Many of his young followers are fervent critics of nuclear weapons. As party leader, he has declared that if he becomes prime minister he will never push the 'nuclear button'. Although the official party line (reflecting the influence of labour unions and members of parliament) is still in favour of *Trident* renewal, the consequences of Brexit and economic stagnation may work to overturn that earlier decision given the high opportunity costs that renewal will entail. The Greens are against, and Liberal Democrats are also lukewarm about maintaining nuclear weapons and have suggested a recessed nuclear deterrent instead. This leaves only the Conservative Party fully in favour of renewing *Trident*. The entry into force of the ban treaty may help the many advocates of nuclear disarmament in the UK to make their point even more vehemently. If Labour wins the next election, a variety of factors (not least cost) may result in *Trident* renewal being dropped, opening the way for the UK to become a state without nuclear weapons and thus the first NPT nuclear-weapons state to fully realise its Article VI commitment.

If the UK signs the ban treaty, a positive domino effect may follow. At a minimum, it will put pressure on the remaining nuclear-weapons states to explain exactly how they intend to achieve the world without nuclear weapons that they have espoused, at least rhetorically, as a goal.

Advocates hope that the ban treaty will be a wake-up call for the nuclear-weapons states and their allies. If they were previously unaware that nuclear disarmament is viewed as a priority by the rest of the world, they should have received the message now. The ban treaty is nothing less than a heart-felt cry for nuclear abolition. Ignoring it could be a recipe for disaster down the road. If the nuclear-weapons states and their allies do not take substantial steps towards elimination (in the form of deep cuts to arsenals, no-first-use policies, the de-alerting of deployed forces, the withdrawal of nuclear weapons stationed abroad and the halting of modernisation) before the next NPT Review Conference in 2020, the probability of that conference failing will be extremely high. The failure of two such conferences in a row would further erode the authority of what will then be a 50-year-old NPT, and could well lead some of its non-nuclear signatories to abandon it in favour of the more comprehensive provisions of the ban treaty.

The prospect of defections from the NPT is certainly not foreseen in the ban treaty itself, which, in a preambular paragraph, reaffirms 'the full and effective implementation' of the NPT. Nevertheless, if nuclear-weapons states that are party to the NPT are judged not to be implementing their treaty obligations, non-nuclear-weapons states may begin to lessen their engagement with that treaty regime, especially if they are party to a treaty with higher disarmament standards. The weakening of the global nuclear non-proliferation regime that might result from this process would not be in the interest of the nuclear-weapons states, even if their conduct over the decades would have contributed to bringing it about. In this sense, the ban treaty is the most recent manifestation of decades of frustration over the failure of nuclear-weapons states to realise their NPT obligations, and of the determination of the majority of NPT parties to rebel against the status quo and champion another route for nuclear disarmament.

The best way to prevent this scenario is for the nuclear-weapons states to take substantial steps in the direction of nuclear-weapons elimination in the near term.[23] The ban treaty serves as a stark reminder of the unfinished business of the NPT.

Notes

[1] See United Nations, 'United Nations Conference to Negotiate a Legally Binding Instrument to Prohibit Nuclear Weapons, Leading Towards Their Total Elimination', https://www.un.org/disarmament/ptnw/.

[2] See, for example, 'Joint Press Statement from the Permanent Representatives to the United Nations of the United States, United Kingdom, and France Following the Adoption of a Treaty Banning Nuclear Weapons', New York, 7 July 2017, https://usun.state.gov/remarks/7892.

[3] See, for example, Benjamin Valentino and Scott Sagan, 'The Nuclear Weapons Ban Treaty: Opportunities Lost', in Bulletin of the Atomic Scientists, 16 July 2017, http://thebulletin.org/nuclear-weapons-ban-treaty-opportunities-lost10955.

[4] See, for example, Beatrice Fihn, 'The Logic of Banning Nuclear Weapons', Survival, vol. 59, no. 1, February–

March 2017, pp. 43–50.

5   See Nina Tannenwald, *The Nuclear Taboo* (Cambridge: Cambridge University Press, 2007).

6   The significance of the treaty seems to have been overlooked even by many foreign-relations experts. For an exception, see Shatabhista Shetty and Denitsa Raynova (eds), 'Breakthrough or Breakpoint? Global Perspectives on the Nuclear Ban Treaty', ELN Global Security Special Report, December 2017.

7   See Rebecca Johnson, 'Banning Nuclear Weapons', *OpenDemocracy*, 26 February 2013; Beatrice Fihn (ed.), 'Unspeakable Suffering: The Humanitarian Impact of Nuclear Weapons' (Geneva: Reaching Critical Will, February 2013); John Borrie, 'Humanitarian Reframing of Nuclear Weapons and the Logic of a Ban', *International Affairs*, vol. 90, no. 3, 2014, pp. 625–46; Tom Sauer and Joelien Pretorius, 'Nuclear Weapons and the Humanitarian Approach', *Global Change, Peace and Security*, vol. 26, no. 3, 2014, pp. 233–50; and Tom Sauer, 'It's Time to Outlaw Nuclear Weapons', *National Interest*, 28 April 2016.

8   See Tom Sauer, 'The Nuclear Nonproliferation Regime in Crisis', *Peace Review*, vol. 18, no. 3, 2006; Paul Meyer, 'Saving the NPT', *Nonproliferation Review*, vol. 16, no. 3, November 2009, pp. 463–72; Alexander Kmentt, 'How Divergent Views on Nuclear Disarmament Threaten the NPT', *Arms Control Today*, vol. 43, no. 10, December 2013; and Paul Meyer, 'The Nuclear Nonproliferation Treaty: Fin de

Régime?', *Arms Control Today*, vol. 47, no. 3, April 2017, pp. 16–22.

9   For further information about ICAN, see its website at http://www.icanw.org/.

10   '2010 Review Conference of the Parties to the Treaty on the Non-Proliferation of Nuclear Weapons: Final Document', New York, 2010, NTP?CONF.2010/50 (Vol. I), pp. 12, 19, https://www.nonproliferation.org/wp-content/uploads/2015/04/2010_fd_part_i.pdf.

11   See William Potter, 'Disarmament Diplomacy and the Nuclear Ban Treaty', *Survival*, vol. 59, no. 4, August–September 2017, pp. 75–108.

12   Some go even further by advocating the spread of nuclear weapons. See, for example, Kenneth Waltz, 'More May Be Better', in Scott Sagan and Kenneth Waltz, *The Spread of Nuclear Weapons*, second edition (New York: W.W. Norton & Co., 2003), pp. 3–45.

13   See, for example, John Mueller, 'The Essential Irrelevance of Nuclear Weapons', *International Security*, vol. 13, no. 2, Fall 1988, pp. 55–79; Tom Sauer, *Nuclear Arms Control* (New York: Macmillan, 1998); Ken Berry et al., *Delegitimizing Nuclear Weapons* (Monterey, CA: CNS, 2010); Ward Wilson, *Five Myths about Nuclear Weapons* (New York: Houghton Mifflin Harcourt, 2013); and James E. Doyle, 'Why Eliminate Nuclear Weapons?', *Survival*, vol. 55, no. 1, February–March 2013, pp. 7–34.

14   Owen Toon et al., 'Atmospheric Effects and Social Consequences of Regional Scale Nuclear Conflicts and Acts of Individual Nuclear Terrorism', *Atmospheric Chemistry and Physics*, vol. 7, 2007, pp. 1,973–2,002; Michael Mills

et al., 'Multidecadal Global Cooling and Unprecedented Ozone Loss Following a Regional Nuclear War', *Earth's Future*, vol. 2, no. 4, 2014, pp. 161–76.

[15] Matthew McKinzie et al., 'Calculating the Effects of a Nuclear Explosion at a European Military Base', presented at the Vienna Conference on the Humanitarian Impact of Nuclear Weapons, 8 December 2014.

[16] United Nations General Assembly, 'Taking Forward Multilateral Nuclear Disarmament Negotiations', 23 December 2016, https://www.unog.ch/oewg-ndn.

[17] See, for example, Newell Highsmith and Mallory Stewart, 'The Nuclear Ban Treaty: A Legal Analysis', *Survival*, vol. 60, no. 1, February–March 2018, pp. 129–52.

[18] See the report by Pax and ICAN, 'Don't Bank on the Bomb: A Global Report on the Financing of Nuclear Weapons Producers', December 2016, https://www.dontbankonthebomb.com/wp-content/uploads/2016/12/2016_Report_final.pdf.

[19] Peter Stubley, 'World's Largest Wealth Fund Pulls Out of BAE Systems Over Nuclear Weapons Links', *Independent*, 16 January 2018, http://www.independent.co.uk/news/uk/home-news/bae-systems-nuclear-weapons-links-norway-government-pension-fund-defence-arms-manufacturer-a8162521.html; 'Biggest Dutch Pension Fund Drops Tobacco, Nuclear Weapon Investments', DutchNews.nl, 11 January 2018, https://www.dutchnews.nl/news/archives/2018/01/the-netherlands-biggest-pension-fund-drops-tobacco-and-nuclear-weapons/.

[20] Patricia Shamai, 'Name and Shame: Unravelling the Stigmatization of Weapons of Mass Destruction', *Contemporary Security Policy*, vol. 36, no. 1, 2015, pp. 104–22.

[21] Tom Sauer, 'How Will NATO's Non-Nuclear Members Handle the UN's Ban on Nuclear Weapons?', *Bulletin of the Atomic Scientists*, vol. 73, no. 3, May–June 2017, pp. 171–81.

[22] The Canadian Pugwash Group, for example, has recommended that the government of Canada sign the ban treaty now and work on modifying NATO policy to be consistent with its provisions prior to ratification. See http://www.pugwashgroup.ca.

[23] For a discussion of how this might be done, see Lewis Dunn, 'After the Prohibition Treaty: A Practical Agenda to Reduce Nuclear Dangers', *Arms Control Today*, vol. 47, no. 6, July–August 2017, pp. 6–12.

Resisting Impunity for Chemical-Weapons Attacks

Rebecca Hersman

2018 marks the seventh year of a civil war in Syria which, from its very beginning, has been marred by the use of chemical weapons (CW). The Syrian regime – responsible for the vast majority of an estimated 150 attacks or more – has faced little or no penalty for its crimes. The attacks are blatant violations of the Chemical Weapons Convention (CWC), multiple United Nations resolutions and a host of international laws and protocols.

Russia and Iran have done their part to enable this vicious behaviour to continue – running interference in international forums, and perpetuating misleading or false interpretations of events on the ground. The apparent disinterest of other states suggests a collective view that the stakes associated with continued CW use are comparatively low. It also reflects a widespread assumption that accountability for states, entities and individuals perpetrating these attacks is unachievable.

This assumption is wrong. It is true that norms and treaties of all kinds are often violated; that states routinely complain about violations that they have no serious intention of punishing; and that violations are difficult to punish when they are committed by states with their own military forces and, especially, major-power backing. So it is true, in turn, that Syria – enjoying steadfast Russian political and military support – was always likely to

Rebecca Hersman is Director of the Project on Nuclear Issues and Senior Adviser for the International Security Program at the Center for Strategic and International Studies (CSIS). She joined CSIS in April 2015 from the US Department of Defense, where she served from 2009 as deputy assistant secretary of defense for countering weapons of mass destruction.

Survival | vol 60 no 2 | April–May 2018 | pp. 73–90   DOI 10.1080/00396338.2018.1448576

be a very hard case. But this does not mean that meaningful, practical efforts at accountability cannot be made, even if they are partial – and a clear international statement that there can be no impunity for CW attacks also lays the ground for future efforts in Syria and beyond.

On 23 January, foreign ministers from 25 countries met in Paris to launch a new multilateral effort to seek accountability for the use of CW – the International Partnership Against Impunity for the Use of Chemical Weapons (hereafter 'the Partnership').[1] This new international initiative met with little fanfare; media worldwide hardly noticed. The arms-control and non-proliferation communities, preoccupied with leaked versions of the US Nuclear Posture Review, paid no attention. A world numb to the scale of human atrocity in Syria showed little interest. Yet, as the normalisation of CW use continues, the Partnership has arrived not a moment too soon.

Continued CW use in the Syria conflict will encourage the further proliferation and use of such weapons in the Middle East and beyond. As the normalisation of CW use continues, the risks of such attacks by states and non-state actors will only increase. The rapid development of the CW capabilities of the Islamic State (also known as ISIS or ISIL)[2] and the bizarre assassination of North Korean leader Kim Jong-un's half-brother in a Malaysian airport using VX are likely harbingers of what lies on the horizon in a world in which CW use is increasingly normalised.[3]

As ongoing use of CW exposes weaknesses in the international treaty-based regime's ability to prevent and respond to attacks, those fissures will spread beyond chemical weapons and ultimately weaken the non-proliferation regime more broadly. This problem, years in the making, threatens to undo decades of international norms, and could have repercussions for deterrence against the use of other weapons of mass destruction (WMD). Moreover, as obstructionism and patronage effectively immobilise international institutions and protect the violations of these important norms, the use of such techniques will only grow, calling into further question the ability of the international system to address fundamental threats to peace and security.

The stakes are, in other words, very high. But the situation is not hopeless. As the French-led Partnership hopes to demonstrate, effective international responses to raise costs and impose consequences for those who use CW – even in the absence of international consensus and full accountability – are possible. States may attempt to weaken vital international institutions, but they cannot preclude voluntary collective action to preserve and protect these norms.

There are also lessons to be learned from past initiatives to strengthen the non-proliferation regime which can be applied to the challenge at hand. Like-minded countries can work to strengthen compliance with and enforcement of norms and laws, in turn bolstering the broader non-proliferation system. As a source of voluntary collective action, the Partnership provides an important path towards strengthening accountability and demonstrating resolve. This will only happen, however, if the partner nations quickly translate words into meaningful action.

How did we get here?

The scale of CW use in Syria is staggering. Reports on the number of attacks vary depending on the source and assessment criteria. Even by the most conservative estimates, repeated and sustained attacks by the Syrian regime, and to a lesser extent ISIS, in the Syrian conflict are indisputable. A French government evaluation found 130 presumed uses of CW from October 2012 to April 2017.[4] The Syrian American Medical Society reports more than 194 chemical attacks since 2012,[5] and Human Rights Watch counts 16 attacks between December 2016 and April 2017 alone.[6] The majority of these attacks occurred after the August 2013 sarin attack in East Ghouta that killed more than 1,400 people.[7] That attack led to the US–Russia Framework Agreement, Syria's accession to the CWC, and an international removal and destruction effort that eliminated the overwhelming majority of Syria's CW stockpile.

By early 2014, however, even as those efforts were under way, the use of chemicals as weapons in Syria had resumed.[8] In the spring of that year, the Organisation for the Prohibition of Chemical Weapons (OPCW) established a new entity, the Fact Finding Mission (FFM), to investigate the growing number of incidents of alleged use in Syria. The FFM's mandate included confirmation of CW use, but not attribution of responsibility. Since then, the FFM has used video metadata and biomedical samples of victims to confirm the use of chemicals as weapons – chlorine, sarin and sulfur mustard – at least 38 times.[9] Faced with steadily increasing cases of confirmed use, the UN Security Council passed Resolution 2235 establishing the UN–OPCW Joint Investigative Mechanism (JIM) in 2015 to identify, where possible, the perpetrators of FFM-confirmed attacks.[10] The JIM, uniquely, could attribute CW attacks to actors while making use of the technical expertise of the OPCW. Notably, the JIM had Russian support at its inception. Between February 2016 and October 2017, the JIM issued seven different reports and attributed multiple CW attacks to the Syrian regime and ISIS. As with the FFM, the JIM was extremely conservative in its analysis of culpability, and maintained a high threshold for blame.

On 26 October 2017, the JIM issued a report determining Syria's culpability for the April 2017 sarin attack in Khan Sheikhoun that killed more than 100 people, including 27 children.[11] This attack marked the largest use of CW in Syria since the 2013 attack on East Ghouta. The report also assigned responsibility to ISIS for a September 2016 sulfur-mustard attack in Umm Hawsh.[12] Despite the extensive evidence supporting the JIM's conclusions, the Russians, who sought to protect their Syrian allies, called into question its methodology and impartiality. Just three weeks after the October 2017 JIM report was released, the Russian Federation used its tenth Syria-related veto in the UN Security Council to prevent an extension of the JIM's mandate.[13] This shuttered the body before it could issue findings on other attacks already reported by the OPCW, such as the FFM-identified sarin attack on 30 March 2016 in Lataminah.[14] Today, without the JIM, there is no longer an established international mechanism for attributing attacks in Syria.

Results in The Hague, home to the OPCW, have not been much better. Despite the painstaking work of the FFM, the OPCW Executive Council has proven unable to address Syria's multiple compliance issues. Most recently, in November 2017, several attempts within the OPCW's Executive Council to express concerns about Syria's compliance with its CWC obligations failed to muster the necessary 28 votes among the 41 members to bring any treaty-based accountability to Syria for its actions.[15] Instead of enforcing the treaty, the CWC's governing body has taken a step to undermine the most comprehensive arms-control agreement ever brought into force.

Chemical-weapons attacks have escalated again since the beginning of 2018, especially in rebel-held positions in southern Syria. Attacks on 13 and 22 January and 1 February in the Ghouta–Damascus region have caused at least 30 casualties, according to social media and reports from the White Helmets.[16] Additional attacks reportedly occurred in the Idlib–Saraqeb area in the north of Syria on 4 and 6 February.[17] Another alleged attack occurred on 25 February, again in the Ghouta region, where a child was reportedly killed due to symptoms consistent with exposure to chlorine.[18]

The sheer number of incidents, especially those that have occurred recently, shows that the Syrian regime believes there are no boundaries limiting what and how much they can get away with. In January 2018, the United States ambassador to the UN called Russian attempts to discredit the JIM's analysis 'misleading, unprofessional, inconsistent and, at times, completely false'.[19] Yet, public shaming has done little to convince Russia of the need to support the very accountability mechanisms it helped establish. Syria has not been found in non-compliance of a treaty it violates with impunity, thereby calling into question a treaty regime seemingly incapable of enforcing its most fundamental tenets. The global norm of non-use of chemical weapons and the rules-based treaty system that supports it is at risk of dying a slow death.

Syria has not been found in non-compliance

While the UN Security Council and OPCW represent the preferred paths to accountability for the illegal use of chemical weapons, they are not the only routes. The United States and like-minded nations can respond, unilaterally or collectively, to ongoing CW use through the use of force. Such was the case when the United States fired 59 *Tomahawk* missiles in April 2017 at Syrian military targets following the use of sarin in Khan Sheikhoun, which had been attributed to the Syrian Air Force.[20] Similar responses might follow further corroborated attacks. French President Emmanuel Macron has said that France would 'strike the place where these launches are made or where they are organized', once proof was established.[21] US Secretary of Defense James Mattis has also kept the military option open as well, threatening that 'you have all seen how we reacted to [the Khan Sheikhoun attacks], so they'd be ill-advised to go back to violating the chemical convention'.[22] US Secretary of State Rex Tillerson has made similar hints: 'We are serious about our demands that chemical weapons not become regularized or normalized as a weapon in any conflict.'[23]

One-off, military responses are at minimum insufficient and, in many cases, are counterproductive if not accompanied by a range of other actions to ensure sustained, consistent enforcement. For one thing, limited and unilateral US airstrikes intrinsically promote the idea that chemical-weapons usage is an American problem, rather than one for all states. Moreover, following the military strike in 2017, there was little in the way of coordinated follow-up to ensure that Syria did not test international resolve by resuming low-level CW use once attention was focused elsewhere. Military force might not be an appropriate response for every CW attack, but ignoring attacks until they get 'big enough' simply begs the cycle to repeat itself. A more comprehensive strategy would have entailed additional pressure in the Security Council to hold Syria accountable; political, diplomatic and economic means to strengthen the international consensus against Syria's use of CW; and additional threats of military force if Syria employed CW again. This would have imposed consequences more consistently, even if every case of CW use did not warrant military punishment.

International leaders continue to struggle, moreover, to define a threshold for military response that sends clear messages about what constitutes unacceptable CW use. This is partly a question of evidence. During a February 2018 press briefing, for example, Mattis said that 'fighters on the ground have said that Sarin has been used. So we are looking for evidence. I don't have evidence, credible or un-credible.'[24]

More fundamentally, however, punishing sarin attacks with military strikes while allowing chlorine attacks to continue is an inappropriate distinction that undermines prohibitions in international law. The use of chlorine and sarin (or any other chemical) are both equally prohibited by the CWC and the body of related international law. Chlorine was the first chemical used in warfare during the First World War, its use prompting the prohibitions under the Geneva Conventions. The difference between chlorine and sarin is not with regard to the prohibition of their use as a weapon, but rather in terms of how they are treated under the CWC's verification measures. (Sarin, as an identified, traditional military agent of extreme toxicity, cannot be developed, manufactured or stockpiled, and its precursors are subject to controls and verification. Chlorine is nearly ubiquitous, and vital for countless legitimate purposes, and therefore is not subject to verification or control under the CWC.) The more than 100 uses of chlorine as a weapon in the Syrian civil war, including three such cases attributed to the Syrian regime by the JIM, are prohibited just as sarin attacks are, yet incurred no response of any type: military, diplomatic, political or economic.[25]

In any case, striking Syrian military bases is little punishment for the perpetrators, nor much justice or restitution for the victims. Meaningful accountability requires that a wider range of costs – economic, political and legal – are imposed as consistently and comprehensively as possible. Selective accountability for so much CW use could encourage rather than dissuade the smaller-scale use of chemical weapons. And while Russia may have closed the path to accountability through the Security Council and the OPCW for now, nations can fulfil their responsibilities in the face of these ongoing atrocities in other ways.

Non-proliferation precedent

The international non-proliferation community has overcome significant challenges before. By taking a page from earlier playbooks, like-minded states can find new ways to seek collective action in pursuit of accountability. In 2002, the *So San*, a flagless North Korean vessel carrying 15 *Scud* missiles to Yemen, was interdicted in Spanish territorial waters. A few days later, the ship was released and allowed to deliver its cargo because of a lack of any international legal basis to confiscate and dispose of the consignment.[26] While an international legal solution to close this gap – in the form of a treaty or Security Council resolution – would have been the ideal solution, it was politically and practically infeasible. Instead, a group of nations came together in 2003 to form the Proliferation Security Initiative (PSI). Through the endorsement of a statement of principles, participating nations sought 'to establish a more coordinated and effective basis through which to impede and stop shipments of WMD, delivery systems, and related materials flowing to and from states and non-state actors of proliferation concern' by fostering improved capacities, authorities, coordination and collaboration.[27]

Nearly 15 years later, 105 countries have endorsed the Statement of Interdiction Principles, and a 21-member Operational Experts Group meets regularly to guide and coordinate regional multilateral exercises, information-sharing, best practices and training to support WMD-interdiction efforts by nations acting in their national capacities.[28] Since the PSI was established, the transfer of WMD-related cargoes has become vastly more difficult, and nations can detect and cooperate to interdict these shipments more effectively. In part because of the insights and knowledge gleaned through PSI activities and information-sharing, subsequent Security Council resolutions dealing with proliferation issues have helped fill gaps in international law that prevented the successful interdiction of the *So San* cargo in 2002.[29]

The lesson of the PSI is for like-minded states to focus on practical measures which in turn help to reinforce, or repair, global norms through collaborative and voluntary efforts. The case of CW use is a more difficult one than that of interdiction, and the stakes are higher than they were in 2003. But like-minded nations have a more robust international legal basis for action to prevent and respond to CW use than they had then for addressing interdiction. The CWC, to which all but four countries in the world are states parties – including Syria – not only encourages, but in many case requires, countries to cooperate in pursuit of the treaty's implementation and to pursue those who violate the treaty through their respective legal systems. The Geneva Protocol prohibits CW use, the Rome Statute of the International Criminal Court recognises it as a war crime and many countries consider it a crime against humanity due to its indiscriminate nature.[30] In fact, the prohibition on the use of chemicals as weapons of warfare is so widely accepted that it is considered by many nations as customary international law.[31]

A step in the right direction
The establishment of the Partnership emulates the PSI in seeking voluntary collective action to support the non-proliferation and arms-control regimes.[32]

Announced in Paris by French Minister for Europe and Foreign Affairs Jean-Yves Le Drian, it featured several other high-level dignitaries, including Rex Tillerson and OPCW Director-General Ahmet Üzümcü.[33]

Tillerson minced no words at the ceremony: 'This initiative puts those who ordered and carried out chemical weapons attacks on notice. You will face a day of reckoning for your crimes against humanity and your victims will see justice done.'[34] The Partnership recognised that repeated CW use threatens the international norm against such attacks as established in international law, including through the Geneva Protocol, Geneva Conventions and a number of UN Security Council resolutions condemning these attacks in Syria.[35] Additionally, Partnership states committed to the principle that actors who employ CW must be held accountable, and that collective response through national and international measures would be necessary to deter CW proliferation and use.[36]

This initiative aims to do more than just talk, however. The Partnership highlights several core areas of cooperation. Firstly, by collecting, compiling, retaining and preserving relevant information, and facilitating the sharing of such information with participating states and relevant international organisations, the Partnership attempts to overcome the hurdles presented by the JIM's confidentiality rules.[37] Information collected by the JIM was treated with a significant degree of confidentiality to protect states that came forward with information and intelligence related to CW use in Syria. However, when Russia blocked the JIM's renewal, that information remained classified at the UN and may now be kept locked away for 20 years or more.[38] Pushing information-sharing among participating states will help to build a repository for information and analysis that can be used to attribute attacks and take further action against CW users.

Secondly, the partnership seeks to use existing legal structures to sanction individuals, entities, groups and governments involved in the proliferation or use of CW, and to publicise the names of those sanctioned. The partnership also seeks to enhance states' legal and operational capabilities to identify and sanction or prosecute these individuals.[39] The JIM's efforts stopped short of imposing costs on implicated actors or entities, and the Partnership seeks to fill this gap through legal, financial and political means.

Sanctions that freeze an individual's or group's assets could impose a significant financial cost on CW users. The public list serves as a forum to name and shame those involved in executing CW attacks, especially if such lists indicate that these individuals face arrest and prosecution if they transit a participating nation's territory. These factors may deter military officers or scientists seeking to become involved with CW programmes or at least prompt them to think twice when targeting civilians with these weapons. In addition, this capacity-building ensures states have the legal and technical assistance needed to implement political, economic and legal accountability mechanisms. This is consistent with states' obligations under both Security Council Resolution 1540 and the CWC – showing how the partnership complements existing CW accountability institutions and mechanisms. Finally, the states agreed to stand together on the use of CW in other international organisations, including the OPCW and UN.[40] While the impetus for the partnership emanates from inaction at the UN and OPCW, the Partnership states are showing that the fight for accountability is not over.

At the time of writing, there were 26 participating parties in the Partnership: Australia, Belgium, Côte d'Ivoire, Czech Republic, European Union, France, Germany, Italy, Japan, Kuwait, Morocco, Netherlands, Peru, Poland, Senegal, South Korea, Spain, Sweden, Switzerland, Tunisia, Turkey, Ukraine, United Kingdom and the United States.[41] The Partnership is not exclusive, nor does it impose any legally binding constraints on its members, as it is not a treaty. It largely follows the PSI model of voluntary membership, though it requires a serious commitment to reduce the dangers emanating from WMD use.

What next?

The political commitments reflected in the Partnership's statement of principles are vital, but insufficient. Meaningful outcomes require that the endorsing nations move quickly to operationalise the partnership through concrete actions. This means focusing not only on the immediate case of CW use in Syria but also anticipating future crises in which this challenge could re-emerge, which might include use by state and non-state actors. While the Partnership is not the only process through which states should seek to uphold the norm against CW use and hold accountable those who violate the norm, for the time being it is the most viable path for collective action.

Enabling a collective international response

The PSI offers examples of collaborative information-sharing, development of best practices, and operational and table-top exercises. But other efforts offer similar parallels. In the areas of counter-terrorism and counter-piracy cooperation, domestic and international law-enforcement entities such as Interpol and the FBI routinely cooperate to maximise successful apprehension and prosecution of suspects through various legal authorities and national jurisdictions. The models for collective action used during the four Nuclear Security Summits, particularly the use of diplomatic 'gift baskets', demonstrate the option of convening subsets of countries around various issues, efforts and approaches without requiring either consensus or the active contribution of all endorsing nations. These flexible, working-group approaches will be particularly essential as the number of endorsers of the Partnership grows.

Raising awareness and speaking collectively

In the near term, endorsing nations can use the Partnership to raise awareness of CW use and speak with one voice. Current efforts to present a unified international response have not worked. The French, British and Americans have done much of the legwork without being able to develop a coalition broader than those countries with a long-standing concern for CW use. Most of the world has very little awareness of the problem, with many populations and governments alike unaware of the scale of CW use in Syria. To remedy this, the Partnership should develop fact sheets on a range of issues – on proliferation, use and countering CW – for participating nations to help educate other governments and diplomatic representatives. They should also develop a comprehensive list of diplomatic, economic and legal tools and approaches to use nationally and collectively to provide an in-depth understanding of the assets available to hold Syria accountable.

The Partnership has several diplomatic actions at its disposal. Participating states can coordinate diplomatic démarches to key countries on the OPCW

Executive Council and UN Security Council to press for greater account-ability for CW use. Joint statements, press releases and other documents can be used to demonstrate collective will and resolve in the UN General Assembly, UN First Committee, Conference on Disarmament, OPCW meet-ings of states parties and the Australia Group.

The Partnership could also help drive a joint statement declaring CW use a violation of customary international law punishable under multiple inter-national legal agreements, including the ICC's Rome Statute, the Geneva Protocol and humanitarian laws against indiscriminate killing. These efforts should encourage broader engagement with civil society, which has shown its ability to pressure governments through the negotiation of the Treaty on the Prohibition of Nuclear Weapons (TPNW). Non-governmental organisa-tions could encourage the over 150 nations that signed on to the TPNW to protect the norm against CW use.

Finally, the OPCW FFM and JIM have both collected, analysed and val-idated enormous volumes of video, witness accounts, samples and other critical evidence. Much of that information is covered by secrecy rules preventing its release. Partner nations can use their collective efforts to get JIM and FFM information released to other UN mechanisms, such as the International, Impartial and Independent Mechanism on international crimes committed in the Syrian Arab Republic (IIIM), to facilitate prosecu-tion of CW use in appropriate international forums.

Capacity-building on CW use

Technical, operational, legal and financial gaps limit the ability of many states to safely and accurately investigate and respond to CW use. Effective accountability requires that nations possess the capacity to investigate, collect and preserve evidence, perform complex technical analysis and appropriately maintain a chain of custody. Today, many of these capa-bilities are limited to a small number of countries and the OPCW. Further steps must be taken to collect and protect evidence of CW use, such as witness testimony, technical-sample analysis, forensic records and assess-ments, until a trial occurs. It is critical this be done in accordance with international legal standards.

These evidence-collection steps can be used for collective international responses through ad hoc mechanisms. Pre-negotiated protocols or agreements between key nations could help facilitate information exchanges between law-enforcement bodies, diplomats and national-security professionals across borders to apprehend and prosecute suspected or known CW users. These arrangements can be demonstrated through exercises to practice preparedness and capability to act. National authorities should refuse to harbour CW users or facilitators of CW attacks, institute financial and economic sanctions, and engage in criminal and civil prosecution. Such national responses can also be used to act against companies or individuals that sell chemicals used in CW attacks.

Through the Partnership, nations can share lessons learned, best practices and model legislation to help bolster the national legal structures that support CW accountability. Partnership countries can also work through the 1540 Committee to build national capacity to prevent, respond to and prosecute CW attacks. States possessing the expertise could instruct on best practices through the 1540 Committee's matchmaking system. They could offer training academies on legal and technical hurdles, or help publicise 1540 Committee opportunities for helping build capacity to prevent and respond to CW attacks. In addition, Partnership countries should lobby for an extension to the 1540 mandate in 2021 to ensure their important work can continue.

Strengthen and expand the Partnership

The 25 current members of the Partnership are a good start, but are not nearly enough. Adding countries not closely aligned with the P3 could help highlight the violation of international law and make the issue less one of a dispute between the P3 and Russia. Nordic, South Asian and South American countries seem likely supporters.

The Partnership should seek programmatic, as well as geographic, expansion. Specific action items need to be created to ensure that the Partnership remains active and its presence felt, even outside of advocacy in international forums. To date, the defence and diplomatic staffs that cover CW issues in Partnership governments have been doing much of the legwork.

As time goes on, demands on their workloads will likely slow Partnership work, absent a more formalised structure to bring together current partners and incorporate new countries into the initiative. To implement this, some sort of modest Partnership secretariat needs to be established, with either permanent or temporary staff on a volunteer basis. This could provide a point of coordination to facilitate communications and create opportunities to convene around specific efforts outside high-level meetings.

Efforts should also be made to improve the 'stickiness' of the Partnership by connecting it to a variety of different forums and institutions beyond those associated with the non-proliferation system. Countries should lay the groundwork before any Syrian peace process to prosecute those who used CW in civil war – an essential step to uphold the CWC in the post-conflict world. Long-term justice mechanisms, similar to the former Yugoslavia's hybrid tribunals, should be pursued for those involved in Syria's CW programme.

Finally, the Partners can press for institutional reforms and mechanisms that will improve the speed and quality of international responses in the event of future attacks, in Syria and beyond. Pre-established mechanisms to address future CW use should be established and upheld. The format of the UN Monitoring, Verification and Inspection Commission (UNMOVIC) in Iraq can serve as a model, whereby scientists are shielded from political pressure by diplomats, avoiding the politicisation of evidence that hindered the JIM process. Finally, UN tools, such as the invocation of General Assembly Resolution 377A, should be used to bring issues from the Security Council to a full General Assembly vote in the case of a Security Council deadlock. This could empower the Secretary-General's Mechanism to perform attribution in the Syrian conflict after the dismantling of the JIM.

The Partnership is not the only means to respond to CW use: the United Nations and OPCW will continue to play a role in the Syria-accountability picture, and nations are compelled to act in their national capacities to respond to the spread and use of CW. However, it remains the best avenue for action for the time being. The Partnership presents clear alternatives: become a part of the continued obstructionism within international institutions, or work with other nations to take action to protect the norm against

CW use. Nations such as Russia that protect violators of international law will be faced with a choice between working through the United Nations to actually resolve the continued use of CW, or witnessing a stronger reliance on ad hoc measures by nations that want to do what needs to be done to protect these norms.

*   *   *

International silence on Syrian chemical-weapons attacks is profoundly damaging, especially in the face of overwhelming evidence that they continue to occur despite Syria's accession to the CWC. The international arms-control and non-proliferation community, which so effectively engages civil society on nuclear issues, has largely turned a blind eye to these attacks and their implications for the non-proliferation regime. The lack of interest and concern from the broader public has allowed governments to continue in wilful ignorance of these atrocities.

The April 2017 US airstrikes imposed some costs on Syria for these attacks, but in the absence of a more consistent, comprehensive and internationalised approach, the results have been fleeting. The Partnership is a first step towards something better, and France's initiative in establishing it is to be applauded. But much difficult work remains to make the Partnership a reliable and effective tool for responding to CW use in the future. Formalising, expanding and deepening the Partnership will be critical to any effort to hold accountable users of chemical weapons in Syria or elsewhere – and doing so could help ensure that calls for justice will not ring hollow. The victims of these attacks deserve no less.

Acknowledgements

This material is based on research sponsored by the US Air Force Academy (USAFA) and the Center for Strategic and International Studies under agreement number FA7000-17-1-0016. The US government is authorised to reproduce and distribute reprints for governmental purposes notwithstanding any copyright notation herein. The opinions, findings, views, conclusions or recommendations contained herein are those of the authors, and should not be interpreted as necessarily representing the official policies or endorsements, either expressed or implied, of the USAFA or the US government.

Notes

1   French Ministry of Foreign Affairs, 'Fight against proliferation – Launch of International Partnership against Impunity for Use of Chemical Weapons', 23 January 2018, https://www.diplomatie.gouv.fr/en/french-foreign-policy/disarmament-and-non-proliferation/events/article/fight-against-proliferation-launch-of-international-partnership-against.

2   Tom O'Connor, 'ISIS Militants Launch Multiple Chemical Weapons Attacks on Iraqi Troops', *Newsweek*, 17 April 2017, http://www.newsweek.com/isis-militants-chemical-weapons-attack-soldiers-iraq-585174.

3   Joby Warrick, 'The Message Behind the Murder: North Korea's Assassination Sheds Light on Chemical Weapons Arsenal', *Washington Post*, 6 July 2017, https://www.washingtonpost.com/world/national-security/the-message-behind-the-murder-north-koreas-assassination-sheds-light-on-chemical-weapons-arsenal/2017/07/06/998b1c38-5d54-11e7-9fc6-c7ef4bc58d13_story.html.

4   French Ministry of Foreign Affairs, 'Chemical Attack in Syria – National Evaluation presented by Jean-Marc Ayrault following the Defense Council Meeting, Annex', 26 April 2017, https://www.diplomatie.gouv.fr/en/country-files/syria/events/article/chemical-attack-in-syria-national-evaluation-presented-by-jean-marc-ayrault.

5   Louisa Loveluck and Carol Morello, 'New Chemical Attacks Reported in Syria, and Trump Administration Blames Russia', *Washington Post*, 23 January 2018, https://www.washingtonpost.com/world/new-chemical-attacks-reported-in-syria-and-trump-administration-blames-russia/2018/01/23/52167730-005b-11e8-86b9-8908743c79dd_story.html?utm_term=.b3a572321c63.

6   Human Rights Watch, 'Death by Chemicals: The Syrian Government's Widespread and Systematic Use of Chemical Weapons', May 2017, pp. 57–62, https://www.hrw.org/sites/default/files/report_pdf/syria0517_web.pdf.

7   Daryl Kimball, 'Timeline of Syrian Chemical Weapons Activity, 2012–2018', Arms Control Association, February 2018, https://www.armscontrol.org/factsheets/Timeline-of-Syrian-Chemical-Weapons-Activity.

8   French Ministry of Foreign Affairs, 'Chemical Attack in Syria'.

9   See OPCW, 'Report of the OPCW Fact-Finding Mission in Syria Regarding Alleged Incidents in the Idlib Governorate of the Syrian Arab Republic Between 16 March and 20 May 2015', 29 October 2015, https://www.opcw.org/fileadmin/OPCW/Fact_Finding_Mission/s-1319-2015_e_.pdf; OPCW, 'Third Report of the OPCW Fact-Finding Mission in Syria', 18 December 2014, https://www.opcw.org/fileadmin/OPCW/Fact_Finding_Mission/s-1230-2014_e_.pdf; OPCW, 'Report of the OPCW Fact-Finding Mission in Syria Regarding the Incident of 16 September 2016 As Reported In the Note Verbale of the Syrian Arab Republic Number 113

Dated 29 November 2016', 1 May 2017, https://www.opcw.org/fileadmin/OPCW/Fact_Finding_Mission/s-1491-2017_e_.pdf; and OPCW, 'Report of the OPCW Fact-Finding Mission in Syria Regarding an Alleged Incident in Khan Shaykhun, Syrian Arab Republic, April 2017', 29 June 2017, https://www.opcw.org/fileadmin/OPCW/Fact_Finding_Mission/s-1491-2017_e_.pdf.

10 United Nations press release, 'Security Council Unanimously Adopts Resolution 2235 (2015), Establishing Mechanism to Identify Perpetrators Using Chemical Weapons in Syria', 7 August 2015, https://www.un.org/press/en/2015/sc12001.doc.htm.

11 UN Security Council, 'Seventh Report of the Organisation for the Prohibition of Chemical Weapons–United Nations Joint Investigative Mechanism', 26 October 2017, http://undocs.org/en/S/2017/904.

12 *Ibid.*

13 Rick Gladstone, 'In U.N. Showdown, Russian Veto Kills Syria Chemical Arms Panel', *New York Times*, 16 November 2017, https://www.nytimes.com/2017/11/16/world/middleeast/syria-chemical-weapons-united-nations.html.

14 OPCW, 'Report of the Organisation for the Prohibition of Chemical Weapons Fact-Finding Mission in the Syrian Arab Republic Regarding an Alleged Incident in Lataminah, Syrian Arab Republic, 30 March 2017', Technical Secretariat Report to the UN Security Council, 6 November 2017, http://undocs.org/S/2017/931.

15 'US Proposal on Syria Rejected by OPCW Executive Council –

Moscow', Sputnik, 24 November 2017, https://sputniknews.com/world/201711241059415284-us-syria-rejection-opcw/.

16 Eliot Higgins, 'For the Third Time This Year, Chlorine Is Used as a Chemical Weapon in Douma, Damascus', Bellingcat, 1 February 2018, https://www.bellingcat.com/news/mena/2018/02/01/third-time-year-chlorine-used-chemical-weapon-douma-damascus/.

17 'Syria War: "Chlorine Attack" on Rebel-Held Idlib Town', BBC News, 5 February 2018, http://www.bbc.com/news/world-middle-east-42944033.

18 'Chlorine Gas Symptoms Reported in Eastern Ghouta, Syria', NBC News, 26 February 2018, https://www.nbcnews.com/news/world/chlorine-gas-symptoms-reported-eastern-ghouta-syria-n851126.

19 UN Security Council, 'Letter Dated 10 January 2018 from the Permanent Representative of the United States of America to the United Nations addressed to the Secretary-General', 16 January 2018, http://www.securitycouncilreport.org/atf/cf/%7B65BFCF9B-6D27-4E9C-8CD3-CF6E4FF96FF9%7D/s_2018_35.pdf.

20 Everett Rosenfeld, 'Trump Launches Attack on Syria with 59 Tomahawk Missiles', CNBC, 7 April 2017, https://www.cnbc.com/2017/04/06/us-military-has-launched-more-50-than-missiles-aimed-at-syria-nbc-news.html.

21 'France's Macron Threatens Syria Strikes if Chemical Weapon Use Proven', BBC News, 14 February 2018, http://www.bbc.com/news/world-europe-43053617.

22 US Department of Defense, 'Media

Availability by Secretary Mattis at the Pentagon', 2 February 2018, https://www.defense.gov/News/Transcripts/Transcript-View/Article/1431844/media-availability-by-secretary-mattis-at-the-pentagon/.

23 'Tillerson Says Military Action Still Possible for Syrian Chemical Attacks', *60 Minutes*, 15 February 2018, https://www.cbsnews.com/news/secretary-of-state-rex-tillerson-says-military-action-still-possible-for-syria-chemical-attacks/.

24 DoD, 'Media Availability by Secretary Mattis at the Pentagon'.

25 See UN Security Council, 'Fourth report of the Organisation for the Prohibition of Chemical Weapons–United Nations Joint Investigative Mechanism', 21 October 2016, https://www.un.org/ga/search/view_doc.asp?symbol=S/2016/888; and UN Security Council, 'Seventh Report of the Organisation for the Prohibition of Chemical Weapons–United Nations Joint Investigative Mechanism', 26 October 2017, http://undocs.org/en/S/2017/904.

26 Suzanne Goldenberg, John Gittings and Brian Whitaker, 'Sailing On, the Ship with a Hold Full of Scud Missiles', *Guardian*, 11 December 2002, https://www.theguardian.com/world/2002/dec/12/yemen.northkorea.

27 Office of the White House Press Secretary, 'Statement of Interdiction Principles', 4 September 2003, https://www.state.gov/t/isn/c27726.htm.

28 US Department of State, 'Joint Statement from Proliferation Security Initiative (PSI) Partners in Support of United Nations Security Council Resolutions 2375 and 2397 Enforcement', 12 January 2018,

29 *Ibid.*

30 Dapo Akande, 'Can the ICC Prosecute for Use of Chemical Weapons in Syria?', EJIL: Talk! Blog of the European Journal of International Law, 23 August 2013, https://www.ejiltalk.org/can-the-icc-prosecute-for-use-of-chemical-weapons-in-syria/.

31 Thilo Marauhn, 'Chemical Weapons and Warfare', *Max Plank Encyclopedia of Public International Law*, June 2016, http://opil.ouplaw.com/view/10.1093/law:epil/9780199231690/law-9780199231690-e264.

32 French Ministry of Foreign Affairs, 'Fight Against Proliferation'.

33 *Ibid.*

34 Rex Tillerson, 'Remarks on Russia's Responsibility for the Ongoing Use of Chemical Weapons in Syria', US Department of State, 23 January 2018, https://www.state.gov/secretary/remarks/2018/01/277601.htm.

35 International Partnership Against Impunity for the Use of Chemical Weapons, 'Declaration of Principles', 23 January 2018, https://www.noimpunitychemicalweapons.org/.

36 *Ibid.*

37 *Ibid.*

38 UN Secretariat, 'Secretary-General's Bulletin: Information Sensitivity, Classification, and Handling', 12 February 2007, https://archives.un.org/sites/archives.un.org/files/ST_SGB_2007_6_eng.pdf.

39 Partnership, 'Declaration of Principles'.

40 *Ibid.*

41 Partnership, 'Participants', 23 January 2018, https://www.noimpunitychemicalweapons.org.

https://www.state.gov/r/pa/prs/ps/2018/01/277419.htm.

Smart Cities: A New Age of Digital Insecurity

Yu-Min Joo and Teck-Boon Tan

Smart cities that capitalise on the power of digital technology to improve the urban experience are multiplying across the globe. While these cities offer a promising solution to many contemporary urban challenges, they are also ushering in a new age of digital insecurity in which cyber-security loopholes can be exploited by malicious hackers to wreak substantial digital and physical damage. To counteract this threat, cities need to identify their digital-security gaps and introduce a risk-management approach that puts priority on key city assets and services for protection. What is more, because cyber attacks tend to be transboundary in nature, smart cities around the world must work in partnership to fend off such attacks.

A new era of digital insecurity

Humanity is becoming an urban species.[1] In 1950, a mere 746 million people lived in cities. Today, that figure is close to four billion, representing more than half of the world's population. Unless some catastrophic event, such as a war or pandemic, reverses this trend, the number of people living in cities will surpass six billion, or 66% of the world's population, by 2050.[2]

A downside of this rapid urban growth is that it has created a globally shared set of complex and unwanted consequences, such as environmental degradation, resource depletion, overcrowding and poor security.[3]

Yu-Min Joo is Assistant Professor at the Lee Kuan Yew School of Public Policy, National University of Singapore. **Teck-Boon Tan** is Research Fellow and Coordinator of the Science and Technology Studies Programme at the S. Rajaratnam School of International Studies, Nanyang Technological University, Singapore.

Survival | vol. 60 no. 2 | April–May 2018 | pp. 91–106   DOI 10.1080/00396338.2018.1448577

Consuming close to two-thirds of the world's energy and producing large amounts of waste, cities are responsible for more than 70% of global greenhouse-gas emissions.[4] Additionally, spatial inequality and skyrocketing housing prices are forcing many city-dwellers to settle for poor living conditions.[5] Meanwhile, rising crime rates have rendered many cities unsafe for their residents.[6] With three million people leaving the countryside every week and flooding into cities in search of a better life, the urban experience has deteriorated dramatically.[7]

To improve this experience, city governments around the world, working in collaboration with the corporate sector, are turning to the techno-utopian vision of smart cities. Broadly defined as urban centres that harness the power of digital technology – information and communication technologies, mobile apps, cloud computing and so forth – to monitor, understand and manage the urban environment, smart cities are widely viewed as a positive and transformational solution to the assorted challenges facing cities today.[8] In these high-tech urban settings, digital technology drives almost every aspect of city life, including healthcare, public transportation, power supply, water management, e-government and telecommunications.[9] Practically everything – from complex systems such as physical infrastructure and automobiles to everyday devices such as mobile phones and refrigerators – are digitally connected to help improve a city's liveability. (These internet-enabled gadgets are sometimes referred to collectively as the 'internet of things'.) In addition, a heterogeneous collection of smart sensors are embedded in city structures not just to collect real-time information on a whole host of urban processes, but also to automatically trigger remedial action when problems are detected.[10]

Yet smart cities have a dark side too. It is becoming increasingly apparent that malicious hackers can exploit smart cities' hitherto unknown digital vulnerabilities to inflict substantial damage.[11] Several scenarios are possible in which hackers, whether state-sponsored or working on their own, breach the cyber defences of a smart city. For example, hackers may gain unauthorised access to sensitive city-level data from core networks and servers.[12] In what is known as a 'distributed denial of service' (DDoS) attack, they could also commandeer systems to send an overwhelming number of queries to websites and services, causing them to crash.[13] Even worse, attackers could subvert critical infrastructure, including power plants and banks, either by shutting them down or operating them in a dangerous and unpredictable manner.[14] With the number of attacks on critical infrastructure increasing from 200 to 300 between 2012 and 2015, it is clear that malicious hackers have turned their attention to these complex systems, and it is only a matter of time before they succeed in doing severe damage.[15]

Despite this danger, research into the digital vulnerabilities of smart cities remains in its infancy, with the field mostly limited to a small cadre of cyber-security researchers and professionals operating largely within the confines of their own disciplines.[16] The corporate sector, meanwhile, has continued to portray the smart city as a transformational innovation, potentially blinding municipal governments to the seriousness of the threat.[17]

Cyber–physical threats

We have identified four critical digital vulnerabilities endemic to all smart cities worldwide (see Table 1). These cyber-security loopholes stem from the digital technologies that form the backbone of such cities. The first pertains to how a city's infrastructure can be undermined by malicious actors via its computer control systems. The second relates to how smart cities have become susceptible to DDoS attacks after being retrofitted with poorly secured 'resource-constrained' devices (digital systems with limited computing power, anti-virus protection and firewall applications). The third arises from the extensive application of wireless connectivity – a communication technology that exposes digital data to interception and modification. The fourth stems from the widespread adoption of cloud-based data storage, a course of action that has created an additional pathway for malicious hackers to gain unauthorised access to sensitive city-level data.

A whole host of modern infrastructure systems – including traffic lights and street lamps, power plants and water-treatment facilities – in smart cities are operated over the internet, allowing city managers to implement changes remotely before minor problems turn critical.[18] This is possible only because an industrial control system (ICS) has been added to the infrastructure systems to facilitate command and control. (An ICS is a

Table 1: **Summary of critical digital vulnerabilities**

Vulnerability	Key features
Industrial control systems	• Hackers can subvert critical infrastructure by attacking insecure industrial control systems. • Failure in one system can shut down other systems if they are interconnected.
Resource-constrained units	• Rudimentary digital devices that lack anti-virus or firewall applications can be commandeered by hackers to launch DDoS attacks on other systems. • Attacks on units that were mass-produced can easily be replicated across other identical units. • Units may be physically insecure due to their deployment in wide-open conditions.
Wireless communication	• Wireless communication exposes digital devices to MitM attacks. • Content broadcast through the air can be intercepted and modified.
Cloud storage	• Cloud storage is becoming a target for hackers as more city-level data is transferred to the cloud. • Data security is wholly dependent on cloud service providers.

small computer system that makes the remote monitoring and operation of its host possible over the internet.[19]) The automation, convenience and efficiency that come with ICS-controlled infrastructure entail considerable risks, since any computer system connected to the internet can, in theory, be hacked.[20] To make matters worse, the recent move away from proprietary standards to open ones for ICS communications protocols has made it easier for hackers to gain detailed knowledge of the operations of these computer systems from the public domain.[21] Akin to how Android's open platform has exposed the Google operating system to more malicious applications – as opposed to iPhone's proprietary OS operating system, which tends to be more secure because of the tight grip Apple maintains on its platform – the move to open standards has rendered many systems susceptible to cyber attacks and digital manipulation.[22] Some might argue that the move to open standards enhances digital security by allowing more cyber-security researchers to study the codes for weaknesses. While that is certainly true, it is important to recognise that this openness also enables more malicious hackers – from sophisticated state-sponsored outfits to run-of-the-mill cyber criminals – to study the codes for exploitable vulnerabilities. Overall, our research suggests that the open-source nature of industrial control systems increases the vulnerability of their host systems to cyber attacks.

Figure 1: **Hyper-connected critical-infrastructure systems**

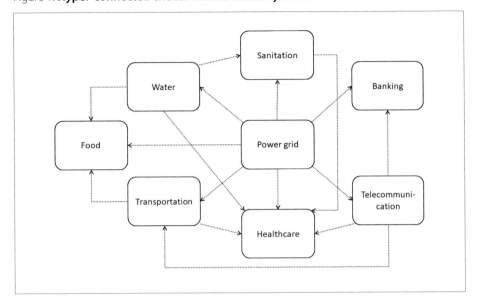

Specifically, hackers can take over a given piece of infrastructure simply by subverting its ICS.[23] A recent example of such an attack occurred in 2015, when pro-Russia hackers took down Ukraine's power grid after armed conflict broke out between the two countries.[24] The hackers were able to do so precisely because they had subverted the ICS controlling the power grid.[25] Leaving nearly 230,000 Ukrainians without power for hours, the attack demonstrated the kind of physical destruction malicious hackers are capable of creating with a cyber weapon. It is worth emphasising that the Ukrainians' ability to revert to manual control likely limited the severity of the attack. In smart cities, that remedial step might not be possible, since ICS-controlled infrastructure often does not have manual backup features. In addition, the outcome of such an attack is likely to be more severe in smart cities because the infrastructure systems in these high-tech urban areas rarely exist in isolation. Hence, a failure in one system is likely to cause near-simultaneous shutdowns in others.[26] The power grid, as a case in point, is connected not only to the banking sector, but also to critical city services such as water treatment, hospitals, telecommunications and transportation (see Figure 1).[27] It is clear that a failure in the power grid could set off a chain reaction causing significant collateral damage.[28]

Our research has also revealed that many of the sensors, devices and systems that have been embedded in smart cities have not been secured from manipulation and tampering by malicious actors.[29] Smart parking sensors that help drivers locate parking spaces with their phones are a prime example.[30] Implanted beneath each parking space, the digital sensors detect whether the space is occupied and then broadcast that information to nearby drivers. The benefits of smart parking sensors are easily grasped: not only do they save drivers time, but they also help to reduce carbon emissions, since people no longer have to drive around aimlessly looking for parking spaces. Even so, the relatively simple designs of smart parking sensors preclude them from having security features, such as authentication protocols, anti-virus applications and firewalls.[31] Without such features, these resource-constrained units are particularly vulnerable to cyber attacks. Once these units have been subverted, hackers can turn them into platforms for launching DDoS attacks on other systems in the same network.[32] Specifically, by injecting malicious software or malware such as *Mirai* into these units, hackers can turn them into 'botnets' – infected devices that send repeated queries to websites and services.[33] In practice, patching resource-constrained units with security updates is not possible given their basic designs.[34] Once they are off the assembly line, little can be done, even when a security flaw is discovered.

Resource-constrained units are vulnerable

Compounding the problem of resource-constrained units is the fact that many of these poorly secured devices are mass-produced, thus making it possible for a successful cyber attack on one unit to be replicated across all other identical units.[35] That is to say, once hackers figure out how a unit can be breached, they will be able to use the same method of attack on an entire product line by virtue of its homogeneity.[36] Were that to happen, the only way out would be for the manufacturer to issue a massive recall – an expensive prospect considering that there may well be hundreds of thousands, or even millions, of units deployed in smart cities worldwide.

Not only are the digital sensors, devices and systems of smart cities digitally insecure, they are physically insecure as well. Deployed under wide-open conditions, they tend to lack the kind of physical protection provided by enclosed premises. As a result, they are vulnerable to tampering and unauthorised modifications by malicious actors, who may be able to access them with little difficulty through an unlocked panel, for example.[37] A case in point would be the smart street light. Sophisticated enough to automatically adjust their brightness to match ambient conditions, smart street lights are clearly susceptible to physical tampering by virtue of being accessible to all.[38] A hacker might choose to switch them off at will – disrupting traffic and potentially endangering the lives of road users. Other examples of exposed technologies include smart electricity and gas meters, surveillance (CCTV) cameras, traffic lights and the aforementioned parking sensors.[39]

A third digital vulnerability arises from the extensive use of wireless communications.[40] Synonymous with 4G, Bluetooth, Wi-Fi and Near Field Communication, wireless communications allow cities to expand their networks and incorporate more electronic devices without having to simultaneously increase physical IT resources by, for example, installing Ethernet crossover cables and access points.[41] More importantly, they offer the benefit of mobility: wireless communications allow people to make use of their digital devices wherever there is wireless connection. At the same time, however, this mode of communication exposes smart devices to so-called 'man in the middle' (MitM) attacks.[42]

Unlike hard-wired communications, wireless communications involve the transmission of digital content through the air between endpoints, making them more prone to data interception by unauthorised parties.[43] Anyone situated between two endpoint devices and equipped with a special interception device could capture the data flowing between the endpoints. If the data is unencrypted, the hacker would be able to see all the intercepted content.[44] For example, if one of the endpoint devices was fitted with a wireless Internet Protocol camera, the hacker would be able to see whatever the camera sees.[45] If the device in question was a Wi-Fi printer, the hacker would be able to intercept any document sent to it for printing.[46] Although MitM attacks clearly have profound implications for privacy and intellectual-property rights, the threat has so far been confined mostly to homes and businesses. That is likely to change, however, with the rise of smart cities.

Given that smart sensors have a tendency to broadcast their data through the air without partnering devices, hackers no longer have to position themselves between two endpoint devices to intercept the digital information being transmitted. Simply placing an interception device in the range of the transmitting device and boosting its signal would be sufficient to spoof the first device into 'believing' that the second was a legitimate receiving device.[47] Smart parking sensors are prime examples of this security vulnerability, since they do not relay information over private channels of communication with other devices, but broadcast their data openly to other in-range devices, such as smart phones and tablets. Other examples of devices that openly broadcast their data include air-pollution sensors and flood detectors. These gadgets are designed to send out alerts to subscribers when environmental anomalies such as poor air quality or rising water levels are detected.[48]

It is not difficult to envision a situation in which a malicious actor might try to feed bogus content to receiving stations in order to disrupt smart-city services. Smart CCTV cameras, for example, could be compromised by MitM attacks to transmit doctored images to law-enforcement agencies to impede police surveillance or investigation.[49] Alternatively, hackers could intercept data sent out by flooding sensors and re-transmit fake information to receiving stations, indicating that water levels are not rising when in fact they are. In an era of smart cities, malicious digital acts can have serious physical consequences.

By far the most effective method of countering MitM attacks on endpoint devices is to build strong encryption and authentication protocols into them. However, this is not always possible due to the fact that many smart sensors, devices and systems are precluded from retaining strong digital-security features by virtue of their minimalist designs.

The final digital vulnerability stems from the decision of smart-city governments to embrace cloud-based data storage – a decision that has created an additional pathway for malicious hackers to gain unauthorised access to sensitive city-level data. Smart cities generate a massive amount of data that needs to be stored efficiently. City managers have turned to the cloud – a network of computer servers designed for data storage and running

Table 2: **Cyber attacks on the cloud**

Year	Nature of the intrusion
2013	Breach of Target's point-of-sale networks.
2014	Breach of Apple's iCloud. About 500 private pictures, including those of celebrities, are leaked.
2016	500 million Yahoo accounts hacked.
2016	World Anti-Doping Agency database is hacked by Russian group Fancy Bear. Confidential medical data is released to the public.
2016	Phishing operations by Russian groups Cozy Bear and Fancy Bear target 60,000 private emails, including those of top US Democrats.
2016	Major DDoS attacks on Dyn's DNS (Domain Name System) infrastructure. Companies including Twitter, Netflix and Reddit experience service disruptions.
2016–17	Breach of toy company CloudPets's database. Users' data leaked.
2017	Security bug ('Cloudbleed') found in Cloudflare, a US-based CSP. The bug allows users to access other users' private information.
2017	Google phishing scam affects about one million Google Docs cloud-storage users.

applications – to cope with the upsurge in data generated. The Seoul metropolitan government, for example, has plans to migrate *all* city-level data to the cloud by 2020.[50]

The benefits of cloud storage are well documented.[51] A cost-effective solution offering pay-as-you-use data storage, the cloud eliminates the need for city governments to expand their own in-house storage infrastructure as the volume of data generated by smart-city technologies swells. This means that cities no longer have to bear the numerous costs associated with hardware maintenance, regular software updates, data-centre security and so on. Given the cost benefits, it is no surprise that smart-city governments are turning to commercial cloud-based services.[52]

Yet in their rush to take advantage of the benefits of cloud-based data storage, city governments may have overlooked the security implications. The biggest weakness of the mass migration of city-level data to the cloud is that the responsibility for data security now depends solely on the cloud service providers (CSPs). In other words, if the CSPs fail to put in place rigorous data-security standards to protect their servers, they risk exposing their storage hardware to malicious attacks and data theft.[53] With no jurisdiction or direct ownership over these servers, smart-city governments have to rely extensively on CSPs to secure their data.[54] This is problematic, since CSPs have demonstrated that they have a tendency to fail in this regard (see Table 2). Indeed, the high-profile breaches of Apple's iCloud in 2014, which resulted in the leaking of nude images of dozens of female celebrities, underlined the pitfalls of cloud-based data storage provided by companies that have not done enough to protect their clients' sensitive data from malicious hackers.[55]

While it is fair to assume that other digital vulnerabilities exist, the four identified here are likely to be among the most serious. No matter how well smart cities may address contemporary urban challenges, they cannot improve the urban experience for their residents if they are not safe to live in. The future of smart cities hinges on how well their governments manage these digital vulnerabilities. Cyber security has traditionally fallen under the jurisdiction of national governments; city governments rarely, if ever, pay much attention to it. With the rise of smart cities, the question of how city governments can cope with an ever-increasing cyber threat will only become more pressing. Dealing with cyber attacks may no longer be a matter of choice for city governments, but rather a necessity.

Cyber security for smart cities

How might smart-city governments respond to the digital vulnerabilities discussed here? Considering the sheer number of smart sensors, devices and systems in place, a plan to shield every one of them from malicious attacks is neither realistic nor practical. An estimated 8.4 billion 'connected things' are currently deployed worldwide, a number that is expected to reach a staggering 20.4 billion by 2020.[56] The question, then, is not how the problem of cyber security can be *solved*, but rather how it can be *managed*.

Given finite public resources, smart-city governments need to consider cyber security through the lens of risk management – a process in which the probability of an unwanted outcome, or more appropriately a hazard, is systematically and meticulously assessed, evaluated and then managed. A key feature of this approach is the weighing of the projected impact of a breach against the resources required to stop it. In other words, the more critical a system is, the more resources it should receive to keep it digitally secure. The advantage of this approach is that it will force governments to thoroughly examine their digital systems in order to zero in on those assessed to be the most critical. This methodical exercise will, in turn, pave the way for a more informed process of securing those systems. Failing to adopt this calibrated approach will inevitably result in the misallocation of valuable resources for the protection of less essential systems.

In addition, this risk-based approach reduces the monumental task of securing the smart city into something that is more manageable. By streamlining and ranking what needs to be protected, cities can begin to undertake a task that might otherwise prove impossible. To be sure, this approach will leave some systems open to digital intrusion. Even so, by determining which systems ought to be assigned the highest priority, cities can begin to implement a cyber-defence policy that will not result in complete failure. After all, the danger of trying to secure everything is that nothing gets sufficiently protected in the end.

Apart from securing the most critical systems, the risk-management approach also calls for measures to deter hackers from launching cyber attacks. In the same way that burglars are more likely to be deterred by homes with strong security systems, hackers too prefer to take the path of least resistance. A coherent cyber-defence policy for smart cities should therefore aim to raise the costs of hackers' activities.[57] In theory, smart-city governments could deter cyber attacks by making them more painful, challenging and expensive for the perpetrators. In practical terms, this strategy calls for two distinct sets of activity.

Firstly, smart-city governments need to introduce more rigorous preventive security measures to make it more difficult for hackers to intrude into municipal infrastructure and core networks. Such measures should include adopting best practices to protect smart-city technologies, keeping abreast with the latest technologies and the most recent security patches, putting in place a recovery plan in the event of a breach, and ensuring that city employees and contractors follow strict cyber-security guidelines, such as not connecting their personal USB flash drives to the city's core networks, and not opening suspicious emails.[58]

Secondly, smart-city governments could deter cyber attacks by increasing the penalties for hackers, thus signalling that perpetrators will be held accountable for their crimes. However, the problem of attribution – defined as the process of establishing the identity and location of an attacker – can often hamper efforts to bring those responsible for cyber crimes to justice. Moreover, cyber attacks are often transboundary in nature, meaning that hackers are frequently located far away from their targets. This not only complicates law-enforcement investigations into cyber attacks, but also compounds the challenge of indicting the perpetrators.[59]

That being said, smart-city governments can improve their chances of bringing cyber criminals to justice by working in concert with international law-enforcement agencies and national governments. Given the transboundary nature of the problem and the unpleasant fact that successful cyber attacks on mass-produced devices can be easily replicated worldwide, it is only logical for smart cities around the world to come together as a collective to fend off malicious hackers. By hardening their cyber defences through joint investigations and prosecutions, smart-city governments, as a global collective, can force malicious hackers to expend more time and resources to adapt, thus raising the cost of launching attacks. Sharing information about new cyber threats and, more importantly, cyber-security solutions will also strengthen the ability of smart-city governments to stay ahead of an ever-evolving digital threat.

*   *   *

Smart cities may well make it possible for humanity to thrive even in relentlessly growing urban areas. Yet such cities are currently exposing their residents to the possibility of a large-scale cyber attack, with the attendant possibility of substantial digital and physical damage. This being the case, one might argue that smart cities may not be worth the risk. The urban experience will hardly be improved if a cyber attack unleashes a large-scale disaster.

Even so, turning away from smart cities will also mean giving up on a potentially viable solution to the complex set of urban challenges facing cities today. It is also unclear if there are other workable solutions. Smart cities may pose significant risks, but may also set humanity on a sustainable development path as it transforms into an urban species. Resolving this policy dilemma will not be an easy task.

Fortunately, smart-city governments can begin to improve the trade-off between the risks of digital intrusion and the rewards of smart cities by responding to the four digital vulnerabilities identified here with a cyber-defence strategy that draws on the principles of risk management. By identifying key city assets and services for protection, city governments will be in a stronger position to cope with this new era of digital insecurity. Doing so would surely be the smarter move.

Acknowledgements

The authors wish to thank Professor Simon A. Chesterman, Dean and Professor of Law at the National University of Singapore, for reading an earlier draft of this article and providing helpful comments. Any error of fact, analysis or judgement remains entirely the authors' own. This research has been financially supported by the Lee Kuan Yew School of Public Policy, National University of Singapore, and the S. Rajaratnam School of International Studies, Nanyang Technological University of Singapore.

Notes

1   Edward Glaeser, *Triumph of the City* (New York: Penguin Books, 2011), p. 1.

2   The United Nations, 'World's Population Increasingly Urban with More than Half Living in Urban Areas', 10 July 2014, http://www.un.org/en/development/desa/news/population/world-urbanization-prospects-2014.html.

3   Leo Hollis, *Cities Are Good for You: Genius of the Metropolis* (New York: Bloomsbury Press, 2013), p. 7.

4   The World Bank, 'Urban Development Overview', 29 March 2017, http://www.worldbank.org/en/topic/urbandevelopment/overview.

5   Kevin Lui, 'Move Over, New Yorkers: You Have No Idea How Small an Apartment Can Really Get', *Time*, 9 December 2016, http://time.com/4581230/hong-kong-apartments-property-sale-rent-small-housing/.

6   Josh Sanburn and David Johnson, 'Violent Crime Is On the Rise in U.S. Cities', *Time*, 30 January 2017, http://time.com/4651122/homicides-increase-cities-2016/.

7   International Organization for Migration, 'World Migration Report 2015, Migrants and Cities: New Partnerships to Manage Mobility', 2015, p. 15, http://publications.iom.int/system/files/wmr2015_en.pdf.

8   See, for example, A. Townsend, *Smart Cities: Big Data, Civic Hackers and the Quest for a New Utopia* (New York: W.W. Norton & Company, 2014); and Rob Kitchin, 'Making Sense of Smart Cities: Addressing Present Shortcomings', *Cambridge Journal of Regions, Economy and Society*, vol. 8, no. 1, 2015, pp. 131–6.

9   Amirhosein Ghaffarianhoseini et al., 'The Essence of Future Smart Houses:

From Embedding ICT to Adapting to Sustainability Principles', *Renewable & Sustainable Energy Reviews*, vol. 24, August 2013, pp. 593–607.

10 Rob Kitchin, Tracey P. Lauriault and Gavin McArdle, 'Knowing and Governing Cities Through Urban Indicators, City Benchmarking, and Real-time Dashboards', *Regional Studies, Regional Science*, vol. 2, no. 1, 2015, pp. 6–28.

11 See, for example, Cesar Cerrudo, 'Hacking Smart Cities', paper presented at RSA Conference 2015, San Francisco, CA, 20–24 April, https://www.rsaconference.com/writable/presentations/file_upload/hta-t10-hacking-smart-cities_final.pdf; and William Woo, 'IT/OT Security in the Digital Economy', conference address, NCS TechConnect, 5 May 2017.

12 Cerrudo, 'Hacking Smart Cities'.

13 'How Vulnerable Are Your Devices to Hackers?', *Straits Times*, 31 May 2017, http://www.straitstimes.com/singapore/how-vulnerable-are-your-devices.

14 Vice Admiral (Retd) Mike McConnell, 'The Future of Cyber Security: Threats, Implications and Strategies', keynote address, Singapore International Cyber Week, 11 October 2016.

15 Todd Thibodeaux, 'Smart Cities Are Going to Be a Security Nightmare', *Harvard Business Review*, 28 April 2017, https://hbr.org/2017/04/smart-cities-are-going-to-be-a-security-nightmare.

16 Rob Kitchin, *Getting Smarter About Smart Cities: Improving Data Privacy and Data Security* (Dublin: Data Protection Unit, Department of the Taoiseach, 2016), p. 9.

17 Andrés Luque-Ayala and Simon Marvin, 'Developing a Critical Understanding of Smart Urbanism?', *Urban Studies*, vol. 52, no. 12, 2015, pp. 2,105–16.

18 Kitchin, Lauriault and McArdle, 'Knowing and Governing Cities Through Urban Indicators, City Benchmarking, and Real-time Dashboards'.

19 Igor Calzada and Cristobal Cobo, 'Unplugging: Deconstructing the Smart City', *Journal of Urban Technology*, vol. 22, no. 1, 2015, pp. 23–43.

20 Bruce Schneier, 'Want to Evade NSA Spying? Don't Connect to the Internet', *Wired*, 7 October 2013, https://www.wired.com/2013/10/149481/.

21 Vinay M. Igure, Sean A. Laughter and Ronald D. Williams, 'Security Issues in SCADA Networks', *Computer and Security*, vol. 25, no. 7, 2006, pp. 498–506.

22 Kim Zetter, '10K Reasons to Worry About Critical Infrastructure', *Wired*, 24 January 2012, https://www.wired.com/2012/01/10000-control-systems-online/.

23 James Barrat, *Our Final Invention: Artificial Intelligence and the End of the Human Era* (New York: St. Martin's Press, 2013), p. 256.

24 Kim Zetter, 'Inside the Cunning, Unprecedented Hack of Ukraine's Power Grid', *Wired*, 3 March 2016, https://www.wired.com/2016/03/inside-cunning-unprecedented-hack-ukraines-power-grid/.

25 *Ibid.*

26 Kevin Soo Hoo, Seymour Goodman and Lawrence Greenberg, 'Information Technology and the

Terrorist Threat', *Survival*, vol. 39, no. 3, Autumn 1997, pp. 135–55.

27 Filipe Caldeira et al., 'Towards Protecting Critical Infrastructures', in Jean-Loup Richet (ed.), *Cybersecurity Policies and Strategies for Cyberwarfare Prevention* (Hershey, PA: IGI Global, 2015).

28 David Clark, Thomas Berson and Herbert S. Lin (eds), *At the Nexus of Cybersecurity and Public Policy: Some Basic Concepts and Issues* (Washington DC: National Academies Press, 2014).

29 Luque-Ayala and Marvin, 'Developing a Critical Understanding of Smart Urbanism?'.

30 Regan Schoultz, 'Smart Technology Ends Search for City Centre Parking Spots', *NZ Herald*, 7 January 2016, http://www.nzherald.co.nz/nz/news/article.cfm?c_id=1&objectid=11570293.

31 David West, 'Achieving Security for Resource-Constrained Devices', *Sensors*, 17 March 2017, http://www.sensorsmag.com/components/achieving-security-for-resource-con-strained-sensors.

32 Jason Nurse et al., 'Smart Insiders: Exploring the Threat from Insiders Using the Internet-of-Things', International Workshop on Secure Internet of Things, 2015.

33 David E. Sanger and Nicole Perlroth, 'A New Era of Internet Attacks Powered by Everyday Devices', *New York Times*, 22 October 2016, https://www.nytimes.com/2016/10/23/us/politics/a-new-era-of-internet-attacks-powered-by-everyday-devices.html?_r=0.

34 Paulo Shakarian, Jana Shakarian and Andrew Ruef, *Introduction to Cyber-Warfare: A Multidisciplinary Approach*

(Cambridge, MA: Elsevier, 2013), p. 202.

35 Andrea Noble, 'Chinese Company to Recall Digital Devices that Hackers Hijacked to Launch Cyberattack', *Washington Times*, 24 October 2016, http://www.washingtontimes.com/news/2016/oct/24/hackers-used-chi-nese-devices-to-target-us-firm-ann/.

36 US Department of Homeland Security, National Protection and Programs Directorate – Office of Cyber and Infrastructure Analysis, 'The Future of Smart Cities: Cyber-Physical Infrastructure Risk', August 2015, p. 12, https://ics-cert.us-cert.gov/sites/default/files/documents/OCIA%20-%20The%20Future%20of%20Smart%20Cities%20-%20Cyber-Physical%20Infrastructure%20Risk.pdf.

37 Ian Hardy, 'Are Smart City Transport Systems Vulnerable to Hackers?', BBC, 5 August 2016, http://www.bbc.com/news/business-36854293.

38 Tomas Kellner, 'Smart Streets Are Made of These: San Diego Deploys America's First Intelligent Lighting System', GE Reports, 24 September 2015, http://www.gereports.com/smart-streets-are-made-of-these-san-diego-deploys-americas-first-intelli-gent-lighting-system/.

39 Interview with a senior IT official in the Seoul Metropolitan Government, South Korea, 9 June 2017; Nicole Kobie, 'Why Smart Cities Need to Get Wise to Security – and Fast', *Guardian*, 13 May 2015, https://www.theguard-ian.com/technology/2015/may/13/smart-cities-internet-things-security-cesar-cerrudo-ioactive-labs.

40 Discussion with a senior executive

of a multinational IT company in Singapore, 24 June 2016.

41 Chris Anderson, 'The Wi-Fi Revolution', *Wired*, 1 May 2003, https://www.wired.com/2003/05/wifirevolution/.

42 Kim Zetter, 'Hacking Wireless Printers with Phones on Drones', *Wired*, 5 October 2015, https://www.wired.com/2015/10/drones-robot-vacuums-can-spy-office-printer/.

43 Nurse et al., 'Smart Insiders: Exploring the Threat from Insiders Using the Internet-of-Things'.

44 'How Vulnerable Are Your Devices to Hackers?'.

45 Andrei Costin, 'Security of CCTV and Video Surveillance Systems: Threats, Vulnerabilities, Attacks, and Mitigations', Proceedings of the 6th International Workshop on Trustworthy Embedded Devices, Vienna, Austria, 28 October 2016, pp. 45–54.

46 Zetter, 'Hacking Wireless Printers with Phones on Drones'.

47 Kobie, 'Why Smart Cities Need to Get Wise to Security – and Fast'.

48 Steven Melendez, 'A New Generation of Smart Sensors Aim to Track the Air You Breathe', *Fast Company*, 23 February 2015, https://www.fastcompany.com/3042504/a-new-generation-of-smart-sensors-aim-to-track-the-air-you-breathe; PUB, 'Water Levels Sensors and CCTVs', 2017, https://app.pub.gov.sg/waterlevel/pages/waterlevelsensors.aspx.

49 Discussion with a senior IT official in the Seoul Metropolitan Government, South Korea, 2 June 2017.

50 Seoul Metropolitan Government, 'Seoul, 2020 "Global Digital Capital" 4 Strategy Presentation', press release, 3 February 2016, http://english.seoul.go.kr/seoul-2020-global-digital-capital-4-strategy-presentation/.

51 Petra Maresova, Vladimir Sobeslav and Ondrej Krejcar, 'Cost–Benefit Analysis – Evaluation Model of Cloud Computing Deployment for Use in Companies', *Applied Economics*, vol. 49, no. 6, 2017, pp. 521–33.

52 Discussion with a senior sales executive from Cisco (Cloud Solutions) in Singapore, 4 August 2017.

53 Discussion with a senior Singapore government IT official, 24 June 2016.

54 Steve Gold, 'Protecting the Cloud: Attack Vectors and Other Exploits', *Network Security*, December 2010, pp. 10–12.

55 Issie Lapowsky, 'We'd All Benefit if Celebs Sue Apple Over the Photo Hack', *Wired*, 4 September 2014, https://www.wired.com/2014/09/law-apple-photo-hack/.

56 Rob van der Meulen, 'Gartner Says 8.4 Billion Connected "Things" Will Be in Use in 2017, Up 31 Percent From 2016', 7 February 2017, http://www.gartner.com/newsroom/id/3598917.

57 'Cybersecurity Strategies in Power Generation: Defence or Resilience', roundtable discussion, Singapore International Energy Week, 13 December 2016.

58 James P. Farwell and Rafal Rohozinski, 'The New Reality of Cyber War', *Survival*, vol. 54, no. 4, August–September 2012, pp. 107–20.

59 Lily Hay Newman, 'Hacker Lexicon: What Is the Attribution Problem?', *Wired*, 24 December 2016, https://www.wired.com/2016/12/hacker-lexicon-attribution-problem/.

American Military Superiority and the Pacific-Primacy Myth

Van Jackson

Does the United States seek primacy in Asia? The belief that it does is widespread and long-standing. Scholars and pundits in the United States and around the world routinely reference the condition of primacy in Asia – defined here as unrivalled influence over strategic life[1] – as either a means or an end of US strategy, or both. But is it accurate? This matters as much more than a semantic dispute. The presumption of Asian primacy features prominently in debates about US grand strategy. Some see it as a normative good for the United States, the only adequate means for securing US interests abroad.[2] Others give the unsustainability of a condition of primacy as reason to favour retrenchment from the United States' international commitments.[3]

An assumption of American primacy in Asia also appears in strategic discourse outside the United States, among US allies and competitors alike. China has long claimed that the United States is trying to strategically encircle it – a belief difficult to separate from the expectation that the United States either has or seeks primacy in a broad sense – and Chinese officials believe the United States both has and seeks primacy.[4] In South Korea, policy arguments urging greater distance from the United States presume that the

Van Jackson is a Senior Lecturer in International Relations at Victoria University of Wellington, and the Defence and Strategy Fellow at the Centre for Strategic Studies in Wellington, New Zealand. He was previously a Council on Foreign Relations International Affairs Fellow, and from 2009–14 served as a strategist and Asia policy adviser in the Office of the US Secretary of Defense. An earlier version of this article was presented at the 6th Annual Australia–Japan Dialogue in Tokyo on 9 December 2016. This version draws from the author's chapter in Michael Heazle and Andrew O'Neil (eds), *China's Rise and Australia–Japan–US Relations: Primacy and Leadership in East Asia* (Edward Elgar Publishing, forthcoming 2018).

Survival | vol. 60 no. 2 | April–May 2018 | pp. 107–132   DOI 10.1080/00396338.2018.1448578

US and China are locked in a contest for dominance of Asia. This premise is only possible if the United States seeks primacy in the region even as China's ambitions expand.[5] In Australia, those urging an accommodation of China's foreign-policy preferences explicitly assume that the United States seeks to maintain a 'strategic primacy' whose all-encompassing nature is untenable in the face of an ascendant and revisionist China.[6]

Crucially, the pursuit of primacy is a plausible path to conflict with China. Scholars and pundits who envision a Sino-American war frequently expect it to arise from a power transition,[7] security dilemma,[8] or China's expanding geographic definitions of its security interests.[9] But the eruption of deliberate conflict is most likely when, within particular conditions identified in those theories, the United States takes a rigidly adversarial stance toward China, which is what primacy as either a strategy or an object of strategy calls for.

The claim that the US seeks primacy in the Asia-Pacific is fundamentally wrong. Since at least the end of the Cold War, the United States has sought to sustain its Asian alliances, maintain a forward military presence for purposes of deterrence and readiness, and preserve its military superiority over potential adversaries.[10] The primacy assumption mistakenly extrapolates from the last of these objectives – preserving military superiority over plausible competitors – that the United States seeks primacy. But military superiority is an issue of force-structure planning, involving long-term capability development, not foreign-policy decision-making per se. Even some of the apparent smoking-gun evidence of US primacist ambitions, the most notable of which appeared during the George H.W. Bush administration at the end of the Cold War, was widely misattributed as foreign policy rather than force-planning policy.

Pursuing primacy requires policies that attempt to contain and curb the rising power of others. American military superiority, by contrast, is better seen as a strategic hedge against undesirable yet foreseeable circumstances of war with competitors. It is also a necessary but insufficient condition for credible US threat-making and war fighting. Without military superiority, America's alliance commitments would, at best, be unreliable. Nothing about this force-planning posture determines US foreign policy, however.

This line of reasoning – about US military superiority in Asia without primacy – seems to be quite durable, emerging as a major feature of the US rebalance to Asia under former president Barack Obama, and has even survived the early days of President Donald Trump, who signalled much to the contrary on the campaign trail.

What the United States has actually done in the Asia-Pacific mostly – albeit not entirely – diverges from what we should expect if it were seeking primacy. Rather than trying to contain China, the United States has so far actively facilitated its rise. Even the US approach to areas in which it acknowledges China as a competitor shows few signs of attempting to hobble China's power. If the Trump administration decides to ratchet up *competition* with China, doing so would not by itself be proof of a US strategy or goal of primacy in Asia. For that to be the case, we would need to see other evidence that the United States' foremost strategic concern is to circumscribe China's capabilities, wealth or influence in the region while maximising its own.

Primacy: what it is, and what it takes

American primacy is popularly characterised as a relative state of affairs that the United States inherited after the Soviet Union's demise.[11] The term 'primacy' is often used colloquially as a synonym for American leadership, military superiority or the liberal international order.[12] All of this, taken together, captures aspects of how the term is conceived in academic literature: as unrivalled – not uncontested – influence over strategic life, in its political, military and economic aspects. The narrowest definition equates primacy to unipolarity, arguing it is necessary and sufficient for US dominance of strategic affairs.[13] Unrivalled material power gets you hegemony, or domination: 'primacy *is* world order', in this view.[14]

But most scholars recognise primacy as what could be called 'unipolarity-plus', with some room for debate about what constitutes the plus. In Barry Posen and Andrew Ross's description, for example, primacy is an ideal-type grand strategy aimed at 'politically, economically, and militarily outdistancing any global challenger'.[15] Stephen Brooks and Bill Wohlforth, among others, have emphasised that the instrumental ability to 'cash out' unipolarity for political influence depends on the perceived legitimacy of the unipolar power's actions. The United States 'had primacy' at the end of the Cold War, in this reading, but the instrumental value of the unipolarity on which it was based diminished after the 2003 invasion of Iraq, which many secondary states opposed.[16] Similarly, Robert Jervis has argued that primacy 'implies that the state has greater ability than any rival to influence a broad range of issues and a large number of states'.[17] Samuel Huntington further clarifies: 'International primacy means that a government is able to exercise more influence on the behavior of more actors than any other government can.'[18]

Even Hedley Bull, who distinguishes primacy from hegemony and domination, agrees that unipolarity (which he calls 'preponderance') is a necessary attribute of primacy.[19] Bull describes primacy as a hierarchy granted by 'lesser states', rather than something that can be an object of the preponderant power's purposive action.[20] Indeed, because Bull claims that primacy only exists where force and coercion do not, his interpretation is conceptually problematic, especially for our purpose here, which is to specifically enquire into the ultimate aims of America's purposive action in Asia, making any definition that does not permit instrumental pursuits untenable. Yet even Bull shares an overlapping understanding with others: unrivalled (not uncontested) influence over strategic life. It involves the ability and willingness to wield influence – military and otherwise – to achieve political ends consistent with preserving the ability and willingness to remain in a superior position of influence. Relative military power is a central concern, but strategic affairs know no bounds, and the military is only one domain of importance, as even Posen and Ross acknowledge. This seeming boundlessness makes primacists eternally revisionist.

How, then, does a state attain or retain a position of primacy? Indicators that the United States seeks primacy in Asia would include depriving rising powers of opportunities for economic or military growth; excluding rising powers from regional security and economic institutional arrangements; maximising the regional military balance in favour of the United States; containing rising powers through geopolitical encirclement that pre-empts their ability to influence neighbours; and, at the extreme end of policy considerations, preventively attacking or sabotaging the nuclear-weapons facilities or industrial centres of rising powers. Primacy need not involve all of the above policies at once, but the more we see evidence of these indicators, the more confident we can be that the United States has its eye on a position of Pacific primacy.

The logical extreme of primacist imperatives is what Posen and Ross call 'strangling the baby in the cradle' – that is, primacy 'carries the logical implication that the United States should be willing to wage preventive war'.[21] Such considerations, public or private, would not be unprecedented for the United States. In the early days of the Cold War, for example, a time when the United States had de facto and short-lived nuclear primacy, many in the US military and president Dwight Eisenhower's cabinet advocated a preventive attack against the Soviets and the Chinese based on this rationale, and even had the backing of some public intellectuals.[22] Short of military options, the

The dominant power could isolate the rising power

United States might also pursue arms-control agreements, or alternatively, engage in an arms-race dynamic with China. In the former case, the United States would seek to lock in a favourable military balance through negotiated restrictions on arms development. In the latter case, the United States would likewise seek a favourable military balance with China, but would pursue it by ensuring it keeps ahead in the quantity and quality of specific categories of weapons.

It is of course possible to subvert or challenge the growing power of competitors in non-military ways, many of which have been discussed in the context of China's challenge to US dominance.[23] The dominant power could isolate the rising power from institutional architectures to hamper its ability to exert influence. It could employ punitive or restrictive economic measures on the rising power directly, ensuring that its trade and investment assets do not fuel the rising power. It could also politically box in the rising power by establishing exclusionary political agreements with states surrounding it, pre-emptively foreclosing on the rising power's ability to penetrate its neighbours and exert influence too deeply. Recent research argues that China is pursuing this approach to its geographic periphery, establishing arrangements with smaller neighbours that compel them to forswear political and military partnerships with the United States, including operational access for US military assets.[24] And a dominant power could wield its economic advantage by doing whatever it takes to preserve its economic and political centrality to the rising power's neighbours.

Finally, some of the clearest signs of primacy are not positive, but would involve evidence of absence. Specifically, a primacist America would do everything it could to oppose conditions of interdependence or mutual vulnerability with China, because accepting either would link the fate of the United States with the rising power it was seeking to marginalise or weaken.

Whatever the means, many realist scholars would call a policy toward a rising China based on non-zero-sum expectations (that is, engagement, trade, interdependence or mutual vulnerability) wrong-headed. The United States should 'reverse course and do what it can to slow the rise of China'.[25] Any policy that enhances China's economic clout, military capabilities, geographic span of control or political influence would undermine US interests if it seeks primacy in the Pacific.

Primacy and Obama's Asia strategy

To put it briefly, policies aimed at primacy should largely resemble the aggressive containment policies of the early Cold War.[26] As applied to China, we would expect to see US attempts to isolate China from institutional architectures, exclusionary political agreements with China's neighbours, a mercantilist economic policy designed to subvert and further isolate China, and even talk of preventive war.

How do such expectations compare with US word and deed during the Obama administration? Poorly. Scant evidence supports the claim that the United States sought primacy under Obama. The theory of US strategy toward Asia – and toward China in particular – has involved a mixture of liberal economic, institutional and socialisation logics, in addition to (but not supplanting) strategic competition in the development and geographic posturing of military capabilities.[27]

Deterrence and alliance

US military activities, commitments and investments in Asia constituted the most visible part of US strategy towards Asia under Obama. This involved building the military capacity of allies and partners through various forms of security cooperation and military exercises. It emphasised credible extended deterrence commitments to allies – that is, maintaining a US military presence in the region that allies and competitors alike deem reliable and persistent. And it required maintaining a military capable of projecting power anywhere in Asia, despite competitor strategies designed to prevent the United States from doing so.

A much-touted pillar of the US rebalance to Asia focused on enhancing the military capacity of allies and partners in the region through security cooperation, weapons sales and training. In the first official articulation of the rebalance, a 2011 *Foreign Policy* article, then-secretary of state Hillary Clinton established security-cooperation networks as an anchor of US strategy toward the region,[28] which secretary of defense Ash Carter reiterated in 2016.[29] The US defence strategy announced in January 2012, which president Obama signed, further added that the Department of Defense (DoD) would work with allies and partners in the Asia-Pacific 'to ensure collective capability and capacity for securing common interests'.[30] Numerous US officials subsequently repeated this refrain of enhancing the military capacities of its regional partners, defining in greater detail how it was doing so.[31]

A second element was sustainment of a reliable military presence that states in the region judge as capable and willing to deter aggression and defend treaty allies. Clinton's 2011 article described US treaty alliances as the 'fulcrum' that made the rebalance possible, having 'underwritten regional peace and security for more than half a century, shaping the environment for the region's remarkable economic ascent'.[32] To this end, Clinton continued, the United States was committed to establishing a 'more geographically distributed, operationally resilient, and politically sustainable force posture',[33] something reiterated in the January 2012 defence strategy. In a more active sense of 'presence', Clinton and subsequent officials have included military-to-military diplomatic engagement and military training exercises – bilateral and multilateral – as a means of signalling US commitment.[34]

In a major speech at the 2012 Shangri-La Dialogue, then-secretary of defense Leon Panetta repeated the US commitment to deter aggression in the region and defend treaty allies, but also described a commitment to gradually redistributing US Navy aircraft carriers, ships and submarines from a 50/50 division between Asia and the rest of the world to having 60% of such capabilities resident in the Pacific by 2020.[35] In a 2013 speech designed to remove doubts about US staying power in Asia, then-national security advisor Tom Donilon echoed prior official statements, adding that the 'Pentagon is working to prioritize the Pacific Command for our most modern capabilities – including submarines, fifth-generation fighters … and reconnaissance platforms'.[36]

The third military pillar of the US rebalance was preservation of 'power-projection capabilities' – that is, the capabilities, organisational capacity and military doctrine sufficient to employ US forces anywhere in Asia as a means of underwriting US threats and promises relating to regional security.[37]

By any meaningful measure of capability, the United States has long maintained military superiority in Asia,[38] but for more than a decade prior to it becoming a priority in the rebalance, the US defence community raised concerns about China's rapid military–technical advances and its asymmetric strategy explicitly designed to nullify the traditional advantages of the US military – to rapidly, overwhelmingly and precisely project power far from US territory.[39] If US military superiority is eroding in relative terms, then the United States and, by extension, its treaty allies are becoming vulnerable to military adventurism or coercion by states seeking to exploit military advantages for political gain. Thus, in his 2012 Shangri-La Dialogue speech, Panetta explicitly noted that the 'joint operational access concept' and 'air–sea battle' – adjoining organisational and doctrinal concepts for how the US military plans to cope with competitor military–technical advances – were meaningful parts of US thinking about strategy toward Asia.[40] Two years later, secretary of defense Chuck Hagel and his deputy, Robert Work, reiterated all these points, describing the imperative of making the investments necessary to maintain military–technical superiority.[41]

Economic liberalism and interdependence

Obama-era officials stressed that the rebalance was not primarily a military strategy. To the contrary, even the importance of the rebalance's military dimension was judged in relation to its contribution to fostering the stabilising conditions that allowed Asia's economies to prosper.[42] Economic prosperity, then, was seen as both a desirable end of, and a crucial means for, the rebalance. Under Obama, if not under Trump, this dimension of US Asia strategy emphasised free trade, open markets and cross-border investment flows. Other than a botched policy response to the China-proposed Asian Infrastructure Investment Bank (AIIB), the economic rebalance to Asia was remarkably inclusive of China: US officials repeatedly welcomed China's rise; economic ties with China deepened; and, far from contemplating preventive war, the Obama White House went so far as to direct the Department of Defense to not describe the Sino-US relationship in terms of great-power competition.[43] (The Trump administration has fundamentally rejected this linguistic reticence, but the departure has been much more rhetorical than material, as discussed below.) Annual US summit meetings with Chinese leaders, such as the Strategic and Economic Dialogue, involved Obama administration officials taking pains to frame areas of Sino-US competition within a larger relational context that it defined as being based on shared interests and economic interdependence.[44]

The Trans-Pacific Partnership (TPP) became the principal economic initiative that US policymakers promoted in hopes of locking in a level regulatory playing field for US businesses. Without denying a self-serving benefit to the US economy, Obama-era officials believed that increased trade through lowered tariffs and other barriers would lead to 'more inclusive development outcomes in the region itself'.[45] The TPP, or a TPP-like trade arrangement that included the United States, was necessary because it would serve as a 'regional economic architecture that can sustain shared prosperity', the implication being that an illiberal set of economic arrangements – based on mercantilist principles, an anarchical patchwork or a neo-tributary system – would be unsustainable and therefore fail to increase shared prosperity in the region.[46] It is on this basis that US officials reportedly encouraged allies to initially oppose Chinese economic initiatives such as the BRICS Development Bank and the AIIB,[47] both of which would offer development loans and balance-of-payment support without requiring the same political or economic contingencies as the International Monetary Fund, World Bank programmes or even the Asian Development Bank.

Institutional convergence

The US rebalance strategy focused on institutions as part of what might be described as the construction of a 'regional architecture'. Institutions, understood broadly as formal and informal rules and reliable patterns of interaction among states,[48] were at the centre of three types of activities that US officials believed allowed the region to escape from unceasing great-power competition: building and sustaining cooperative patterns or regimes; legitimising regional institutions; and opposing challenges to extant institutions.

Building on existing bilateral alliances and partnerships, US officials actively promoted reliable configurations of trilateral and multilateral cooperative relationships, especially among Australia, Japan, India, South Korea, Indonesia and China.[49] President Obama, secretary Clinton and others described the purpose of these configurations broadly as a foundation for 'small groupings of interested states to tackle specific challenges'.[50] And although the United States did not see it as necessary to be part of every configuration, Clinton made plain that 'we are seeking to shape and participate in a responsive, flexible, and effective regional architecture … that not only protects international stability and commerce but also advances our values'.[51] To this end, Tom Donilon added: 'an effective regional architecture lowers the barriers to collective action on shared challenges. It creates dialogues and structures that encourage cooperation, maintain stability, resolve disputes through diplomacy and help ensure that countries can rise peacefully.'[52]

US officials also sought to increase the legitimacy of existing regional institutions such as the ASEAN Regional Forum, APEC, EAS and others. Toward this end, the Obama administration not only actively participated in the region's patchwork of institutions, but also appointed the first resident US ambassador to ASEAN and signed the grouping's Treaty of Amity and Cooperation. It also continued the tradition of making the APEC Summit and EAS presidential-level commitments.[53] The United States additionally sought to lend legitimacy to these institutions by encouraging their use as venues for peaceful dispute resolution, arguing that they seek to enhance the symbolic and material capacity of multilateral institutions to 'better handle territorial and maritime disputes such as in the South China Sea'.[54]

The United States also openly used institutions in Asia instrumentally to promote normative liberal content. Involving positive agenda setting and socialising norms of peaceful interaction, the United States resisted indigenous proposals or initiatives for institutions that undercut the liberal elements of regional order, such as freedom of navigation, protection of human rights and conformity with international law. For example, the United States openly supported the work of the China–Japan–Republic of Korea Trilateral Secretariat,[55] while harbouring scepticism about the Shanghai Cooperation Organisation (of which China is a founding member) – an institution comprising illiberal states brought together by a shared concern for what it describes as 'terrorism, separatism, and extremism'.[56] This opposition to illiberal content may also help explain why US officials initially opposed Chinese efforts to establish the BRICS Development Bank and AIIB, which seemed to 'route around' liberal economic institutions.[57] Opposition to Chinese regional economic institutions may appear as an attempt to bolster American primacy, but had those initiatives reinforced, rather than undermined, the liberally oriented economic institutions that already existed, and not smacked of illiberal potential, the United States would have been much more likely to back them.

Primacy and Trump's Asia strategy

To what extent does the central claim of this article – that the United States seeks military superiority but not primacy in Asia – still apply during the Trump administration? The history of US Asia strategy under President Trump is largely unwritten, yet some might expect that changing the chief steward of US strategy would also change the aim of it, especially given the differences in general character and world view between Trump and Obama.

Notwithstanding the president's inconsistent word and deed, Asia has still seen more continuity than change from the United States. Military superiority remains central to US policy; the United States has shown a willingness to cooperate with China on issues of mutual interest; and US security alliances remain in place with no looming signs of the patron's intention to abandon its clients. There have, of course, been two types of observable divergences between the Trump and Obama eras. The first has involved the de-emphasising of regional institutions and the wilful abandonment of US regional economic influence in favour of rectifying trade, currency and investment imbalances. The second is the rhetorical rejection of interdependence with China and a corresponding willingness to prioritise great-power competition. Yet, neither type shows much sign of either embracing or trending towards a goal of primacy in the Pacific.

Military superiority continues

During its first year, the Trump administration prioritised the military as its principal tool of US foreign policy in several observable ways. Firstly, it called for Congress to end sequestration caps on defence spending, submitted a defence budget that requested a 9.8% increase over the previous year, and proposed a 28% spending cut for the US Agency for International Development and the State Department.[58] Secondly, Trump's own rhetoric about nuclear weapons emphasises the importance of nuclear superiority to US security. He claimed in a tweet that 'The United States must greatly strengthen and expand its nuclear capability until such time as the world comes to its senses regarding nukes', and when asked by a journalist to clarify, responded: 'Let it be an arms race. We will outmatch them at every pass and outlast them all.'[59] The administration has partially followed through on Trump's controversial tweets about nuclear superiority by using the 2018 Nuclear Posture Review to promise a modernisation overhaul of the entire nuclear arsenal, hint at lowering the threshold for US nuclear use and announce new types of nuclear weapons (including low-yield devices).[60]

Thirdly, essentially making the decision that Obama rejected in 2013, Trump ordered the launch of 59 *Tomahawk* cruise missiles against a Syrian air base in response to the Syrian regime's use of sarin.[61] Administration officials, including Vice President Mike Pence, linked the strikes on Syria to North Korea, stating: 'The world witnessed the strength and resolve of our new president in Syria and Afghanistan … North Korea would do well not to test his resolve or the strength of the armed forces of the United States.'[62] The similarity of the circumstances of Trump's Syria strike with that which Obama faced in 2013 suggests that the Trump administration sees greater value in the military as an instrument of policy than did Obama. This interpretation is buttressed by the prominence of military officials in Trump's national-security team, as well as the controversial and offence-heavy 'formula' for deterrence success that the commander of US Pacific Command has repeatedly embraced, claiming threat credibility was a function of 'Capability × Resolve × Signaling'.[63] All of this suggests the continuation – even the accentuation – of the military instrument in US political and strategic thinking.

New type of great-power relations

Trump's campaign rhetoric about China suggested he was going to take a hard line against Asia's next-largest power. He said he would label China a currency manipulator, criticised the country for its militarisation and artificial island-building in contested portions of the South China Sea, and blamed it for failing to curb North Korea's nuclear-weapons programme.[64] Just prior to assuming the presidency, Trump also raised the possibility of abandoning America's 'One China' policy,[65] and broke a decades-long symbolic precedent by accepting a congratulatory phone call from Taiwan's president, Tsai Ing-wen.[66] He even claimed he was willing to entertain a trade war with China.[67]

Despite these early signs of a hawkish approach, Trump invited China's Xi Jinping to his Mar-a-Lago residence in Florida less than two months after taking office. During the visit, Trump and Xi agreed to a 100-day economic action plan, issued on 11 May 2017, that identified several new economic initiatives that would increase – not curb – trade and investment ties between the United States and China.[68] Since then, Trump has withheld criticism about China's contested activities in the South China Sea,[69] avoided contact with Taiwan out of deference to China's sensitivity,[70] declared the

United States and China collaborative partners in resolving the North Korean nuclear issue (though with little progress) and publicly claimed that he would not label China a currency manipulator when they were collaborating together.[71] What is more, Secretary of State Rex Tillerson met with Chinese leaders in Beijing on 19 March 2017 and came out of his meetings reportedly accepting some variant of a 'new type of great power relations', a highly controversial phrase that not only implies sphere-of-influence diplomacy among the great powers,[72] but is also a relationship description that China repeatedly pressed the Obama administration to accept. Obama refused because of the adverse implications for both regional institutional architecture and the preferences of smaller regional powers.[73]

Far from a trade war, militarised crisis or a containment posture, the first year of the Trump presidency has seen the United States mostly engaging China as a strategic partner, not a threatening rival. Admittedly, Trump's National Security Strategy (NSS) and National Defense Strategy have emphasised the strategic-competition frame for viewing China, but there has been very little follow-through to date on that rhetoric, which in itself does not equate to an ambition for primacy. On the contrary, a careful reading casts the goal as maintaining a balance of power that prevents Chinese hegemony. The United States, according to the NSS, seeks 'a balance of power that favors US interests', while 'revisionist powers' like China seek to 'shift regional balances of power in their favour'.[74] Sustaining a regional balance of power, not strategic primacy, has been a continuous US priority for more than a century.[75]

Shortening the shadow of the future

Where the Trump administration has so far deviated the most from Obama-era policy is in the economic and institutional logics of US strategy toward Asia. Trump's approach to foreign policy is often characterised as transactional, but transactionalism itself is not what makes him different; rather, it is that he assumes a very short 'shadow of the future' in his pursuit of transactions. Liberally oriented policies involving free trade and institutions require a long shadow of the future: that is, the ability to assume repeated interactions over time in a particular domain. Unilateralist policies, institutional scepticism and mercantilism – Trump's foreign-policy brand, in essence – do not. If we take Trump's world view seriously, we can trace many policy differences compared with Obama to the length of the shadow of the future each assigned to their decisions. Obama's was long to the point of occasional decision paralysis; Trump's has been exceedingly short.

As promised during the presidential campaign, Trump signed an executive order shortly after taking office withdrawing the United States from TPP negotiations. This move was significant both because it was a direct repudiation of a core initiative in Obama's rebalance to Asia, and because TPP was widely interpreted as a move toward assuring US economic leadership in Asia. TPP had excluded China, and some viewed TPP as an attempt to undermine China, which is not entirely accurate.[76] But to the extent TPP was an attempt at retaining a superior US position in Asia, its wilful abandonment suggests a move away from, not towards, primacy. Also consistent with the broader scepticism that Trump displayed toward international institutions and liberal economic policies during his presidential campaign, the United States sent its senior director for Asia on the National Security Council to attend China's 'One Belt, One Road' conference, which was interpreted in China and around the world as tacit US endorsement of China's bid for economic leadership of Asia.[77]

If not primacy, why military superiority?

Military superiority is a necessary condition for primacy, so it is understandable that observers might incorrectly deduce from US attempts to retain military superiority that it seeks primacy. Military superiority features prominently in US strategic thinking for two interlinked reasons having nothing to do with a desire to dominate strategic life: force-planning imperatives, and the credibility of US commitments. US officials' descriptions of the rationale for what the Obama administration called the 'third offset' strategy, which seeks military superiority, supports these lines of reasoning. As the Trump administration's National Defense Strategy reveals, retaining America's military–technical edge over plausible competitors remains a foremost priority, though the moniker 'third offset' is no longer used. Military superiority, as Evan Montgomery notes, is not only necessary for primacy, but also for multiple ideal-type grand strategies involving much less ambitious goals.[78] Identifying a goal of military superiority, therefore, cannot be sufficient to conclude a goal of primacy.

Force planning does not determine policy

Force planning is a strategic hedge against an uncertain future. It constitutes a bureaucratic exercise far removed from, yet highly consequential for, foreign policy. The US Department of Defense plans its needs in five-year increments known as the Future Years Defense Program (FYDP). Most weapon systems are developed over multiple FYDPs. The programmes that populate the FYDP are, analytically, a product of force-planning processes that assess what the joint force should be. Force planning involves looking into the future – sometimes as far as 20 years or more – making assumptions about what the security environment will look like, and determining the operations and missions that ultimately drive military requirements of size (how many) and shape (what kinds).[79] Given the long horizons involved and the potentially existential consequences of being militarily unprepared for future operations and missions, force planning either grants future policymakers greater decision-making latitude, or forecloses on certain future decisions, depending on how the size and shape of the military they inherit fits with the demands of the security environment at the time.

This differs significantly from the form and function of foreign policy, which deals with the actions, rituals and reactions oriented toward foreign actors in world politics today. Foreign policy can be based on some future expectation or an aim to shape the long-term security environment,[80] but even then it encompasses determinations about one state's present posture toward another. As Iver Neumann observed first-hand, foreign-policy officials tend to 'concentrate on the here and now, on keeping the wheels turning, and … intervene if and only if they seem to be in the process of slowing down'.[81] By contrast, force planning deals with long-term decisions that serve as a subordinate input to defence policy and strategy, which may or may not be a subordinate input of foreign policy depending on how well orchestrated US policy is at any given time.[82]

Ensuring the US military's ability to deter or defeat all potential future adversaries is the writ of defence strategists who engage in force planning.[83] The demand for military superiority is rooted in this perceived need, because a force that lacks military superiority over plausible adversaries by definition lacks the ability to deter or defeat them.[84] Whether the United States ever tries to deter or defeat anyone is a foreign-policy decision that belongs to the president and other policymakers; force planners, who in practice are asked to design military superiority, help make sure future policymakers have the option to make such decisions.

The distinction between force planning and foreign policy also matters for debunking what was otherwise once seen as smoking-gun evidence of US primacy ambitions – a famously leaked copy of the 1992 US Defense Planning Guidance (DPG). Media coverage at the time reported key passages from the document as evidence that the George H.W. Bush administration sought primacy, including the statements that 'Our first objective is to prevent the re-emergence of a new rival', and 'we endeavor to prevent any hostile power from dominating a region whose resources would, under consolidated control, be sufficient to generate global power'.[85] This sounds like a straightforward description of a primacy strategy, and popular scholarship subsequently amplified that misperception by citing it as illustrative of one.[86] Despite the breathless DPG coverage, however, the 1993 NSS – which the Bush administration issued just before leaving office – made no mention of primacy, preventing the emergence of new rivals or maintaining dominance.[87]

The best way to understand this otherwise unexplained tension between DPG and NSS is by understanding that the DPG is a DoD force-planning document, not a statement or directive of foreign policy. The DPG is one of several internal defence documents that guide the Pentagon's complex budgetary process; the draft document itself required neither coordination with nor approval from the Department of State.[88] When the DPG lays out visions of defence strategy, it does so not on behalf of the US government, but for the sake of guiding the next defence budget-proposal submission to Congress and the next FYDP. This is evident upon reading the full text of the later declassified 1992 DPG,[89] but also in the opening paragraphs of other declassified DPGs as well.[90] The entire misrepresentation of the 1992 DPG originated from the misrepresentation of internal force-planning statements (the DPG) as external foreign-policy statements (the NSS). This is not to say that everyone in the Bush administration was opposed to primacy. The DPG clearly reflected a prevalent view within the Pentagon that the United States should pursue a strategy of primacy. But the DPG was merely one input into the larger national-security strategy, and the White House did not support extending it to become an administration position.

Commitment credibility and the third-offset strategy

A rationale for military superiority intrinsically related to the bureaucratic task of hedging against an uncertain future described above is the role it plays in the credibility of US threats and promises. Credibility involves some combination of the capability to follow through on a commitment, an interest in following through and a perceived reputation for following through. While the literature on credibility has debated the variable weight of the latter two factors,[91] the importance of capability is not in dispute. This is intuitive; promises to protect an ally or attack an adversary under some specified conditions must be executable to be believable, and if the United States lacks the capability to execute such commitments, then they are not believable. US commitments in Asia – both narrowly, to treaty allies, and diffusely, to principles such as freedom of navigation or assured access to the 'global commons' – require the United States to be capable of prevailing in worst-case scenarios involving competitors who violate its commitments.

Since it is plausible that China may take future aggressive actions that activate US commitments, China's military capabilities must be taken into account. And since China is the next-strongest power in Asia, treating China as a pacing competitor for US force planning (again, because conflict is plausible, not probable or desirable) necessarily entails developing a military capable of defeating Chinese forces in foreseeable circumstances. None of the thinking behind military superiority is determinative of a US policy stance toward China in the present, which involves elements of competition, cooperation, interdependence and mutual vulnerability.[92] But without military superiority, future US options will be narrower, and its commitments hollower.

In US discussions about the third-offset strategy, the force-planning and credibility reasons for US military superiority are on full display, while none of the markers of strategic primacy appear in either word or deed. The military–technical challenge to US military superiority involves the rise and spread of precision-guided munitions (PGMs) – 'battle networks' that integrate sensors and weapons to attack US targets precisely, quickly and from far distances.[93] Whereas PGMs were once the sole advantage of the United States, and used to great effect during the Gulf War in the 1990s, barriers to adoption are much lower today and China already fields some of these technologies.[94] This is the vulnerability that US defence thinkers believe must be offset. In public remarks about the third-offset strategy, Robert Work noted that 'The pacing competitors – not adversaries – are Russia and China, because they're developing advanced capabilities that potentially worry us.'[95] In a separate speech several months earlier, also addressing the third offset, Work claimed 'we're looking at the capabilities being developed by both Russia and China, two great powers, not because we think we're going to go to war with them … We want to make sure that we have overmatching capabilities to make the chance of us having a war infinitesimally small.'[96] And speaking to the credibility dimension of the third offset, Ashton Carter asserted 'We must ensure we, and our partners, are postured to defeat threats from high-end opponents in a complex set of environments.'[97] Carter's predecessor as secretary of defense, Chuck Hagel, gave the same characterisation of the third offset: 'Without our superiority, the strength and credibility of our allies will suffer … Questions about our ability to win future wars could undermine our ability to deter them'.[98] Even Defense Secretary James Mattis, whose priority for the Pentagon has been readiness and current operations, still touted the innovative technological work of offices such as the Defense Innovation Unit Experimental (DIUx) in Silicon Valley as a growth area for the Department of Defense in order to keep up in military–technological competition with China.[99]

Each of these statements stresses that the third offset does aim at military superiority, but that it is not a determinant of policy; they are addressing material vulnerabilities in relation to plausible competitors in future imag-ined scenarios in which the United States might be called on to make good on its commitments. The force-planning credibility explanation makes sense of a goal of military superiority without primacy, especially when paired with the lack of evidence that the United States is seeking containment of a rising China and positive evidence that it has heretofore facilitated China's rise.

*   *   *

Challenging the myth that America seeks Pacific primacy is important. If President Trump, or any future US administration, did decide to seek primacy in Asia, it would not be a continuation of US strategic or policy traditions – on the contrary, it would be a dramatic departure. A more accurate picture of US regional strategy would significantly deflate certain long-standing fears of allies and competitors alike.

For US allies, the notion that the rise of China and the relative decline of the United States requires a strategic recalculation follows from a corresponding assumption that the United States seeks primacy, in direct conflict with China's ever-enlarging interests. Those urging an accommodation of China argue that as China's interests expand, so does its resolve to fight. Since, by this reading, the United States would not ultimately be willing to run the same risks as the Chinese to preserve US dominance of Asia, the regional order will eventually shift in Beijing's favour. But if the United States seeks only to maintain a balance of power undergirded by military superiority, then the only deliberate clash with China would come from Chinese overreach via military occupation or invasion somewhere beyond its borders.

Similarly, Chinese fears that the United States seeks to strategically encircle it have no merit unless the United States seeks primacy, because only a primacy strategy would call for that kind of containment posture. Of course, if China does indeed seek either hegemony or primacy in Asia, then the great powers probably are destined to clash. And admittedly, what matters most is not US intentions but rather Chinese perceptions of them. But the only way to avoid strategic misperceptions is to reconcile images with evidence, as I have done here. Military superiority has a rationale distinct from primacy. Characterisations of US thinking about Asia should thus engage with US policy as it is and as it has been – not with false images of American strategy in the Pacific. That is the best hope for stability in a fluid security environment.

Acknowledgements

The author would like to thank Andrew O'Neil and Michael Heazle for their helpful comments.

Notes

1   As I discuss in more detail below, 'strategic life' attempts to capture more than just military affairs, including inputs that contribute to, amplify or substitute for military power.

2   See Zalmay Khalilzad, 'Losing the Moment? The United States and the World after the Cold War', *Washington Quarterly*, vol. 18, no. 2, 1995, pp. 85–107; and Jakub J. Grygiel and A. Wess Mitchell, *The Unquiet Frontier: Rising Rivals, Vulnerable Allies, and the Crisis of American Power* (Princeton, NJ: Princeton University Press, 2016).

3   See Barry Posen, *Restraint: A New Foundation for U.S. Grand Strategy* (Ithaca, NY: Cornell University Press, 2014); Barry Posen, 'Stability and Change in U.S. Grand Strategy', *Orbis*, Fall 2007, pp. 561–7; Eugene Gholz, Daryl G. Press and Harvey M. Sapolsky, 'Come Home, America: The Strategy of Restraint in the Face of Temptation', *International Security*, vol. 21, no. 4, 1997, pp. 5–48; T.V. Paul, 'Soft Balancing in the Age of U.S. Primacy', *International Security*, vol. 30, no. 1, 2005, pp. 46–71; and Stephen M. Walt, *Taming American Power: The Global Response to U.S. Primacy* (New York: W.W. Norton, 2005).

4   See, for example, Wang Jisi, 'China's Search for Stability with America', *Foreign Affairs*, September/October 2005, pp. 39–48; Hu Qingyun, 'US to Increase Troops Stationed in Australia: Deal Seen as Move to "Encircle" China', *Global Times*, 13 August 2014, http://www.globaltimes.cn/content/875836.shtml; and Felix Chang, 'China's Encirclement Concerns', *Geopoliticus*, 24 June 2016, http://www.fpri.org/2016/06/chinas-encirclement-concerns/.

5   Jae Ho Chung and Jiyoon Kim, 'Is South Korea in China's Orbit? Assessing Seoul's Perceptions and Policies', *Asia Policy*, vol. 21, no. 1, 2016, pp. 123–45.

6   See, for example, Hugh White, *The China Choice: Why We Should Share Power* (Oxford: Oxford University Press, 2013).

7   Graham Allison, *Destined for War: Can America and China Escape Thucydides's Trap?* (New York: Houghton Mifflin Harcourt, 2017).

8   Thomas J. Christensen, 'The Contemporary Security Dilemma: Deterring a Taiwan Conflict', *Washington Quarterly*, vol. 25, no. 4, 2002, pp. 5–21.

9   John J. Mearsheimer, 'The Gathering Storm: China's Challenge to US Power

in Asia', *Chinese Journal of International Politics*, vol. 3, no. 4, 2010, pp. 381–96.

10 For overviews, see Michael J. Green, *By More Than Providence: Grand Strategy and American Power in the Asia Pacific Since 1783* (New York: Columbia University Press, 2017), pp. 429–540; and Van Jackson, 'Red Teaming the Rebalance: The Theory and Risks of US Asia Strategy', *Journal of Strategic Studies*, vol. 39, no. 3, 2016, pp. 365–88.

11 See, for example, Richard N. Hass, 'What to Do with American Primacy', *Foreign Affairs*, vol. 78, no. 5, September/October 1999, pp. 37–49.

12 See Hass, 'What to Do with American Primacy'; Hal Brands, 'The Era of American Primacy Is Far from Over', *National Interest*, 26 August 2016; Walt, *Taming American Power*; and Evan Braden Montgomery, 'Contested Primacy in the Western Pacific: China's Rise and the Future of US Power Projection', *International Security*, vol. 38, no. 4, 2014, pp. 115–49.

13 See Christopher Layne, 'The Unipolar Illusion: Why New Great Powers Will Rise', *International Security*, vol. 17, no. 4, 1993, pp. 5–51; Christopher Layne, 'What Comes after U.S. Primacy', *National Interest*, 8 September 2016; and Christopher Layne, 'From Preponderance to Offshore Balancing: America's Future Grand Strategy', *International Security*, vol. 22, no. 1, 1997, pp. 86–124.

14 Layne, 'From Preponderance to Offshore Balancing', p. 94.

15 Barry Posen and Andrew Ross, 'Competing Visions for U.S. Grand Strategy', *International Security*, vol. 21,

no. 3, 1996/97, pp. 5–53.

16 Stephen Brooks and William Wohlforth, *A World Out of Balance: International Relations and the Challenge of American Primacy* (Princeton, NJ: Princeton University Press, 2008), pp. 1–2.

17 Robert Jervis, 'International Primacy: Is the Game Worth the Candle?', *International Security*, vol. 17, no. 4, 1993, pp. 52–3.

18 Samuel Huntington, 'Why International Primacy Matters', *International Security*, vol. 17, no. 4, 1993, pp. 68–83.

19 Hedley Bull, *The Anarchical Society: A Study of Order in World Politics*, third edition (New York: Columbia University Press, 2002). Curiously, US literature on primacy rarely references Bull's canonical work, and usually defines primacy in a manner partly at odds with Bull's understanding of it – specifically, Bull argues primacy cannot be achieved by 'force or threat of force', while for American scholars the ability to wield force is crucial to attaining and sustaining primacy. See, for example, Michael E. Brown, Owen R. Cote, Sean M. Lynn-Jones and Steven E. Miller (eds), *Primacy and Its Discontents: American Power and International Stability* (Cambridge, MA: MIT Press, 2008). This is the dominant text on primacy in US security studies and makes no mention of Bull or his understanding of primacy.

20 Bull, *Anarchical Society*, p. 208.

21 Posen and Ross, 'Competing Visions for U.S. Grand Strategy', p. 41.

22 Marc Trachtenberg, 'A "Wasting Asset": American Strategy and the Shifting Nuclear Balance, 1949–1954', *International Security*, vol. 13, no. 3,

1988/89, pp. 5–49.

23 Thomas J. Christensen, 'Fostering Stability or Creating a Monster? The Rise of China and U.S. Policy toward East Asia', *International Security*, vol. 31, no. 1, 2006, pp. 81–126.

24 Van Jackson, 'Asian Security after US Hegemony: Spheres of Influence and the Third Wave of Regional Order', Asan Forum, 14 October 2016, http://www.theasanforum.org/asian-security-after-us-hegemony-spheres-of-influence-and-the-third-wave-of-regional-order/.

25 John J. Mearsheimer, *The Tragedy of Great Power Politics* (New York: W.W. Norton and Co., 2001), pp. 401–2.

26 Portions of this section originally appeared in Jackson, 'Red Teaming the Rebalance'.

27 This point is made most thoroughly in Jackson, 'Red Teaming the Rebalance'.

28 Hillary R. Clinton, 'America's Pacific Century', *Foreign Policy*, vol. 189, no. 1, 2011, http://foreignpolicy.com/2011/10/11/Americas-pacific-century/.

29 Ashton Carter, 'Asia-Pacific's Principled Security Network', remarks at 2016 IISS Shangri-La Dialogue, Singapore, 4 June 2016.

30 US Department of Defense, *Sustaining U.S. Global Leadership: Priorities for 21st Century Defense* (Washington DC: US GPO, 2012), p. 2.

31 See Samuel J. Locklear III, 'A Combatant Commander's View on the Asia-Pacific Rebalance: The Patch-Work Quilt', speech to the Asia Society, New York, 6 December 2012; and Jonathan Greenert, 'The Navy's Rebalance to Asia: Challenges and Opportunities', presentation at the Center for Strategic and International Studies, Washington DC, 15 May 2014.

32 Clinton, 'America's Pacific Century'.

33 *Ibid.*

34 *Ibid.*

35 Leon Panetta, 'The U.S. Rebalance toward the Asia-Pacific', remarks at the IISS Shangri-La Dialogue, Singapore, 2 June 2012.

36 Tom Donilon, 'The United States and the Asia-Pacific in 2013', remarks at the Asia Society, New York, 11 March 2013.

37 Dennis C. Blair, 'Military Power Projection in Asia', in Ashley Tellis, Mercy Kuo and Andrew Marble (eds), *Strategic Asia 2008–9: Challenges and Choices* (Seattle, WA: National Bureau of Asian Research, 2008).

38 Evan Braden Montgomery, 'Contested Primacy in the Western Pacific: China's Rise and the Future of U.S. Power Projection', *International Security*, vol. 38, no. 4, 2014, pp. 115–59.

39 *Ibid.*

40 Panetta, 'The U.S. Rebalance toward the Asia-Pacific'.

41 See Chuck Hagel, 'Developing a Third, Game-Changing Offset Strategy', keynote address to the Southeastern New England Defense Industry Alliance, Newport, RI, 3 September 2014; and Robert Work, 'A Technological Edge over Our Adversaries', remarks at the National Defense University, Washington DC, 5 August 2014.

42 See Clinton, 'America's Pacific Century'; and Donilon, 'The United States and the Asia-Pacific in 2013'.

43 David B. Larter, 'White House Tells the Pentagon to Quit Talking about "Competition" with China', *Navy Times*, 26 September 2016.

44 Thomas Fingar and Fan Jishe, 'Ties that Bind: Strategic Stability in the U.S.–China Relationship', *Washington Quarterly*, vol. 36, no. 4, 2013, pp. 125–38.

45 Joseph Y. Yun, statement before the Senate Committee on Foreign Affairs Subcommittee on East Asian and Pacific Affairs, 25 April 2013, p. 3, https://www.foreign.senate.gov/imo/media/doc/Yun_Testimony2.pdf.

46 Donilon, 'The United States and the Asia-Pacific in 2013'.

47 Jane Perlez, 'U.S. Opposing China's Answer to World Bank', *New York Times*, 9 October 2014.

48 Robert O. Keohane, 'International Institutions: Two Approaches', *International Studies Quarterly*, vol. 32, no. 4, 1988, pp. 379–96.

49 Clinton, 'America's Pacific Century'.

50 *Ibid.*

51 *Ibid.*

52 Donilon, 'The United States and the Asia-Pacific in 2013'.

53 *Ibid.*

54 Yun, statement before the Senate Committee on Foreign Affairs.

55 Andrew Yeo, *China, Japan, Korea Trilateral Cooperation: Implications for Northeast Asian Politics and Order* (Seoul: East Asia Institute, 2013).

56 The United States applied for membership to the SCO and was rejected in 2006.

57 Nazneen Barma, Ely Ratner and Steven Weber, 'Welcome to the World without the West', *National Interest*, 12 November 2014, http://nationalinterest.org/feature/welcome-the-world-without-the-west-11651.

58 See Ryan Brown and Jeremy Herb, 'Congressional Republicans See Trump's Defense Budget Hike as Insufficient', CNN, 23 May 2017, http://edition.cnn.com/2017/05/23/politics/trump-defense-budget-increase/index.html; and Arshad Mohammed, 'Trump Plans 28 Percent Cut in Budget for Diplomacy, Foreign Aid', Reuters, 16 March 2017.

59 Max Fisher, 'Trump's Nuclear Weapons Tweet, Translated and Explained', *New York Times*, 22 December 2016.

60 US Department of Defense, 'Nuclear Posture Review', February 2018.

61 Harriet Alexander, Danny Boyle and Barney Henderson, 'US Launches Strike on Syria – How It Unfolded', *Telegraph*, 7 April 2017.

62 Anna Fifield, 'White House Warns North Korea Not to Test US Resolve, Offering Syria and Afghanistan Strikes as Examples', *Washington Post*, 17 April 2017.

63 Van Jackson, 'Why Mattis versus Kim Jong-Un Will End Badly for Us All', War on the Rocks, 20 April 2017.

64 See Javier Hernandez, 'Trump's Mixed Signals on South China Sea Worry Asian Allies', *New York Times*, 10 May 2017; and 'Everything Trump Has Tweeted (and What It Was About)', *Los Angeles Times*, entry from 29 May 2017.

65 Caren Bohan and David Brunnstrom, 'Trump Says U.S. Not Necessarily Bound by "One China" Policy', Reuters, 12 December 2016.

66 Tom Phillips, Nicola Smith and Nicky Woolf, 'Trump's Phone Call with Taiwan President Risks China's Wrath', *Guardian*, 3 December 2016.

67 Trump has not deployed the exact phrase 'trade war', but he has threat-

ened massive tariffs on Chinese imports, which are widely viewed as a catalyst for a trade war. See Wendy Wu, 'Just How Badly Could Trump's Threatened 45% Tariff Hurt China?', CNBC, 15 January 2017.

68 US Department of Commerce, 'Initial Results of the 100-Day Action Plan of the U.S.–China Comprehensive Economic Dialogue', 11 May 2017, https://www.commerce. gov/news/press-releases/2017/05/ joint-release-initial-results-100-day-action-plan-us-china-comprehensive.

69 Ankit Panda, 'The US Navy's First Trump-Era South China Sea FONOP Just Happened: First Takeaways and Analysis', *Diplomat*, 25 May 2017.

70 Jeff Mason, Stephen Adler and Steve Holland, 'Exclusive: Trump Spurns Taiwan President's Suggestions of Another Phone Call', Reuters, 28 April 2017.

71 Donald Trump (@realDonaldTrump), tweet, 16 April 2017, https://twitter. com/realdonaldtrump/status/85358341 7916755968?lang=en.

72 Hannah Beech, 'Rex Tillerson's Deferential Visit to China', *New Yorker*, 21 March 2017, http://www. newyorker.com/news/news-desk/ rex-tillersons-deferential-visit-to-china.

73 Andrew Erickson and Adam Liff, 'Not-So-Empty-Talk: The Danger of China's "New Type of Great Power Relations" Slogan', *Foreign Affairs*, 9 April 2014, https://www. foreignaffairs.com/articles/142178/ andrew-s-erickson-and-adam-p-liff/ not-so-empty-talk.

74 See 'National Security Strategy of the United States of America' (Washington DC: The White House, December 2017), pp. 25 and 49.

75 Green, *By More Than Providence*.

76 Even president Obama reframed TPP in these competitive terms with China after it started losing domestic political support. Barack Obama, 'The TPP Would Let America, Not China, Lead the Way on Global Trade', *Washington Post*, 2 May 2016.

77 Echo Huang, 'Trump Just Gave China What It Wanted for Its New Silk Road: A Credibility Boost from the U.S.', *Quartz*, 15 May 2017, https:// qz.com/983477/trump-just-gave-china-what-it-wanted-for-its-new-silk-road-a-credibility-boost-from-the-us/.

78 Montgomery, 'Contested Primacy in the Western Pacific'.

79 For a primer on US force planning, see Henry C. Bartlett, Paul Holman, Jr and Timothy E. Somes, 'The Art of Strategy and Force Planning', in *Strategy and Force Planning*, third edition (Newport, RI: US Naval War College, 2000), pp. 18–34.

80 Future-oriented foreign policy is conventionally referred to as 'policy planning' in the United States.

81 Iver Neumann, 'To Be a Diplomat', *International Studies Perspective,* vol. 6, no. 1, 2005, p. 90.

82 Stephen J. Hadley and William J. Perry, *The QDR in Perspective: Meeting America's National Security Needs in the 21st Century* (Washington DC: US Institute of Peace Press, 2010), p. 7.

83 Henry C. Bartlett, Paul Holman, Jr and Timothy E. Somes, 'The Spectrum of Conflict: What Can It Do for Force Planners?', in Bartlett et al., *Strategy and Force Planning*, pp. 435–47.

84 Montgomery, 'Contested Primacy in the Western Pacific'.

85 'Excerpts from Pentagon's Plan: Prevent the Re-Emergence of a New Rival', *New York Times*, 8 March 1992, http://www.nytimes.com/1992/03/08/world/excerpts-from-pentagon-s-plan-prevent-the-re-emergence-of-a-new-rival.html?pagewanted=all.

86 See, for example, Posen and Ross, 'Competing Visions for U.S. Grand Strategy', pp. 31–2; and Barry Posen, 'Command of the Commons: The Military Foundation of U.S. Hegemony', *International Security*, vol. 28, no. 1, 2003, pp. 19–20.

87 'National Security Strategy of the United States', (Washington DC: National Security Strategy Archive, 1 January 1993).

88 Memorandum from Donald Rumsfeld to President George W. Bush, 'Defense Planning Guidance', 7 September 2001, available at http://library.rumsfeld.com/doclib/sp/2802/2001-09-07%20to%20President%20George%20W%20Bush%20re%20Defense%20Planning%20Guidance.pdf.

89 'Defense Planning Guidance, FY 1994–1999', 16 April 1992, available at https://www.archives.gov/files/declassification/iscap/pdf/2008-003-docs1-12.pdf.

90 See, for example, Rumsfeld to Bush, 'Defense Planning Guidance'.

91 For details on this debate, see Van Jackson, *Rival Reputations: Coercion and Credibility in US–North Korea Relations* (Cambridge: Cambridge University Press, 2016), pp. 16–23; and Alex Weisiger and Keren Yarhi-Milo, 'Revisiting Reputation: How Past Actions Matter in International Politics', *International Organization*, vol. 69, no. 2, 2015, pp. 473–95.

92 Fingar and Jishe, 'Ties that Bind'.

93 Robert O. Work and Shawn Brimley, *20YY: Preparing for War in the Robotic Age* (Washington DC: Center for a New American Security, 2014).

94 Thomas G. Mahnken, 'Weapons: The Growth and Spread of the Precision-Strike Regime', *Daedalus*, vol. 140, no. 3, 2011, pp. 45–57.

95 Quoted in Cheryl Pellerin, 'Deputy Secretary: Third Offset Strategy Bolsters America's Military Deterrence', *DoD News*, 31 October 2016.

96 Robert Work, remarks on the Third Offset Strategy, Brussels, 28 April 2016, https://www.defense.gov/News/Speeches/Speech-View/Article/753482/remarks-by-d%20eputy-secretary-work-on-third-offset-strategy.

97 Ash Carter, 'Strategic and Operational Innovation at a Time of Transition and Turbulence', remarks to the Reagan National Defense Forum, Ronald Reagan Presidential Library, Simi Valley, CA, 7 November 2015, https://www.defense.gov/News/Transcripts/Transcript-View/Article/628147/remarks-on-strategic-and-operational-innovation-at-a-time-of-transition-and-tur/.

98 Chuck Hagel, speech to the Reagan National Defense Forum, Ronald Reagan Presidential Library, Simi Valley, CA, 15 November 2014, https://www.defense.gov/News/Speeches/Speech-View/Article/606635/.

99 Tom Simonite, 'Defense Secretary James Mattis Envies Silicon Valley's AI Ascent', *Wired*, 11 August 2017, https://www.wired.com/story/james-mattis-artificial-intelligence-diux/.

Iran and Saudi Arabia in the Age of Trump

Hassan Ahmadian

Iran and Saudi Arabia appear fated to be rivals. Their controlled competition in the 1970s, organised around common threats, gave way to intense rivalry after the Iranian Revolution of 1979. Over the ensuing four decades there have been ups and downs, but the constant feature has been competition. The 2011 Arab Spring added a new dimension to previous disputes, turning the traditional Iran–Saudi rivalry into a fierce regional confrontation.

International actors have always been crucial in determining the character of the relationship. Foremost among these is the United States. The American role has, at times, superseded bilateral calculations. Washington's posture has affected events in the Middle East ever since the Second World War, when British withdrawal left the United States as the bulwark against Soviet influence. Soon, Washington became the main international partner of both the Iranian and the Saudi monarchies. As Iran and Saudi Arabia became more influential, thanks to the oil boom of the early 1970s and the simultaneous demise of pan-Arabism, the United States' engagement with both countries, and its inclination to manage their relationship, increased. America's conduct in the Middle East after 1979, including its containment of Iran and security support to Saudi Arabia, has been pivotal to both nations' strategic calculations – and hence to their bilateral relationship.

Hassan Ahmadian (ahmadian@ut.ac.ir) is an Assistant Professor in the Department of West Asia and North Africa, University of Tehran.

Survival | vol. 60 no. 2 | April–May 2018 | pp. 133–150   DOI 10.1080/00396338.2018.1448579

A rivalry-driven relationship

As the Middle East's Arab-centric order faded away, the victim, in part, of pan-Arabism's defeat on the battlefields of 1967, Iran's and Saudi Arabia's regional roles grew.[1] And when, in the 1970s, Tehran and Riyadh embarked on a cooperative track, much was at stake for both countries. The Cold War's regional projections – a revolutionary Iraq, a pro-USSR People's Republic of South Yemen and an emboldened Dhofar Liberation Front in Oman – threatened a regional status quo that both Iran and Saudi Arabia aimed to protect.[2] Yet, even then, it took the United States to talk both kingdoms into cooperation. Competition over the world oil market and regional leadership remained determinants of the relationship.[3]

Iran's 1979 revolution ended regional cooperation with Saudi Arabia, just as it disrupted the Iran–US partnership. What remained of the traditional relationship was rivalry, now multifaceted and aggravated. In 1981, Saudi Arabia and its allies formed the Gulf Cooperation Council (GCC), a security-focused forum, in the wake of Iran's revolution and the Iran–Iraq War.[4] The public appeal of Iran's revolution, combined with the rhetoric emanating from certain sections of Iranian society, inflated Riyadh's fears and collided with the regional role the Saudis sought to play. Iran, meanwhile, was faced with an eight-year war against an enemy backed by many Arab states, including Saudi Arabia.[5]

The tensions of the 1980s relaxed somewhat in the 1990s. Scrambling to normalise Iran's Arab relations, the Hashemi and Khatami administrations embarked on a programme of diplomatic outreach aimed at easing regional tensions and enhancing Iran–Arab relations. As such, in Andrew Terrill's words, 'limited cooperation … [became] possible within an overall atmosphere of suspicion and competition'.[6] Despite some ups and downs, a cooperation agreement (1998) and a security accord (2001) were signed.[7] However, the religious, ideological and identity schisms between the two countries meant that normalised diplomatic relations could only ease, and not end, the rivalry.[8]

In any case, 9/11 derailed the reconciliation, and the US invasion of Iraq in 2003 marked a turning point. A democratic political order in Shia-majority Iraq meant a friendly neighbour for Iran. Riyadh 'harboured deep reservations', as Banafsheh Keynoush puts it, 'about a war that could only increase Iran's regional influence'.[9] As such, Saudi Arabia resisted the new reality in Iraq, and refrained from re-establishing diplomatic relations with Baghdad until 2015.

During the Bush administration, when a US war with Iran seemed all too possible, and the crisis over Iran's nuclear programme escalated, Saudi Arabia aligned itself with Washington as a means to counter Iran's regional influence.[10] According to Adel al-Jubair, then Saudi ambassador to the US, King Abdullah called on Washington to 'cut off the head of the snake' – namely Iran – while his inner circle urged military strikes on Iran's nuclear facilities and tougher sanctions.[11]

Meanwhile, Saudi Arabia, along with its partners in the GCC, massively ramped up arms imports.[12] Iran stepped up its efforts to develop its ballistic-missile programme, and enhanced its regional reach to counter perceived threats.[13] In sum, prior to the Arab Spring, Tehran and Riyadh were competing on many fronts: over influence and presence in the Middle East and the wider Muslim world; via rhetorical rivalry for moral leadership in the Muslim world; and in the acquisition and production of weapons. The worst, however, was yet to come. Until then, both countries broadly followed a set of unwritten rules, such as avoiding personally insulting leaders, and defusing the politicisation of sectarian divides. During and after the Arab Spring, those lines were to be crossed.

From rivalry to confrontation

The Arab Spring made the unspoken explicit. Arab popular uprisings shocked Riyadh and came as a surprise to Tehran. Their mutual antagonism soon sharpened. Bahrain was the first theatre. The Shia-majority country's Sunni monarchy was faced with the popular protests of a Bahraini Spring. Tehran was vocal in its political advocacy of Bahrainis' popular demands, although it decided not to intervene directly.[14] Riyadh, on the other hand, chose to intervene militarily in favour of its allies in Manama.[15]

The rhetoric accompanying Saudi intervention and Tehran's reaction to it raised the level of animosity. Riyadh accused Tehran of intervening in Bahrain and igniting the Shia Bahrainis to topple the regime. Tehran responded furiously, accusing Saudi Arabia of occupying Bahrain. As Simon Mabon argues, 'while the actual level of Iranian involvement within Bahrain is uncertain, both Manama and Riyadh have acted on the assumption that Tehran has offered support to opposition groups'.[16] Still, as Andrew Terrill puts it, 'the ability of the Iranians to influence the majority of Bahrain's Shia citizens is ... in considerable doubt'.[17] Nevertheless, developments in Bahrain marked a sharp increase in tensions between Iran and Saudi Arabia.

Then came Syria, where Iran and Saudi Arabia, for obvious reasons, took opposing sides. For Riyadh, Syria appeared as an opportunity to curb Iran's regional influence while simultaneously advancing its own.[18] After the US administration pronounced its hopes for Syrian regime change in August 2011 and started supporting parts of the Syrian opposition, Saudi Arabia closed down its embassy in Damascus and called on President Bashar al-Assad to leave power.

Iran saw the potential consequences of regime change in Syria as dire. For more than three decades, as Jubin Goodarzi puts it, the Iran–Syria axis had been useful to both countries for 'maximising their autonomy, keeping their local adversaries in check, diluting foreign (particularly US) power and influence in the Middle East and asserting themselves in their respective spheres of influence'.[19] Tehran's strategic goals in Syria were therefore directly opposed to Saudi Arabia's, and, as Ali Ansari and Aniseh Bassiri Tabrizi have written, can be summarised in three parts: the 'defeat of Daesh and Jabhat al-Nusra'; the 'restoration of the status quo ante'; and the 'preservation of state institutions'.[20]

Witnessing its rival's rush towards Damascus, Tehran saw its strategic position endangered, and interpreted Saudi's anti-Assad campaign as anti-Iranian. Iranian officials held that Syria was targeted because of its alliance with Tehran. If Bahrain was the scene of a political and media confrontation, Syria brought the two rivals into an indirect military confrontation.

Yemen was the final case. At various stages, developments in Yemen caught both countries by surprise. Iran was surprised by the Houthi advance on Sana'a and beyond. Houthi leaders 'flatly ignored' Tehran's advice not to take Sana'a.[21] As Peter Salisbury observes, while the Houthis have some support from Iran, this is not the same as taking orders from

Tehran.[22] Nevertheless, perceiving what Gerd Nonneman has called their 'traditional ... aspiration to hegemony on the Arabian Peninsula' as under threat, the Saudis have regarded the Houthis as Iran's proxy.[23] In any case, Saudi Arabia's war in Yemen, under the pretext of a request from President Abd Rabbo Mansour Hadi, and accompanied by vitriolic anti-Iran rhetoric, has brought the two countries to cross all previous limits short of direct war.

At present, the rivalry is ethnic (Arab/Persian), sectarian (Sunni/Shia) and geopolitical.[24] The Arab Spring heightened a regional disequilibrium in which both parties felt threatened. For a weakened camp of 'Arab moderates', led by Saudi Arabia, Iran's regional position in itself became a matter of concern. Countering Iran became the focus of Riyadh's anti-revolutionary posture and rhetoric. For Iran, Riyadh's anti-Assad push constituted an anti-Iran policy. Tehran reacted by redoubling its efforts to protect its regional position. Flashpoints spread across Syria, Iraq and Yemen. The rhetorical confrontation went even further.

The American effect

Were it not for the role of the United States, the Iran–Saudi relationship might have gone in a different direction. Since the Second World War, Washington's Middle East policies have affected the perceptions and behaviours of both countries, and the United States has been present for most, if not all, of the significant developments in their relations.

America and Saudi

For the United States and Saudi Arabia, oil changed the game. Prior to its discovery on the Arabian Peninsula, American interest in the Kingdom was negligible. But thereafter, engagement with the United States reshaped Saudi's economic status, security calculus and strategic behaviour. The founding and nationalisation of Aramco brought Riyadh unprecedented wealth, enabling its regional ambitions. And as Saudi Arabia rose to become a regional power, the American security umbrella became a critical factor in its strategic calculations. 'Saudi Arabia's religiosity', as author Rachel Bronson puts it, made 'the kingdom a reliable Cold War partner ... providing its leaders with a perception of global threats similar to the one held by the United States'.[25]

Despite the two countries' closeness, at times things have been rocky. Two main disturbances troubled the relationship. The first was the Saudi-led Arab oil embargo on Washington for its support of Israel during the Arab–Israeli War of 1973. The embargo's psychological impact on America exceeded its material effect. It caused 'mass panic',[26] in Bronson's words, and gave the impression of anti-Americanism as a driving force in Saudi politics and foreign policy,[27] increasing the level of mistrust between the two partners.

The second was 9/11.[28] The fact that 15 out of 19 hijackers were Saudi citizens could not have been smoothed over, were it not for the mutual interest in continued energy trade and intelligence cooperation. Even the findings of the congressional investigation into the Saudi role in 9/11 were initially held back as too sensitive to publish.[29]

US troops on Saudi soil provided some security but also proved a liability – a rallying cry for jihadists returned from Afghanistan.[30] In welcoming the US security umbrella, as a Congressional Research Service report puts it, Saudi leaders have left themselves 'increasingly vulnerable to domestic and regional criticism for appearing to side with the United States against fellow Arab and Muslim regimes'.[31] And although al-Qaeda's Saudi campaign was 'a reflection less of discontent with the Saudi regime than of extreme anti-westernism', as Thomas Hegghammer observes, the jihadist group gradually merged the fight against the US with its anti-Saudi rhetoric and actions.[32]

US–Iran relations

US–Iranian relations started with an occupation, but also an American contribution to Iran's liberation. Soviet and British forces occupied the country in August 1941; US forces, in smaller numbers, came later.[33] At war's end, and in an early crisis of the emerging Cold War, Moscow looked like it might renege on its commitment to withdraw. US President Harry Truman's hard line may or may not have been the reason that the Soviets ultimately did withdraw their troops, but it certainly gave Washington some credit with Iran's public.[34]

That credit was ruined, however, by the Anglo-American-engineered coup against the democratically elected, and popular, government of

Mohammad Mosaddegh in 1953.[35] Few world leaders would be more loyal to the United States than Shah Mohammad Reza Pahlavi after the coup returned him to power. America's public image suffered, certainly in Iran, but the Shah's reliance on Washington to counter the Soviet threat grew.[36] This continued, with minor ups and downs corresponding with changing US administrations, until Iran's revolution of 1979.

Over the ensuing four decades, Iran–US relations have been character-ised by mistrust, contradiction and animosity in both directions. Iran sees itself as on 'a quest for survival, not expansion', as Hossein Mousavian puts it, and its leaders are worried about American ambitions to isolate Iran and change its regime.[37] US officials, meanwhile, 'believe that Iran is constantly undermining U.S. efforts in the Middle East', in Mahmood Sariolghalam's words.[38] And while there are differing narratives explain-ing the root causes of mistrust, the outcome is less debatable: the two sides have forged rival alliances and embarked on policies at odds with the other.

The growth in animosity has not been linear, however; the relationship has had its freezes and thaws. The sharpest improvement was the Joint Comprehensive Plan of Action (JCPOA) signed by Iran and the United States along with China, Russia, France, Britain and Germany in July 2015.[39] Interaction before and during the intense negotiations leading up to the agreement cooled down many other differences between the two sides.

Effects of US policy

During the Cold War, especially under the Nixon administration, the United States encouraged Iran and Saudi Arabia to cooperate against common threats, guided by the US tendency to interpret regional affairs through the lens of the global East–West rivalry.[40] A strategic partnership emerged between the two countries, and despite covert and sometimes overt rivalry, the two pro-Western monarchies served as the 'twin pillars' of regional order until the revolution of 1979 and the redirection of Iran's foreign policy brought cooperation to an end.[41]

Post-1979 Iran–Saudi relations were to a great extent a by-product of Washington's continued alliance with Saudi Arabia and its tense relations with Iran. The extension of a security umbrella to Saudi Arabia kept its ruling elites on board with Washington's anti-Iranian policies. As such, the Iran–Saudi rivalry accelerated or eased in step with American attitudes. Whenever US policy hardened, Saudi Arabia distanced itself from Iran; when it softened, Saudi Arabia moved towards more cooperative behaviour.

During the 1980s and early 1990s, in line with continued Iran–US tensions, Saudi Arabia ratcheted up its anti-Iran policies, supporting Iraq's war against Iran and siding with anti-Iran forces across the region, downing an Iranian fighter jet in the Persian Gulf, imprisoning Iranian civilian sailors and fishermen, supporting Iraq in its rivalry with Syria (Iran's only Arab ally) and supporting anti-Hizbullah parties in Lebanon. Iran's international breakthrough during Mohammad Khatami's years in office in the late 1990s and early 2000s, on the other hand, diminished Iran–US hostilities and provided Riyadh with an incentive to engage with Tehran. The inclusion of Iran in George W. Bush's 'axis of evil',[42] by contrast, brought an end to Iran–Saudi rapprochement.[43]

The exception to this pattern was Saudi Arabia's reaction to Barack Obama's Middle East policy. Saudi Arabia had three main complaints. Firstly, Riyadh was displeased by Obama's support for popular uprisings against US allies in Tunisia, Egypt, Yemen and even in Bahrain.[44] Secondly, Washington's diplomatic approach towards Iran, aimed at resolving the nuclear issue peacefully, signalled a huge change in the United States' regional engagement. And thirdly, the US shift to a strategy of balancing between Middle Eastern powers was at odds with a tradition of preferential treatment for American allies.[45]

The previous pattern – of warmer US–Iran relations leading to a thaw between Saudi Arabia and Iran – thus did not hold. Moreover, the timing of the nuclear agreement, well into Obama's second term, reduced US leverage over regional allies to buy in to the new approach. Riyadh chose to wait for the next administration.

The Trump factor

President Donald Trump's Middle East policy represents a break from his predecessor's. While Iran's de-escalation policy led it to conclude the JCPOA, that policy of engagement is falling victim to the Trump administration's eagerness to undo Obama's achievements and to reshape Washington's conduct in the Middle East.[46]

Trump is not interested in preserving the status quo. However, 'the strategic bottom line', as Leon Hadar concedes, 'is that Iran and its Shia partners, such as Hezbollah and Shia allies in Iraq, are stronger today than they were 16 years ago, a reality that Obama recognized in reaching the nuclear deal'.[47] Defying that logic means Trump is fighting against the facts on the ground in the region. Whereas Obama struggled to bring about a more balanced regional policy as a means of establishing and strengthening regional stability, Trump is focused on backing the United States' traditional allies and countering its traditional rivals.[48]

Trump's regional policy has three main objectives. Firstly, the president intends to counter or push back against Iran's regional presence and influence.[49] 'The administration's heated rhetoric and recent actions', as Ellie Geranmayeh puts it, 'indicate US strategy is primarily focused on isolating and containing Iran'.[50] Secondly, Trump intends to limit or even halt Iran's gains from the JCPOA. So far, Trump is doing that by 'rocking the boat, not sinking it', to use Peter Feaver's phrase.[51] His decertification of the deal will not in and of itself abrogate it, but, according to the International Crisis Group, it 'seriously, unnecessarily and recklessly undermines it'.[52] Thirdly, Trump's policy aims at reinvigorating traditional alliances.[53] And while the Obama administration distinguished among different points of contention between Iran and the United States in order to achieve the JCPOA, Trump tends to look at Iran and its policies as a package that shouldn't be disaggregated, and rejects issue-by-issue engagement.[54]

Washington cannot achieve all these goals – countering Iranian influence, limiting Iran's gains from the JCPOA and undoing Obama's rebalancing – alone, however. It cannot, for example, undo the JCPOA and expect its partners' agreement. This is why Trump has singled out Iran for criticism at every possible juncture. Trying to link the JCPOA's flaws to Iran's regional behaviour, Trump aims at accumulating regional and international support for the pushback against Iran. Still, at the time of writing, the US was in practice adhering to the distinction between the two issues.[55]

Trump has also been insistent on curbing Iran's ballistic-missile tests. The US negotiating team in the P5+1 dropped the subject of Iran's missile programme, however, when it became apparent that the talks were getting nowhere, and that there was no international support for the US position.[56] It is doubtful how much international support or Iranian acceptance Trump will get.

Trump's Saudi policy, on the other hand, accommodates Riyadh's strategic concerns about Iran and its gripes about Obama's record. Trump's first foreign visit was to Saudi Arabia, where his hosts acted quickly to shape his Middle East vision. Riyadh gave Trump the media and political attention he eagerly sought and received in return his approval and support for the anti-Iran struggle. Accusing Iran of 'fueling the fires of sectarian conflict and terror' and being 'responsible for so much instability in the region', Trump has, as Fareed Zakaria puts it, 'adopted the Saudi line on terrorism, which deflects blame from the kingdom and redirects it toward Iran'.[57] Or, in former Obama administration official Rob Malley's words, 'Saudi–Iranian tensions are rising and bin Salman is determined to depict Tehran as the source of all regional evils'.[58] Saudis have enthusiastically embraced the rebirth of their strategic partnership with Washington.

*   *   *

The change in American policy has had a range of negative effects on Saudi–Iran relations. These negative effects are likely to continue. Siding with Riyadh against Tehran regionally can only exacerbate an imbalance in which both parties act to preserve their own regional interests.[59] Historically, this has tended to increase tensions, leading to greater escalation. The media campaign surrounding cases such as the Lebanese Prime Minister Saad Hariri's resignation and the Yemeni ballistic missile supposedly intercepted above Riyadh could have been different had Trump taken a balanced posture toward the Iranian–Saudi rift.[60] Knowing that it has Trump's support has emboldened Riyadh.

Meanwhile, the Middle East is as unstable ever. Countries are being torn apart and civil wars are ravaging the social and political fabric of the region.

What an anti-Iran Trump adds to the equation is a sense of new opportunity for the Saudis, and deep insecurity for the Iranians. The Arab Spring is a prime example of how such a dynamic can play out.[61] Regional instability is an outcome of regional rivalries which are, in turn, partly derived from international (in this case, American) policies. And the more unstable the region becomes, the more incentive there is for Saudi Arabia and Iran to intensify their rivalry.

To further complicate this picture, Trump's policies are interpreted differently around the region. His Iran-threat inflation is working, but it only adds to the wider ambiguity surrounding his agenda, making regional calculations of his intentions more difficult.[62] Besides Trump's hostile attitude toward Iran and the JCPOA, and his support for Israel, there is little to be sure of.[63] Even Trump's hostility toward Iran and the JCPOA have yielded unclear policy. The ambiguity is deterring big businesses from entering the Iranian market.[64] In such an environment, every regional party behaves according to its own understanding of the new administration's posture, and this in turn brings about more uncertainty.

These features of the regional situation are made worse by a developing arms race. While Trump may hold the exclusion of Iran's ballistic-missile programme from the JCPOA as one of its biggest flaws requiring repair, his administration has inked huge military deals with regional actors, including Saudi Arabia.[65] To counter the regional imbalances emanating from those purchases, Iran has little option but to enhance its ballistic-missile programme for deterrence and defence.[66] Trump's arms sales to Washington's traditional partners and his animosity toward Tehran are augmenting the arms race that the US claims to oppose.

Lastly, sectarian division is at an all-time high. Geopolitical rivalry coalesced around the Arab uprisings, deepening the Shia–Sunni divide and leading to direct conflict.[67] While Obama's balancing policy distanced the US from sectarian rhetoric and its effects on the ground, Trump's anti-Iran policy risks making Washington a sectarian actor. As the Harvard professor Stephen Walt puts it, Trump is trying to create a 'sort of Sunni axis'.[68] Iran and its regional allies, for a variety of reasons, have long resisted being labelled sectarian.[69] With Trump buying into the Saudi regional line, however, he seems more anti-Shia and pro-Sunni to those involved in the Middle East's regional conflicts.

The Trump administration's bilateral and regional policies are heightening Iran–Saudi rifts. The president's bilateral policies are increasing regional reluctance to hold direct talks. This is especially true for Riyadh, which is banking on Trump to strengthen its regional position vis-à-vis Iran before embarking on any engagement. Meanwhile, Trump's ambiguous regional policy is destabilising an already volatile situation. Iran sees a new threat, Saudi Arabia a new opportunity.

Notes

1   See Fouad Ajami, 'The End of Pan-Arabism', *Foreign Affairs*, vol. 57, no. 2, Winter 1978, pp. 355–73.

2   On Iraq's disruptive policies for the United States and its regional allies and partners, see Bryan R. Gibson, *Sold Out? US Foreign Policy, Iraq, the Kurds, and the Cold War* (New York: Palgrave Macmillan, 2015), chapters 6 and 7. South Yemen's presence in the Arabian Peninsula and its support of Marxist and leftist movements in that area was a disruptive factor for anti-Soviet, pro-status quo states in the region. For a detailed study on South Yemen's regional policies and behaviour, see Fred Halliday, *Revolution and Foreign Policy: The Case of South Yemen 1967–1987* (Cambridge: Cambridge University Press, 1990). During the years 1970–76, Oman was a theatre of operations in which the Sultan's forces, supported by pro-Western powers, succeeded in defeating the insurgent forces seeking to destroy the country's established power structure. See S. Monick, 'Victory in Hades: The Forgotten Wars

of The Oman 1957–1959 and 1970–1976, Part 2: The Dhofar Campaign 1970–1976', *Scientia Militaria: South African Journal of Military Studies*, vol. 12, no. 4, 1982. See also Clive Jones, 'Military Intelligence and the War in Dhofar: An Appraisal', *Small Wars and Insurgencies*, vol. 25, no. 3, 2014, pp. 628–64.

3   Ali Fatollah-Nejad, 'The Iranian–Saudi Hegemonic Rivalry', *Iran Matters*, 25 October 2017, https://www.belfercenter.org/publication/iranian-saudi-hegemonic-rivalry.

4   Christian Koch, 'The GCC as a Regional Security Organization', *KAS International Reports*, no. 11, 2010, p. 23, http://www.kas.de/wf/doc/kas_21076-544-2-30.pdf?1011101.

5   See Barry Rubin, 'The Gulf States and the Iran–Iraq War', in Efraim Karsh (ed.), *The Iran–Iraq War: Impact and Implications* (London: Palgrave Macmillan, 1989), pp. 121–32.

6   W. Andrew Terrill, 'The Saudi–Iranian Rivalry and the Future of Middle East Security', in Mackenzie Tyler and Anthony M. Boone, *Rivalry in the*

Middle East: Saudi Arabia and Iran (New York: Nova Publishers, 2012), p. 4.

7   Adel Altoraifi, 'Understanding the Role of State Identity in Foreign Policy Decision-Making: The Rise and Demise of Saudi–Iranian Rapprochement (1997–2009)', PhD thesis, London School of Economics and Political Science, October 2012, pp. 209–22.

8   Stanley Foundation, *The United States, Iran, and Saudi Arabia: Necessary Steps Toward a New Gulf Security Order*, Policy Dialogue Brief, 46th Strategy for Peace Conference, 20–22 October, 2005, https://www.stanleyfoundation. org/publications/pdb/SPC05PGpb.pdf.

9   Banafsheh Keynoush, *Saudi Arabia and Iran: Friends or Foes?* (London: Palgrave Macmillan, 2016), p. 175.

10 See, for instance, Philip Sherwell and Tim Shipman, 'Bush Setting America Up for War With Iran', *Telegraph*, 16 September 2007, http://www.telegraph.co.uk/news/ worldnews/1563293/Bush-setting-America-up-for-war-with-Iran.html.

11 'Saudi King Abdullah and Senior Princes on Saudi Policy toward Iraq', released by WikiLeaks, 20 April 2008, https://wikileaks.org/plusd/ cables/08RIYADH649_a.html.

12 According to the Center for Strategic and International Studies (CSIS), the GCC received arms transfers worth $38.5 billion between 2004 and 2011, 35 times Iran's deliveries of only $1.1bn. The quantity of new orders during 2004–11 was less favourable, but the Gulf states still ordered $106bn-worth of arms to Iran's $9bn – a spending ratio of almost twelve to one. Anthony H. Cordesman, 'Military Spending and Arms Sales in the Gulf', CSIS, 28 April 2015.

13 See Nasser Hadian, 'Iran Debates its Regional Role', Atlantic Council South Asia Center, 14 September 2015, http:// www.atlanticcouncil.org/publications/ issue-briefs/iran-debates-its-regional-role; and Kayhan Barzegar, 'Iran and the Shiite Crescent: Myths and Realities', *Brown Journal of World Affairs*, vol. 15, no. 1, Fall/Winter 2008, pp. 87–99.

14 In response to Bahrain's accusation of Iranian intervention, Iran's Supreme Leader said 'that's a lie, wherever we get involved we announce it'. Still, he continued to extend political support to the Bahraini protesters, calling them 'most oppressed'. See 'Full Text of Friday Prayer Sermon in Tehran', Supreme Leader's Information Office, 3 February 2012, http://www.leader.ir/ fa/speech/9093/leader.ir.

15 Endeavouring to preserve what was left of the so-called 'Arab Moderate' camp in the Middle East after the fall of Egypt's Hosni Mubarak and Tunisia's Zine al-Abidine Ben Ali, Saudi Arabia intervened, despite US opposition. See Guido Steinberg, 'Leading the Counter-Revolution: Saudi Arabia and the Arab Spring', *SWP Research Paper*, June 2014, https://www.swp-berlin. org/fileadmin/contents/products/ research_papers/2014_RP07_sbg. pdf; Joshua Teitelbaum, 'Saudi Arabia, Iran and America in the Wake of the Arab Spring', *BESA Center Perspectives*, no. 140, 23 May 2011, http://archives.cerium.ca/IMG/pdf/ Saudi_Arabia_Iran_and_America_ in_the_Wake_of_the_Arab_Spring___

Dr_Joshua_Teitelbaum.pdf; and René Rieger, 'In Search of Stability: Saudi Arabia and the Arab Spring', *GRM Paper*, Gulf Research Center, 2013, available at https://www.files.ethz.ch/isn/182104/GRM_Rieger_final__09-07-14_3405.pdf.

16 Simon Mabon, 'The Battle for Bahrain: Iranian–Saudi Rivalry', *Middle East Policy*, vol. 19, no. 2, Summer 2012, pp. 84–98.

17 Terrill, 'The Saudi–Iranian Rivalry and the Future of Middle East Security', pp. 17–18.

18 Neil Quilliam, 'Saudi Arabia's Syria Policy', in Ioannis Galariotis and Kostas Ifantis, *The Syrian Imbroglio: International and Regional Strategies* (Florence: European University Institute, 2017), p. 20.

19 Jubin M. Goodarzi, *Syria and Iran: Diplomatic Alliance and Power Politics in the Middle East* (London and New York: Tauris Academic Studies, 2007), p. 292.

20 Ali Ansari and Aniseh Bassiri Tabrizi, 'The View from Tehran', in Aniseh Bassiri Tabrizi and Raffaello Pantucci (eds), 'Understanding Iran's Role in the Syrian Conflict', Royal United Services Institute for Defence and Security Studies (RUSI), Occasional Paper, August 2016, pp. 6–8.

21 Joost Hiltermann and April Longley Alley, 'The Houthis Are Not Hezbollah', *Foreign Policy*, 27 February 2017, http://foreignpolicy.com/2017/02/27/the-houthis-are-not-hezbollah/.

22 Peter Salisbury, 'Yemen and the Saudi–Iranian "Cold War"', Chatham House, February 2015, p. 1, https://www.chathamhouse.org/sites/

files/chathamhouse/field/field_document/20150218YemenIranSaudi.pdf.

23 See Gerd Nonneman, 'Determinants and Patterns of Saudi Foreign Policy: "Omnibalancing" and "Relative Autonomy" in Multiple Environments', in Gerd Nonneman and Paul Aarts, *Saudi Arabia in the Balance: Political Economy, Society, Foreign Affairs* (London: Hurst & Co., 2005), p. 332; and Ibrahim Farihat, *Unfinished Revolutions: Yemen, Libya, and Tunisia after the Arab Spring* (New Haven, CT and London: Yale University Press, 2016), p. 49.

24 Frederic Wehrey and Karim Sadjadpour, 'Elusive Equilibrium: America, Iran and Saudi Arabia in a Changing Middle East', Carnegie Endowment for International Peace, 22 May 2014, http://carnegieendowment.org/2014/05/22/elusive-equilibrium-america-iran-and-saudi-arabia-in-changing-middle-east-pub-55641.

25 Rachel Bronson, 'Rethinking Religion: The Legacy of the U.S.–Saudi Relationship', *Washington Quarterly*, vol. 28, no. 4, 2005, p. 133.

26 Rachel Bronson, *Thicker than Oil: America's Uneasy Partnership with Saudi Arabia* (Oxford: Oxford University Press, 2006), p. 119.

27 Josh Pollack, 'Anti-Americanism in Contemporary Saudi Arabia', *Middle East Review of International Affairs*, vol. 7, no. 4, December 2003, p. 30.

28 Josh Pollack, 'Saudi Arabia and the United States, 1931–2002', *Middle East Review of International Affairs*, vol. 6, no. 3, September 2002, p. 89.

29 Simon Henderson, 'What We Know

About Saudi Arabia's Role in 9/11', *Foreign Policy*, 18 July 2016, http://foreignpolicy.com/2016/07/18/what-we-know-about-saudi-arabias-role-in-911/. See also Lawrence Wright, 'The Twenty-Eight Pages', *New Yorker*, 9 September 2014. https://www.newyorker.com/news/daily-comment/twenty-eight-pages.

30 See Thomas Hegghammer, *Jihad in Saudi Arabia: Violence and Pan-Islamism Since 1979* (Cambridge: Cambridge University Press, 2010). See also Hassan Ahmadian, 'Al-Qaida in Saudi Arabia: The Experience of "Internal Jihad" and the Future Outlook', in *Middle East 9th Book: Saudi Arabia's Internal Issues* (Tehran: Abrar Moaser Tehran, 2012), pp. 395–420 [Persian].

31 Alfred B. Prados, 'Saudi Arabia: Current Issues and U.S. Relations', Congressional Research Service, 15 September 2003, p. 5.

32 Thomas Hegghammer, 'Islamist Violence and Regime Stability in Saudi Arabia', *International Affairs,* vol. 84, no. 4, July 2008, p. 714.

33 T. H. Vail Motter, *The Persian Corridor and Aid to Russia* (Washington DC: Center of Military History, 2000), p. 20.

34 On January 1942, the tripartite (Anglo-Soviet-American) alliance guaranteed the integrity of Iran and the withdrawal of foreign troops after the fighting had ended. *Ibid.*, p. 13. See also Joseph J. St Marie and Shahdad Naghshpour, *Revolutionary Iran and the United States: Low-Intensity Conflict in the Persian Gulf* (Burlington, VT: Ashgate Publishing Company, 2011), p. 84.

35 See Jalil Roshandel and Nathan Chapman Lean, *Iran, Israel, and the*

United States: Regime Security vs. Political Legitimacy (Santa Barbara, CA: Praeger Security International, 2011), p. 123. See also James F. Goode, *The United States and Iran: In the Shadow of Musaddiq* (New York: Palgrave Macmillan, 1997), pp. 109–24; and St Marie and Naghshpour, *Revolutionary Iran and the United States*, p. 85.

36 Alethia H. Cook and Jalil Roshandel, *The United States and Iran: Policy Challenges and Opportunities* (New York: Palgrave Macmillan, 2009), p. 18.

37 Seyed Hossein Mousavian and Shahir Shahid Saless, *Iran and the United States: An Insider's View on the Failed Past and the Road to Peace* (New York: Bloomsbury, 2014), p. 261.

38 Mahmood Sariolghalam, 'Understanding Iran: Getting Past Stereotypes and Mythology', *Washington Quarterly*, vol. 26, no. 4, 2003, p. 70.

39 'Joint Comprehensive Plan of Action', Vienna, 14 July 2015, https://www.state.gov/documents/organization/245317.pdf.

40 See Martin Harrison, 'Saudi Arabia's Foreign Policy: Relations with the Superpowers', *CMEIS Occasional Paper*, no. 46, February 1995, p. 19; and Faisal bin Salman al-Saud, *Iran, Saudi Arabia and the Gulf: Power Politics in Transition 1968–1971* (London and New York: I.B. Tauris, 2003), chapter 4.

41 Helia Ighani, 'Managing the Saudi–Iran Rivalry', Council on Foreign Relations, 25 October 2016, https://www.cfr.org/sites/default/files/pdf/2016/10/Workshop_Report_CPA_Saudi_Iran_Rivalry_OR.pdf.

42 Sasan Fayazmanesh, *The United States and Iran: Sanctions, Wars and the Policy*

of Dual Containment (London and New York: Routledge, 2008), pp. 113 and 164.

43 This model has ignited a debate over Iran's foreign policy in Tehran. The two sides of the debate are the internationalists and the regionalists. According to internationalists, the US-effect model suggests that Iran should prioritise engaging the international community and this will lead to regional rapprochement with Iran's Arab neighbours. Regionalists, however, hold that Iran's Arab neighbours are now in a far better position than they were two or three decades ago and they no longer simply follow US policies. The inability of Obama to pressure Saudi Arabia to buy into the 2015 nuclear deal is held up as an example.

44 See Emiliano Alessandri and Hassan T. Reinerti, 'U.S. Democracy Promotion from Bush to Obama', EUSpring, April 2015, http://aei.pitt. edu/66143/1/us_dem_promotion_ april15.pdf.

45 For more on Obama's Middle East shifts, see Jeffrey Goldberg, 'The Obama Doctrine', *Atlantic*, April 2016, https://www.theatlantic. com/magazine/archive/2016/04/ the-obama-doctrine/471525/.

46 See, for instance, Peter Baker, 'Can Trump Destroy Obama's Legacy?', *New York Times*, 23 June 2017, https:// www.nytimes.com/2017/06/23/ sunday-review/donald-trump-barack-obama.html. See also David Lauter, 'Trump Set Out to Uproot Obama's Legacy. So Far, That's Failed', *Los Angeles Times*, 18 July 2017, http://beta. latimes.com/politics/la-na-pol-trump-obama-legacy-20170718-story.html.

47 Leon Hadar, 'Give Trump a Chance in the Middle East', *Foreign Policy*, 27 June 2017, http://foreignpolicy. com/2017/06/27/give-trump-a-chance-in-the-middle-east/.

48 The two goals that Donald Trump made quite clear during his JCPOA decertification speech were: 'neutralizing the Government of Iran's destabilizing influence and constraining its aggression, particularly its support for terrorism and militants' and revitalising the United States' 'traditional alliances and regional partnerships as bulwarks against Iranian subversion and restore a more stable balance of power in the region'. The White House, 'President Donald J. Trump's New Strategy on Iran', 13 October 2017, https://www.white-house.gov/the-press-office/2017/10/13/ president-donald-j-trumps-new-strategy-iran.

49 See David E. Sanger, 'Trump Signals He Will Choose Approach on Iran That Preserves Nuclear Deal', *New York Times*, 14 September 2017, https:// www.nytimes.com/2017/09/14/ world/middleeast/trump-iran-deal-sanctions-deadline.html. See also Emma Ashford, 'The Trump Administration's Iran policy Is Dangerous and Flawed', *Guardian*, 23 May 2017, https://www.theguardian. com/commentisfree/2017/may/23/ trump-administrations-iran-policy-dangerous-flawed.

50 Ellie Geranmayeh, 'The Coming Clash: Why Iran Will Divide Europe from the United States', European Council on Foreign Relations, October 2017, http://www.ecfr.eu/ page/-/ECFR-236_-_Why_Iran_Will_

Divide_Europe_From_The_US_
GERANMAYEH.pdf.

51 Peter Feaver, 'Trump Has an
    Iran Strategy — But It Will Be
    Very Tough to Pull Off', *Foreign
    Policy*, 13 October 2017, http://
    foreignpolicy.com/2017/10/13/
    trump-has-an-iran-strategy-but-it-
    might-be-too-tough-to-pull-off/.

52 International Crisis Group, 'Saving
    the Iran Nuclear Deal, Despite
    Trump's Decertification', 13 October
    2017, https://www.crisisgroup.
    org/middle-east-north-africa/
    gulf-and-arabian-peninsula/iran/
    saving-iran-nuclear-deal-despite-
    trumps-decertification.

53 Roberta Rampton and Ayesha Rascoe,
    'Trump to Wade into Middle East
    Politics on First Foreign Trip', Reuters,
    4 May 2017, http://www.reuters.com/
    article/us-usa-trump-trip/trump-to-
    wade-into-middle-east-politics-on-
    first-foreign-trip-idUSKBN1801XV.

54 See White House, 'President Donald J.
    Trump's New Strategy on Iran'.

55 Moritz Pieper, 'What President
    Trump's Latest Move Means for the
    Iran Nuclear Deal', World Economic
    Forum, 17 October 2017, https://
    www.weforum.org/agenda/2017/10/
    what-president-trumps-latest-move-
    means-for-the-iran-nuclear-deal.

56 Richard Nephew, 'How the U.S. Can
    Deal With Iran's Ballistic Missile
    Program', *Foreign Affairs*, 3 November
    2017, https://www.foreignaffairs.com/
    articles/iran/2017-11-03/how-us-can-
    deal-irans-ballistic-missile-program.

57 See White House, 'President
    Trump's Speech to the Arab
    Islamic American Summit', 21 May
    2017, https://www.whitehouse.

gov/the-press-office/2017/05/21/
president-trumps-speech-arab-islamic-
american-summit; and Fareed Zakaria,
'How Saudi Arabia Played Donald
Trump', *Washington Post*, 25 May 2017,
https://www.washingtonpost.com/
opinions/global-opinions/saudi-arabia-
just-played-donald-trump/2017/05/25/
d0932702-4184-11e7-8c25-44d09f-
f5a4a8_story.html. See also Jamie
Tarabay, 'Donald Trump Just Got
Played in Saudi Arabia "Bigly"',
Vocativ, 23 May 2017, http://www.
vocativ.com/432034/donald-trump-
saudi-arabia-yemen-violence/index.
html.

58 Robert Malley, 'The Middle
    East Is Nearing an Explosion',
    Atlantic, 8 November 2017,
    https://www.theatlantic.com/
    international/archive/2017/11/
    lebanon-saudi-iran-hezbollah/545306/.

59 According to RAND Corporation
    research on Iran–Saudi relations, in
    order to strengthen regional stability
    and security, Washington should view
    Saudi Arabia less as a bulwark against
    Iran and more as an interlocutor. See
    Frederic Wehrey et al., *Saudi–Iranian
    Relations Since the Fall of Saddam:
    Rivalry, Cooperation, and Implications for
    U.S. Policy* (Santa Monica, CA: RAND
    Corporation, 2009), p. 100. The Trump
    administration is doing the opposite.

60 In both cases Riyadh accused Iran
    of destabilising regional activities.
    Hariri's resignation, announced
    from Riyadh, was coupled with
    a furious attack on Iran's role in
    Lebanon and the region, assert-
    ing among other things that there
    was an assassination plot against
    him. Angus McDowall, Tom Perry

and Sarah Dadouch, 'Lebanon PM Hariri Resigns, Assails Iran and Hezbollah', Reuters, 4 November 2017, http://www.reuters.com/article/us-lebanon-politics-hariri/lebanon-pm-hariri-resigns-assails-iran-and-hezbollah-idUSKBN1D4oDY. The Yemeni missile targeting Riyadh was claimed by Saudi Arabia to be Iranian, and Riyadh accused Iran of an 'act of war'. David D. Kirkpatrick, 'Saudi Arabia Charges Iran With "Act of War," Raising Threat of Military Clash', *New York Times*, 6 November 2017, https://www.nytimes.com/2017/11/06/world/middleeast/yemen-saudi-iran-missile.html. Iran denied both claims.

61 See Keynoush, *Saudi Arabia and Iran: Friends or Foes?*, p. 227.

62 'Threat inflation … is the attempt by elites to create concern for a threat that goes beyond the scope and urgency that a disinterested analysis would justify.' Trevor Thrall and Jane Cramer, *American Foreign Policy and the Politics of Fear: Threat Inflation since 9/11*. (Abingdon: Routledge, 2009), p. 1.

63 See White House, 'President Donald J. Trump's New Strategy on Iran'; and White House, 'President Trump's Speech to the Arab Islamic American Summit'.

64 See Ladane Nasseri, 'Trump's Iran Policy Is a Headache for EU Business', Bloomberg, 17 October 2017, https://www.bloomberg.com/news/articles/2017-10-17/trump-gave-eu-business-a-new-iran-headache-whatever-leaders-say.

65 See White House, 'President Donald J. Trump's New Strategy on Iran';

and 'U.S. Official Says Nearly $110 Billion Worth of Military Deals Inked with Saudi Arabia', Reuters, 20 May 2017, https://www.reuters.com/article/us-usa-trump-saudi-deals/u-s-official-says-nearly-110-billion-worth-of-military-deals-inked-with-saudi-arabia-idUSKCN18GoKU?il=0.

66 Iran's foreign minister detailed its view of its missile capabilities, and the programme's historical background. See Javad Zarif, 'Why Iran Is Building Up Its Defenses', *Washington Post*, 20 April 2016, https://www.washingtonpost.com/opinions/zarif-what-critics-get-wrong-about-iran-and-the-nuclear-agreement/2016/04/20/7b542dee-0658-11e6-a12f-ea5aed7958dc_story.html.

67 Geneive Abdo, *The New Sectarianism: The Arab Uprisings and the Rebirth of the Shi'a–Sunni Divide* (New York: Oxford University Press, 2017), p. 63.

68 Stephan M. Walt, 'Making the Middle East Worse, Trump-Style', *Foreign Policy*, 9 June 2017, http://foreignpolicy.com/2017/06/09/making-the-middle-east-worse-trump-style-saudi-arabia-qatar-iran-israel/.

69 As a minority living in a Sunni-majority Muslim world, Shi'ites have historically feared persecution and have therefore tended to refrain from pursuing sectarian behaviour. Additionally, Iranian leaders have been cautious lest their rhetoric be labelled sectarian, alienating the rest of the Muslim world. And pursuing policies on sectarian lines would diminish Iranian regional influence and reach – not a rational course of action.

The Future of al-Qaeda: Lessons from the Muslim Brotherhood

Barak Mendelsohn

Despite its failure to mount a spectacular attack on the US homeland in 16 years, interest in al-Qaeda is back in fashion. This is not entirely surprising: the United States' account with the group responsible for the 9/11 attacks will remain open as long as al-Qaeda exists. For its part, al-Qaeda still proclaims its hatred of the United States, views the fight against the US as a necessary step toward the attainment of its political and strategic objectives, maintains a forward presence in Syria and actively plots to attack American interests.

Yet we should not exaggerate al-Qaeda's prowess, or the strategic threat it poses. In an American public debate that emphasises threats – both real and overstated – the search for a bogeyman never stops. With its primary jihadi rival, the Islamic State (otherwise known as ISIS or ISIL), losing its last strongholds in Iraq and Syria, al-Qaeda is likely to reclaim some of its aura, though not necessarily its primacy within the jihadi ranks.

A particularly important part of current warnings about al-Qaeda is its ability to expand through franchises. Although it lost its Iraqi branch when the Islamic State of Iraq (ISI, the precursor to ISIS) chose to follow an independent path, al-Qaeda still features formal branches in Yemen, North Africa, Somalia and the Indian subcontinent, and a strong contingent

Barak Mendelsohn is an Associate Professor of Political Science at Haverford College and a Senior Fellow at the Philadelphia-based Foreign Policy Research Institute (FPRI). He is the author of *The al-Qaeda Franchise: The Expansion of al-Qaeda and Its Consequences* (Oxford University Press, 2016) and *Combating Jihadism: American Hegemony and Interstate Cooperation in the War on Terrorism* (University of Chicago Press, 2009).

Survival | vol. 60 no. 2 | April–May 2018 | pp. 151–178   DOI 10.1080/00396338.2018.1448580

in Syria. But an uncritical view of franchises as force multipliers can be deceptive. Those who see a strong al-Qaeda are in danger of assuming that the group is a cohesive organisation, while ignoring the problems that al-Qaeda's franchising strategy exacerbates.

Transnationalism is difficult. Firstly, it is a feature of the state-centric international system that groups tend to prioritise – or succumb to – local identities and aspirations. This, in turn, limits the ability of transnational movements pursuing territorial self-determination to challenge the state-based order.[1] Localisation through franchising may be an appealing tactical response to the difficulties of operating across borders, but it weakens trans-national (or more accurately, non-national) identification, thus undermining group identity and ideological coherence. Secondly, the principal–agent problem – particularly across borders – limits the ability of a clandestine transnational organisation to lead an effective campaign. Security concerns require delegation and give regional managers at the branch level the ability to pursue an agenda and strategy that often emphasises local considerations and diverges from the central leadership's preferences.[2]

We can learn about the process of al-Qaeda's localisation and decentrali-sation, and the consequences of that process, from the case of the Muslim Brotherhood (MB), another Islamist movement straddling the line between the national and the transnational. Founded in 1928 by the Egyptian Hassan al-Banna, the group began expanding outside Egypt's borders as early as the mid-1930s. Decentralisation and localisation are compatible with the Brotherhood's bottom-up approach, and facilitated the group's remarkable growth. However, in the face of a resilient state-based order, those trends undermined the group's ability to promote an Islamic, non-national iden-tity. Rhetorically, the MB remains committed to a transnational agenda; but it has evolved into a loose network of state-based branches that share general ideological tenets, each operating according to its unique circum-stances and based on its own choices.

Since its inception, al-Qaeda has been a transnational group, committed to violence as its central mode of action, and rejecting political participa-tion as a path for change. In contrast, the Muslim Brotherhood began as an Egyptian organisation that has emphasised *Dawa* (proselytising) and political action over violence. Notwithstanding these differences, important insights can emerge from the comparison. The two groups share end-state aspirations and face similar dilemmas as they attempt to resolve the incompatibility between their universalising visions and the harsh reality of operating within a state-based order.

If al-Qaeda is indeed undergoing a similar process to the one the MB has gone through, we will have to recalibrate our assessments of the threat the group poses. Specifically, we should expect the group's localisation to adversely affect the ability of al-Qaeda central to set the course for its composite groups. It could gradually evolve into a sort of advisory board that propagates al-Qaeda's cause but has very limited ability to meaningfully influence its increasingly independent branches. Al-Qaeda central will draw its power from its stature within the jihadi movement rather than from its aggregated capabilities, and will take a back seat to only nominally subordinate franchises.

Attention turns back to al-Qaeda

For most of the Obama presidency, US officials were dismissive of al-Qaeda. In particular, the killing of Osama bin Laden in May 2011 led American spokespeople to express their confidence in al-Qaeda's diminished influence and even to suggest its impending collapse. President Barack Obama declared that the permanent defeat of al-Qaeda was within reach.[3] His secretary of defense, Leon Panetta, similarly expressed his confidence that the strategic defeat of al-Qaeda would be near, if the United States could kill or capture around 10–20 key al-Qaeda leaders of the core group and its affiliates.[4] Obama's counter-terrorism advisor John Brennan suggested that, while it remained a threat through its franchises, al-Qaeda was 'a shadow of its former self' and its core could soon become irrelevant.[5] This optimism was shared by some academics. In a book dedicated to the 'rise and fall of al-Qaeda', Fawaz Gerges declared that al-Qaeda 'has all but vanished, or at least dwindled to the palest shadow of its former self'.[6] But al-Qaeda persisted: not only has it survived 16 years of an American-led global manhunt, it has weathered the ISIS storm and even succeeded in capitalising on the chaos brought by the Arab uprisings.

At first, the Arab revolutions appeared to prove al-Qaeda's irrelevance: the group did not participate in the revolutions in Egypt, Tunisia, Libya or Yemen. Moreover, the toppling of these regimes contradicted the logic behind al-Qaeda's US-first strategy. They demonstrated that at least some of the hated governments could be brought down peacefully and that change in the Middle East was possible even before the collapse of the United States, the alleged protector of the region's regimes. But as remaining auto-crats – Bashar al-Assad in particular – turned to brutal suppression of the challenges to their regimes, and post-revolution transitions in Egypt, Libya and Yemen faltered, al-Qaeda's narrative gained new appeal. Moreover, it soon became evident that the Arab revolutions presented al-Qaeda with new opportunities. The uprisings opened new safe havens for jihadis, made access to weaponry easier (particularly weapons from Muammar Gadhafi's arms depots) and weakened long-time US counter-terrorism counterparts.[7]

The meteoric rise of the Islamic State challenged al-Qaeda's position within the jihadi movement and threatened the group's existence. Al-Qaeda appeared old and stale. While al-Qaeda talked about bringing the caliph-ate back, ISIS was delivering; whereas al-Qaeda focused on a narrative of defence of the oppressed *umma*, the Islamic State promoted an expansionist, offensive agenda, combining it with a message of hope that captured the imagination of young Muslims eager to participate in turning the utopian Islamic order into reality. ISIS was flashier and richer, its media apparatus savvier and better positioned to take advantage of social media and tech-nological advances. In comparison, al-Qaeda leader Ayman al-Zawahiri's messages were long, boring and exhausting.

But the Islamic State's overreach proved a blessing for al-Qaeda. It led the US and the international community to focus on fighting the self-styled caliphate, thus giving al-Qaeda further breathing space and allowing it to rebuild. With global attention turning to ISIS, al-Qaeda was able to improve its image (which had suffered tremendously due to the actions of the Islamic State of Iraq when it was still an al-Qaeda branch), nurture relations with local populations, embed itself within local insurgencies in Syria and Yemen, and deploy high-ranking officials from the Afghanistan–Pakistan arena to a forward base in Syria, closer to the West.[8] In addition, al-Qaeda built a larger footprint in Afghanistan than the US had previously assessed. The comeback of its Somali franchise al-Shabaab, and the increased operational tempo of a sub-branch of al-Qaeda in the Islamic Maghreb (AQIM) in Mali and the Sahel, are further indicators of al-Qaeda's resilience.

Reality caught up with US policymakers. In the last three years, the US has increased its operations against al-Qaeda targets in Yemen, Syria, Somalia and Afghanistan.[9] The rhetoric shifted as well. The May 2017 'Worldwide Threat Assessment' of the US intelligence community notes the success of the United States and its global counter-terrorism partners in significantly reducing al-Qaeda's ability to 'carry out large-scale, mass casualty attacks, particularly against the US home-land'. But it also asserts that the threat posed by the group has evolved and grown since 9/11, and that it remains a significant threat overseas, exploiting local and regional conflicts.[10] Similarly, the new US national-security strategy, released in December 2017, notes that notwithstanding their defeat in Syria and Iraq, the threat posed by ISIS and al-Qaeda will persist due to their global reach and the presence of branches in strategic locations.[11]

Reality caught up with US policymakers

Scholars and pundits, freer than government officials to look beyond the fight against the Islamic State, sound even more alarmed. Bruce Hoffman, for example, maintains that al-Qaeda has used the shifted focus to the Islamic State to recuperate, and is a more dangerous long-term threat than ISIS. According to Hoffman, the deployment of high-ranking al-Qaeda operatives to Syria allowed the group to build an infrastructure for attacks against the West and put it in a position to take advantage of the collapse (even if incomplete) of the Islamic State by absorbing many of its remnants.[12]

Going further, Daveed Gartenstein-Ross and Nathaniel Barr maintain that 'today al-Qaeda seems to be the strongest it has been since 9/11, and is arguably in the best shape it has known in history'.[13] The authors attribute al-Qaeda's fortune to a strategic re-orientation and effective responses to the defeat of its Iraqi branch in 2007–09, the Arab revolutions of 2011 and the rise of the Islamic State. They see the localisation of al-Qaeda, and particularly its attempts to embed itself within local movements, as the most important strategic change that has engendered a positive distinction between al-Qaeda and the IS, assuring its survival and, in fact, its revitalisation.[14]

Not all analysts share this view of al-Qaeda's newly found ascendance, however. While acknowledging that the jihadi movement has known some success in recent years, Daniel Byman maintains that overall, al-Qaeda has been experiencing a real and possibly permanent decline. This decline manifests in the group's inability to carry out a spectacular attack in over a decade, the shift of its branches to fighting the 'near enemy' in contrast to al-Qaeda's America-first strategy, diminished resources and weak popular support. Byman also reminds us that al-Qaeda failed to drive the US out of the Middle East; in fact, American forces and bases now dot the region, making it more 'occupied' than before 9/11.[15] In the same vein, Cole Bunzel challenges the notion that al-Qaeda is strong, noting that it recently lost Jabhat al-Nusra, its strongest and most successful affiliate, after losing its Iraqi branch only two years earlier. He also dismisses the possibility that al-Qaeda would become stronger through reconciliation with the Islamic State, arguing that the conflict between the organisations is rooted in unbridgeable theological and strategic differences.[16]

How to make sense of this complicated picture of achievements and failures? And why do assessments of al-Qaeda's prowess diverge? More importantly, how much of a threat does al-Qaeda really pose?

We must first recall that during its nearly 30 years of existence, al-Qaeda's fortune has known ebbs and flows. In the mid-1990s, its finances were in a shambles,[17] yet in the years leading up to the 9/11 attacks the group rebounded. And while 9/11 was the peak of al-Qaeda's success, it was followed by the quick loss of 70% of its manpower in the American invasion of Afghanistan and years of suffocating dragnet.[18] By the end of the decade, al-Qaeda had lost a staggering 75% of its original leadership.[19] These swings were in no way the result of al-Qaeda's deeds alone. Indeed, as in the past, al-Qaeda's trajectory may depend on factors largely outside of the group's control.[20]

More generally, determining the state of a terrorist organisation is difficult because, as a clandestine entity, it operates in the shadows. The true scope of its capabilities is often revealed only in retrospect. Naturally, even more than states, armed non-state actors have incentives to misrepresent their capabilities in order to enhance their bargaining power.[21] Furthermore, by definition, terrorist groups rely on demonstration of the pain they could inflict upon their opponents rather than on full-force assault, leaving even the best intelligence agencies with considerable information gaps.

Localisation and its consequences

Al-Qaeda's localisation drive began in 2003, with the establishment of a Saudi branch, al-Qaeda in the Arabian Peninsula (AQAP), followed in 2004 by a merger with Abu Musab al-Zarqawi's Tawhid wal-Jihad (TWJ) to form an al-Qaeda branch in Iraq. These early expansions took place against the backdrop of a siege of the group's central leadership in Afghanistan and Pakistan, which debilitated al-Qaeda and prevented it from taking an active role in the resistance to US forces in Iraq. By franchising, al-Qaeda got access to the Iraqi arena. More broadly, branching out allowed al-Qaeda to claim that it was not only relevant but, in fact, successful.

Al-Qaeda's early expansion choices backfired: the launching of the campaign in Saudi Arabia was premature,[22] and the formation of a relationship with the unruly Zarqawi undermined al-Qaeda's image among Sunni Muslims. Over time, however, al-Qaeda's franchising process improved. It added local branches in Algeria (2006), Yemen (2009), Somalia (2010), Syria (2011) and the Indian subcontinent (2014), but its approach in these cases was more cautious. Al-Qaeda carefully examined the groups seeking to join (though caution did not guarantee positive returns from any relationship), and in the cases of Somalia and Syria it even chose to keep the affiliation a secret.[23]

Al-Qaeda's strategy of localisation was not an inevitable derivative of its ideology. Incitement of the Muslim *umma*, often declared by al-Qaeda leaders as the group's primary mission,[24] did not require formal organisational expansion. It did not require forming branches, and could have taken other forms; al-Qaeda could have focused on increasing its operational reach, or entered into other types of relationships with peer jihadi organisations – through either absorption, unification based on organisational equality or collaboration under an umbrella group.[25]

Centre and periphery

Localisation has been a risky strategy for al-Qaeda. Firstly, it forced al-Qaeda central to delegate vast authority to its franchises. Given the precarious position of its core leadership in Pakistan's tribal areas, al-Qaeda central had little ability to provide timely guidance when a branch faced a dilemma. Secondly, localisation brought in groups whose interests sometimes diverged from those of the central leadership, without giving al-Qaeda central effective means of control. Thirdly, it threatened the position of al-Qaeda within the broader jihadi movement by giving ambitious branches and their leaders the opportunity to use the affiliation with al-Qaeda to raise their stature before turning against al-Qaeda central. Finally, it tied the image of al-Qaeda central to perceptions of its branches, making it a hostage to affiliates' actions. When branches overreached, al-Qaeda became complicit in their atrocities, endangering public support.[26]

All of these dangers were manifest in the case of al-Qaeda's affiliation with Zarqawi's TWJ. Al-Qaeda's entry into the prized Iraqi arena, where it had previously lacked an organisation to confront the invading US forces, came at a very high price. Zarqawi and his successors were unreliable partners who ended up severely harming the al-Qaeda brand. Contrary to al-Qaeda's wishes, Zarqawi prioritised a counterproductive sectarian approach that undermined al-Qaeda's US-first strategy.[27] The group brought chaos to Iraq, but the carnage – particularly the indiscriminate killing of innocent Muslim civilians – gradually undermined its image among Sunnis in Iraq and abroad. The jihadis' unrestrained brutality, often directed against other Sunnis, led some important groups among Iraq's Sunni tribes to stand up to the jihadis and unravel what appeared, until 2006, to be a tremendous success story. The TWJ affiliation would end up haunting al-Qaeda for years to come, as the rogue franchise first tarnished al-Qaeda's reputation among Sunni Muslims and later (as ISIS) took advantage of the conditions in Iraq and Syria to challenge and upstage its central leadership.[28]

As Jacob Shapiro and Dan Byman have emphasised, delegation brings a practical problem: maintaining operational security requires keeping communications limited, which means in turn that the centre lacks the ability to effectively supervise the affiliates and assure that their actions are in line with al-Qaeda's objectives and strategy. Absent effective oversight, al-Qaeda has been exposed to reputational damage by branch leaders and the rank and file, who have variously lacked understanding of how violence is expected to advance particular political objectives, disagreed with the methods and targets assigned by al-Qaeda's leadership, or simply acted based on their own self-interest.

Nationalism beats transnationalism

Branching out is not just a practical risk, however, but a political one: it undermines al-Qaeda's ideology and identity. Al-Qaeda views religion, rather than nationalism or ethnic and tribal identities, as the only legitimate foundation for world order. Its world view conflicts with the state-based logic underlying world order: al-Qaeda rejects the legitimacy of states and state borders, seeing them as a ploy to divide the Muslim *umma* and prevent it from realising its true potential. Instead, al-Qaeda wants to overthrow the Westphalian order and replace it with universal Islamic rule.[29]

In its early days, during the 1990s, this perspective distinguished al-Qaeda from other jihadi groups that emphasised local struggles and attempted – each in its own country – to bring down insufficiently Islamic regimes. Bin Laden argued that those separate efforts were futile because the Muslim *umma* faced a system-wide challenge, with the United States backing the oppressive regimes and assuring their survival. The answer, therefore, was to conduct a worldwide struggle against the US and bring about its collapse.[30]

By franchising, al-Qaeda is diverging from its transnational strategy: branches tend to focus on the states in which they emerged. Moreover, franchising has weakened one of al-Qaeda's greatest achievements: the creation of a transnational entity based on religious affiliation, multinational in its composition and anti-nationalist in its orientation. Segmentation diminishes multinational composition. Although multinationalism does remain in the aggregate, membership at the branch level is local. Operationally, the al-Qaeda branches are assigned geographical spheres of responsibility. Consequently, they busy themselves with local targets (or Western targets in their localities) at the expense of targeting the United States. Despite clear instructions from Zawahiri to focus on Western targets, exceptions made for self-defence and a broad view of what could legitimately trigger self-defence have inevitably led al-Qaeda's branches to prioritise local struggles over the global one.[31]

Whatever globalisation's achievements, the world is still divided into states which are granted exclusive authority within their territory. States represent the status quo; transnational groups that seek self-determination are the revisionists. This order of things is deeply entrenched, and most non-state actors tend to pursue a very limited challenge, attempting to revise specific borders and seeking incorporation into the state-based order, rather than pursuing its overthrow.

There is a centuries-old track record of challengers to the state-based order – rare as they are – succumbing to the socialising power of inter-national society.[32] Facing systemic constraints, the Soviet-led communist movement soon abandoned its plan to establish communism as the founda-tion for a new global order. Communism persisted, but instead of serving as an organising principle for world politics, revolutionising the global order, it was relegated to a secondary role as state ideology. States may adopt communism, but whenever the rules of international society clash with communist ideology, international society wins. Religious actors expe-rience similar pressures: although monotheist religions are not anchored in territoriality, most actors interested in promoting religious identity confine themselves to a particular territory and subordinate their religious beliefs to the dominance of the state.[33]

Nationalism is critical to this process. State identity has, over the years, become anchored in national identity,[34] making it extremely difficult for actors who vehemently reject the legitimacy of nationalism to mount a successful challenge. Whether through state institutions or elite-driven efforts to cement national identity, the state puts non-state challengers at a considerable disadvantage. And while it is theoretically possible for actors below or above the state level to develop distinct identities, the dominance of nationalism tends to overshadow alternative identities. Most chal-lenges to nationalism are challenges to particular national identities, not to the idea of nationalism itself. As a result, challengers usually end up solidifying the nation-state as the building block of the world order, and undercutting the alternatives.

So it might be the case that localisation allows for a more effective allocation of al-Qaeda's human resources, deploying them where they can inflict maximum damage. But its benefits are overshadowed by its contribution to the weakening of al-Qaeda's religious ideology, as localisation counteracts Islamic globalism. Instead of promoting a religious order, localisation is likely to undercut al-Qaeda's transnational agenda and even lead to fragmentation. The greater the autonomy of the affiliates, the more likely parochial national, ethnic or tribal identities will interact with and even supersede their religious component. As al-Qaeda branches increasingly respond to local conditions, the impact of al-Qaeda central will decline. This could – though it does not have to – lead to al-Qaeda's disintegration, with franchises extricating themselves from the group, the way the Islamic State of Iraq and Jabhat al-Nusra did. It could also result in decentralisation that would maintain the connection between al-Qaeda central and the franchises, but limit al-Qaeda central to a symbolic and advisory position.

The logic of comparison

On the face of it, much separates al-Qaeda from the Muslim Brotherhood. Firstly, al-Qaeda was established as an armed group and has always been committed to violence as its primary tool. The MB, on the other hand, was established as a social movement focused on *Dawa* and education, in which jihad as violence is largely (though not always) rejected in favour of attempts for peaceful change. Al-Qaeda operates outside the state-based order, whereas the MB operates from within.[35] This difference in attitudes has limited the strategies al-Qaeda can deploy: it can either violently confront those who stand in its way, or (more recently) accept limited truces that delay inevitable armed confrontation.[36] MB branches have more options, including, for example, political participation and grassroots activities to reshape society. MB chapters are also freer to collaborate with other actors, whereas jihadi actors such as al-Qaeda are highly reluctant to cooperate with societal actors that do not subscribe to an Islamist ideology. In fact, al-Qaeda is likely to view such actors as apostates rather than potential partners.

Secondly, al-Qaeda was established as an explicitly transnational organisation. Even after it began its formal expansion efforts, its central leadership remained de-territorialised (as opposed to the branches). In contrast, the MB was established as an Egyptian organisation. While the movement has international leadership and a transnational message focusing on Islamic revival, calls for Muslim collective action and aspires to Muslim unity, the Egyptian branch is still the dominant force within the movement, holding sway over its international institutions.

Thirdly, the decision to branch out came from al-Qaeda's central leadership. Al-Qaeda central also decides which groups to admit as franchises and whose admission to reject. In contrast, the limited information available on the affiliation process within the MB suggests that its expansion, though encouraged, has rarely been directed from the Egyptian core. Fourthly, and relatedly, al-Qaeda is more hierarchical than is the Brotherhood. Though it has decentralised its operations, al-Qaeda has remained essentially hierarchical in command structure. In the MB, the hierarchical dimension is relatively weak and primarily a local feature. Notwithstanding the fraternal relations between chapters, they are formally independent and authorised to determine their own strategies.

Notwithstanding these differences, a careful comparison between these cases of transnational Islamist organisations is warranted, and can produce important insights. After all, both al-Qaeda and the MB are confronted by the tension between transnationalism and localisation: both actors highlight a religious identity while operating within a state-based order that emphasises national identities. They aspire to establish an all-encompassing Islamic polity modelled after the golden days of Islam, but the ideational power of local identities, and the operational constraints of state authority, force them to seek a way to bridge the gap between their universal vision and a reality that calls for segmented efforts. They must overcome the power of localisation even as they find themselves turning to it as a temporary step on the way to creating their transnational Islamic polity.

In argumentative terms, the Muslim Brotherhood is a 'hard case' for the theory of localisation's drawbacks – that is, a case which is harder to demonstrate, but which, if proven, makes the theory stronger. Non-violent groups do not face principal–agent problems as severe as those faced by violent groups. So if nationalism trumps localisation for the Brotherhood, it is even more likely to do so for al-Qaeda.

The Muslim Brotherhood

The Muslim Brotherhood is a global organisation with a transnational scope and a universalising mission.[37] Established in 1928 in Egypt by Hassan al-Banna, the group sought the removal of Western influence from Egypt and the implementation of Islamic law. Notably, al-Banna did not call for the overthrow of Egypt's political order, instead seeking its reform. Al-Banna was also interested in revival of the caliphate, but viewed it as a distant objective.[38] As the group evolved, gaining numerous members in Egypt and admirers outside the country, it sought to spread its ideology and expand the organisation beyond Egypt's borders.[39] It now has branches in more than 70 countries.[40] Since the early 1980s, these affiliates have been linked together through a formal international organisation, the International Organisation of the Muslim Brotherhood (IOMB).

MB branches share the belief that all Muslims are part of one *umma*, that Islam is not just a religion but a comprehensive system of rules that guides every aspect of life – politics included – and that the solution to the problems of the *umma* is the return to Islam's original state. The strategy derived from these fundamental beliefs is to build an alternative Islamic society that would ultimately reform the state and, in a bottom-up process, bring Muslim countries under true Islamic control.[41]

Although the MB's internal statute declares that the group is a 'universal Islamic body', its branches are largely independent. As Barry Rubin puts it, the Brotherhood branches 'operate in silos rather than collectively'.[42] There is little coordination among them, and each chapter makes its decisions based on the particular local conditions it is facing. Branches avoid outright intervention in each other's affairs, normally limiting themselves to offering advice and support.[43] The MB has prioritised flexibility and adaptability over control.

While organisational links may be weak, shared ideological commitments strengthen unity within the Brotherhood. The late MB general guide (the leader of the Brotherhood in Egypt and of the IOMB) Mohammed Akef argued that the MB should be viewed as an ideological movement rather than an organisation. Disparate Muslim organisations follow their own rules, but they share the message of the Brotherhood and its doctrine. The MB, according to one description, is 'a global movement whose members cooperate with each other throughout the world, based on the same religious worldview – the spread of Islam, until it rules the world'.[44] These ideological principles offset some – but not all – of the adverse effects of decentralisation.

Information about the internal considerations behind the Muslim Brotherhood's expansion is hard to come by due to the group's secretive nature. However, it appears that, compared with al-Qaeda's organisational expansion, the Egyptian leadership had a much smaller role in the establishment of affiliates. The Brotherhood's expansion beyond Egypt was largely the result of independent initiatives by admirers of al-Banna, who sought to imitate the original chapter and bring the slogan 'Islam is the solution' to their own countries. While it has at times been assisted by emissaries sent from Egypt (for example, al-Banna's son-in-law was sent to Palestine and Jordan to help set up chapters), there is little evidence to suggest deep Egyptian investment in shaping these branches. Moreover, notwithstanding the broad acceptance of the seniority of the Egyptian branch, its authority – and even more, its level of control – over MB branches outside of Egypt has always been limited. Even as the Palestinian branch initially viewed itself as part of the Egyptian MB, and the Jordanian chapter regarded itself as a branch of the parent organisation in Jordan, the Syrian branch was quite autonomous.[45] Over time, the Jordanian and Palestinian branches also grew more independent.

If there is general agreement about the Brotherhood's fundamental ideology, particularly its view of Islam as an all-encompassing 'total system', the MB's political programme is highly ambiguous, and as a result branches adopt diverging strategies. Roel Meijer traces this vagueness all the way back to al-Banna;[46] it involves questions such as the relationship with the state, what constitutes a legitimate political process, the balance between social and political action (and respective organisations and associations), and how an MB branch should respond to state repression. Such ambiguity makes it easier for each of the branches to chart its own direction while cementing the MB as a big-tent group.

Local circumstances have been highly consequential in shaping each MB branch. Facing particular incentive structures based on unique local conditions and political constraints and opportunities, branches' ability to adopt distinct strategies has been instrumental to their survival. MB branches differ in their relations with the regimes in the countries where they operate, with some characterised as primarily conflictual and others as cooperative.[47] King Abdullah attended the inaugural meeting of the Jordanian branch; six years after its establishment, the branch had already fielded candidates in national elections. MB members assumed positions in Jordan's government, including at the ministerial level. The Kuwaiti MB branch similarly maintained largely cooperative relations with the regime, eschewing violence and attempting to promote Islamisation through the institutions of Kuwaiti society and the state.[48] Syria offers the opposite example: relations between the regime and the MB were primarily conflictual. Conflict reached its peak when an MB-led uprising was brutally quelled in Hama in 1982, with the regime massacring 20,000 people. Some states have alternated between confrontational and cooperative relations with the MB.

Local circumstances have been consequential

Local conditions have also contributed to intra-Brotherhood conflicts. While the Egyptian leadership supported the 1979 Iranian revolution, the main MB leaders in Saudi Arabia did not. Similarly, the MB's Kuwaiti branch opposed the Iraqi invasion in 1990, whereas the Egyptian core supported it. Moreover, despite the call of MB branches to resist US occupation of Iraq, the local branch cooperated with the Americans.[49] Branches have also experienced internal disputes as they faced changing local circumstances.[50]

In the absence of a political programme to articulate the manner in which the movement could overcome the division of the *umma* based on separate nation-states, branches ended up respecting the principle of state sovereignty. With each branch developing separately, attachment to one's own branch appears to surpass the commitment to the broader movement. In fact, not only does the MB not seek to consolidate the branches into a single international movement, when a member relocates to a different country, he does not automatically become a member of the local branch.[51] Membership in the Brotherhood is not seen as international; rather, an MB member belongs to a particular chapter.

The formation of the IOMB in 1982 was an effort to institutionalise relations among MB branches. The new international organisation codified spheres of responsibility, distinguishing between questions that require decisions by the international body, issues requiring the branches to consult with the international organisation and decisions that are the prerogatives of the national branches.[52] It also established the position of the general guide, a 13-member guidance bureau and the 130-member Shura Council. To a certain extent, the IOMB was a natural attempt at formalising and deepening coordination, a necessity given the Brotherhood's tremendous geographical expansion.

According to the internal statute, the national branches are formally bound by the decisions of the IOMB. Alison Pargeter notes that they must adhere to the 'policies and positions of the Muslim Brotherhood toward public issues as determined by the General Guidance Office and the General Shura Council' and obtain the general bureau's approval before making important political decisions. Branches also commit to setting their own local statutes and gain IOMB approval before they enter into force.[53]

While Brotherhood organisations from all over the Muslim world had convened as early as 1954,[54] the impetus for the creation of the IOMB in the 1980s relates to the gradual evolution of Europe from a refuge for exiled Brotherhood leaders to an arena for locally focused Muslim activism. According to Steven Brooke of the University of Louisville, the group was now eager to institutionalise the relations among branches and thus reduce their freedom of action.[55] Other scholars emphasise different motivations behind the shift in the Brotherhood's structure. Saudi scholar Nawaf Obaid views the IOMB as an attempt by the founding Egyptian Brotherhood to exert greater control over the movement (and guarantee the supply of much-needed financial resources to the Egyptian chapter).[56] In the same vein, Pargeter views the IOMB as one in a list of attempts by the Egyptian MB to create alternative centres of activity and sources of funding that could sustain the branch while it weathered a particularly difficult time in Egypt.[57]

Although in theory a non-Egyptian can assume the leadership of the IOMB, normally the role is reserved for the Egyptian general guide.[58] However, regardless of the intentions of the Egyptian MB and the language of the internal statute, the IOMB leadership has been primarily symbolic and confers little meaningful authority. The preference for an Egyptian leader is a nod to the special role of the Egyptian branch of the movement and a result of the dominance of Egyptians within the IOMB's main committees (another sign of the organisation's general deference to the Egyptian MB).[59] Yet these gestures to the founding Egyptian MB did not erase existing tensions between the Egyptian branch and other affiliates. In some cases, the establishment of the IOMB, and the demand for branch leaders to pledge allegiance to the general guide, exacerbated these tensions.[60] As the late Sudanese MB leader Hassan al-Turabi asserted, 'you cannot run the world from Cairo'.[61]

The IOMB has been primarily symbolic

A more equitable division of positions might have improved the IOMB's ability to become a meaningful framework. The unique status of the Egyptian branch increased the burden on the Egyptian leadership, led to a skewed emphasis on Egyptian matters at the expense of international causes, and increased tensions between the Egyptian leadership and MB branches in other countries. The IOMB's ability to engage in international affairs was greatly diminished when the Egyptian government suppressed the MB.[62]

The IOMB has not been a success story. The organisation has rarely been asked to settle difficult internal questions, and the few times that branches have turned to the IOMB they have found it slow to respond and generally ineffective.[63] Additionally, the formation of the international MB failed to lead to the consolidation of the European branches or to their organisational subordination to a central MB leadership. As Lorenzo Vidino explains, the European MB should not be seen as hierarchical branches. Instead, he labels them as MB legacy groups, or 'New European Brothers', because 'rather than an organization of card-carrying members, [the Brotherhood] is a movement whose affiliation is determined by a series of personal contacts and, most importantly, a shared ideology or, in the words of a senior leader in Europe, a "common way of thinking"'.[64]

The fortune of the IOMB further declined following the 9/11 attacks. Fearful that the movement would become entangled in the global war on terrorism, the Brotherhood sought to de-emphasise its global nature and give the impression that the IOMB was no more than a coordinating body.[65] The departure of important branches such as Hamas and most recently, in 2016, of the Jordanian and Tunisian branches from the IOMB despite the marginal obligations membership entails (or perhaps because membership brings few benefits and leaving costs very little) further attests to the weakness of the IOMB as a transnational force.[66]

Confirming that the IOMB lacks meaningful operational value, the general supervisor of the Jordanian branch noted: 'each country has its own exclusive organizational and political nature and relations with the state in which it exists. This gathering has no binding capacity regarding any domestic decision.'[67] The Egyptian deputy general guide Mohamed Habib claimed that 'the aims of the international [organisation] are one and it has one methodology so all the branches aim for the same things but within the framework of the legislation of their own countries'.[68]

To sum up, George Washington University's Nathan Brown argues that the IOMB resembles the Socialist International: 'a tame framework for a group of loosely linked, ideologically similar movements that recognize each other, swap stories and experiences in occasional meetings, and happily subscribe to a formally international ideology without giving it much priority'.[69]

Lessons

What can be learned from the case of the Muslim Brotherhood? Firstly, it would be misleading to assess the strength of a transnational entity based on its cumulative size and its geographic spread. The scope of its network does not reveal the strength of the connections between its different components. In the absence of effective central control, the broader the group, the more likely we are to find internal friction.

Secondly, while decentralisation via localism might be conducive to organisational expansion, it comes at the expense of control. Even as flexible strategies broadened the tent of the MB as a movement, they diminished its ability to act as a centralised organisation and to amalgamate diverging MB voices into one coherent message, let alone turn expansion into a force multiplier. Consequently, the size of the Brotherhood as a movement does not translate to equivalent political effects.

Thirdly, localisation creates dynamics that weaken transnational ties. Steven Brooke encapsulates the inherent dilemma of the MB: 'Part of the attractiveness of Brotherhood ideology was its adaptability across different contexts, but over time this adaptability weakened organizational bonds between the branches.'[70] The success in expanding the organisation comes at a price – shared ties are loose, and transnationalism is diminished. One consequence is that the political value of the formal international organisation is slim; each branch is effectively independent.

Other political constraints further hinder the ability of MB branches to coordinate too openly or extensively: deep coordination would increase regimes' sense of threat, and as a result undermine the efforts of MB chapters to pursue their political and social goals. Moreover, greater coordination between branches could lead to increased friction between corresponding regimes and to pressuring states that have adopted a softer approach to the MB to become more confrontational. Al-Qaeda's emphasis on violent means reduces the importance of such political considerations. Al-Qaeda does not have political parties, and it does not rely on the provision of goods that requires state approval the way the MB does. Yet al-Qaeda, too, must consider how formal expansion would affect a host state's ability to formulate an independent response to the group. In the aftermath of 9/11, publicity may force states – even those that would have preferred a more passive or accommodating approach to the presence of al-Qaeda in their midst – into a direct confrontation to avoid international (particularly American) backlash.

Fourthly, an ambiguous political programme lends itself to organisational expansion, particularly in a decentralised organisation, but it reduces the significance of the movement's transnationalism. The bar for entry for an actor who seeks to become a branch of a transnational movement with a vague plan is relatively low. Local branches need only to agree on shared fundamental ideological commitments such as the implementation of Islamic law; in practice, they are free to interpret the general guidelines set by the movement's leadership as they see fit, design strategies that are tailored to their particular circumstances and even experiment with new strategies. Such flexibility would be particularly useful for groups that see achieving their end goals as distant and arguing over how to reach them as a premature distraction. This factor applies, to some extent, to al-Qaeda. However, this could become a double-edged sword if the group's enemies are able to tie all branches to the unpopular overreaches of one of its components.

On the other hand, the clearer the political strategy designed by the central leadership of the transnational Islamist group, the greater the prospects for organisational coherence, since it is easier for the branches to know what they are expected to do and follow their superiors' plans. Additionally, the constraints on the ability of a branch to choose its own path also increase because the group's central leadership is better positioned to detect shirking.

Finally, the incorporation of European MB branches into the broader MB offers an illuminating example of the manner in which localisation and organisational measures affect group ideology. The rise of MB chapters in Europe as permanent fixtures, and the focus of MB activity in its own right rather than as merely an auxiliary to the MB in the Muslim world, required ideological adjustments. The group had to abandon the common division of the world into *dar al-Islam* (abode of Islam) and *dar al-Harb* (the part of the world that has yet to come under Muslim control) because such a division suggested that Muslims should not live in Europe and certainly should not participate in its social and political life. The solution the MB adopted was to argue that the binary division does not suit an era in which Muslims can live peacefully in non-Muslim countries and practise Islam freely despite being a minority. Thus providing a modern religious interpretation to justify and carve out a special place for Muslims in the West, the MB announced a third category, that of *dar al-Da'awa* (land of preaching).[71]

*   *   *

On the day the Islamic State announced the establishment of its caliphate, it also released a video documenting the destruction of a border crossing between Iraq and Syria. In the video, the group's military commander, Omar al-Shishani, declared: 'Praise be to Allah, we are happy today because we participated in tearing down the border erected by the tyrants in order to prevent the Muslims from traveling to their lands. The tyrants tore apart the Islamic caliphate and made it into countries such as Syria and Iraq, to be ruled by man-made laws.' The group's spokesman, Abu Muhammad al-Adnani, promised more to come: 'surely the borders will be erased from the map'.[72]

The scene encapsulates the problem any transnational movement (Islamic, communist or otherwise) seeking trans-border political control faces: once the state-based order took root, it became an enormous undertaking to erase existing borders,[73] let alone create a new world order that is based on non-territorial affiliation in the nation-state's stead. Those actors seeking to restore Islam to its glory days have found that capturing a state is hard, but uniting territories previously belonging to multiple states under religious rule is much harder. It is not just that the great powers actively prevent any state from rising to great-power status;[74] the challenge is greater because national and sub-national identities are entrenched, and local conditions have greater impact on indigenous populations than do encompassing ideologies that fail to capture locals' particular needs or local power and incentive structures. Arguably, aggregating all its resources, overcoming localisation tendencies and producing systemic effects are the most challenging tasks a transnational Islamist movement faces.

The MB succumbed to these systemic pressures. Its bottom-up strategy requires space to operate in order to Islamise society and makes the group dependent on the consent (active or passive) of host states to its activities. Moreover, lacking a plan to merge cross-border efforts and erase state borders that prevent political Muslim unity, MB efforts focus on local efforts, each branch in its own state. That Muslim unity is seen as a remote objective, which the MB does not expect to attain anytime soon, makes the taming of the group's transnationalism easier to swallow.

Al-Qaeda's approach is different. It is still committed to the creation of a transnational polity and to the overthrow of the state-based order. It doubtless sees the collapse of the Islamic State's self-styled caliphate as a cautionary tale (and a vindication of bin Laden's opposition to the establishment of al-Qaeda-led Islamic emirates[75]), but it cannot be oblivious to the excitement the caliphate project created. Despite the establishment of franchises, al-Qaeda seeks to evade the nationalism trap. Its branches do not assume the names of the states in which they operate (for example, al-Shabaab rather than al-Qaeda in Somalia). Even when a branch is based on local citizens (rather than transnationally composed) and most of its attacks are directed at local targets, it uses names with Islamic connotations or references to geographic areas (for example, al-Qaeda in the Arabian Peninsula). Moreover, branches are seeking to expand regionally: al-Qaeda in the Islamic Maghreb is no longer the Algerian organisation it used to be, operating deep in the Sahel and West Africa and comprising operatives from Mali, Mauritania, Libya, Morocco and elsewhere. Al-Shabaab, too, has expanded its operations into Kenya and includes a far larger number of Kenyans than in the past.

Nevertheless, the localisation problem has not vanished. Branches may expand their reach within their designated regions, but struggles still tend to be local in nature (Malians are the primary AQIM operatives in Mali). Moreover, there is no effort to replicate the Islamic State's experiment in Syria and Iraq, in which it attempted to construct an Islamic identity and dilute local identities by bringing a massive number of foreign fighters to participate in state-building. Al-Qaeda still believes the collapse of the United States to be a necessary step before it can capture states and erase international borders. It lacks a viable plan for overcoming the power of local identities, putting enormous faith in the strength of Islamic identity and al-Qaeda's own ability to bring about political unity in a post-American Middle East.

Yet events on the ground indicate that the stronger an al-Qaeda branch becomes, the greater its inclination to look inward. In Yemen, AQAP has successfully enmeshed itself within a local Sunni movement, but its alliances with tribes and other societal actors do not amount to a successful takeover of these movements or to the adoption of the al-Qaeda world view by its partners. Moreover, the connections it has formed with local populations have restricted its ability to fight its state enemy for fear that the population in which it embedded itself would be targeted.[76] In Syria, Jabhat al-Nusra found the al-Qaeda label to be such a hindrance to its efforts to build lasting relationships that it decided to leave the mother organisation. Interestingly, and as a sign of al-Qaeda central's limitations, while Jabhat al-Nusra consulted Zawahiri's lieutenant in Syria, the al-Qaeda chief himself was unaware of the decision until the public announcement. Despite his disapproval, the defecting Syrian branch did not return to al-Qaeda.[77]

The expansion of the jihadi movement is real and worrying, but it should not be equated with the fortunes of al-Qaeda. Al-Qaeda is still a powerful symbol for jihadi resistance, but it is also a drag on its successful franchises. Therefore, the threat it poses varies by location. Ultimately, its power is not the aggregate of all franchises' capabilities, and its central leadership greatly depends on the branches' willingness to follow it. Rather than a powerful transnational threat, al-Qaeda represents several local – yet meaningful – threats. This trend is likely to continue, making the leadership offered by al-Qaeda central more symbolic than operational.

The United States should resist the temptation to inflate the al-Qaeda threat. It should examine the strength of the ties between al-Qaeda central and each branch, and devise policies that would deepen cleavages within the group as a whole. The United States should assess the threat posed by each affiliate based on its idiosyncratic interests, not just its capabilities. Importantly, Washington's thinking about the jihadi movement should not be informed by its aggregate material capabilities. Understanding the forces influencing politics within the jihadi movement in general, and al-Qaeda in particular, would be invaluable to the formulation of fine-tuned policies.

Acknowledgements

The author would like to thank Stephen Brooke and Marc Lynch for their helpful comments on earlier drafts, and Jessica Blitz for terrific research assistance.

Notes

1   Barak Mendelsohn, *Combating Jihadism: American Hegemony and Interstate Cooperation in the War on* *Terrorism* (Chicago, IL: University of Chicago Press, 2009).

2   Jacob Shapiro, *The Terrorist Dilemma:*

Managing Violent Covert Organizations (Princeton, NJ: Princeton University Press, 2013).

3 The White House, 'Remarks by President Obama in Address to the Nation from Afghanistan', 1May 2012, https://obamawhitehouse.archives. gov/the-press-office/2012/05/01/ remarks-president-obama-address-nation-afghanistan.

4 Phil Stewart, 'Leon Panetta Says al Qaeda's Defeat "Within Reach"', Reuters, 9 July 2011.

5 Lee Ferran, 'Al Qaeda "Shadow of Former Self", US Counter-Terror Official Says', ABC News, 30 April 2012, http://abcnews. go.com/blogs/headlines/2012/04/ al-qaeda-shadow-of-former-self.

6 Fawas Gerges, *The Rise and Fall of al-Qaeda* (New York: Oxford University Press, 2011), p. 3.

7 Aaron Zelin, 'Introduction', in Aaron Zelin (ed.), *How Al-Qaeda Survived Drones, Uprisings, and the Islamic State: The Nature of the Current Threat* (Washington DC: Washington Institute for Near East Policy, 2017), p. 3.

8 *Ibid.*, pp. 4–5.

9 See Bill Roggio, 'US Military Killed 15 AQAP Operatives in 6 Airstrikes', *Long War Journal*, 24 December 2016; Thomas Joscelyn, 'Pentagon: Airstrikes Kill 20 or More al Qaeda Fighters in Northern Syria', *Long War Journal*, 5 January 2017 ; Bill Roggio, 'US Military to Actively Target Shabaab in Somalia', *Long War Journal*, 31 March 2017; and Bill Roggio, 'US Military Kills AQIS Leaders, Fighters in Southern Afghanistan', *Long War Journal*, 26 April 2017.

10 Daniel Coats, Director of National Intelligence, 'Statement for the Record Worldwide Threat Assessment of the U.S. Intelligence Community Senate Select Committee on Intelligence', 11 May 2017, pp. 5–6, https://www. intelligence.senate.gov/sites/default/ files/documents/os-coats-051117.pdf.

11 White House, 'National Security Strategy of the United States of America', December 2017, pp. 10–11, 26, https://www.whitehouse.gov/ wp-content/uploads/2017/12/NSS-Final-12-18-2017-0905.pdf.

12 Bruce Hoffman, 'The Global Terror Threat and Counterterrorism Challenges Facing the Next Administration', *CTC Sentinel 9:11*, November/December 2016, p. 4.

13 Daveed Gartenstein-Ross and Nathaniel Barr, 'How Al-Qaeda Survived the Islamic State Challenge', *Current Trends in Islamist Ideology*, no. 21, March 2017, p. 62.

14 *Ibid.*, pp. 50–68.

15 Daniel Byman, 'Explaining Al Qaeda's Decline', *Journal of Politics*, vol. 79, no. 3, 2017, pp. 1,106–17.

16 Cole Bunzel, 'The Islamic State Will Survive', *Foreign Policy*, 10 July 2017.

17 Peter Bergen and Paul Cruickshank, 'Revisiting the Early Al Qaeda: An Updated Account of its Formative Years', *Studies in Conflict and Terrorism*, vol. 35, no. 1, 2012, pp. 27–9.

18 Lawrence Wright, *The Looming Tower: Al-Qaeda and the Road to 9/11* (New York: Knopf, 2006).

19 Audrey Cronin, *How Terrorism Ends: Understanding the Decline and Demise of Terrorist Campaigns* (Princeton, NJ: Princeton University Press, 2009), p. 167.

20 Seth Jones, 'Will al-Qaeda Make a Comeback? The Factors That Will

Determine Its Success', *Foreign Affairs*, 7 August 2017.

21 James Fearon, 'Rationalist Explanations for War', *International Organization*, vol. 49, no. 3, 1995, pp. 379–414.

22 Thomas Hegghammer, *The Failure of Jihad in Saudi Arabia* (West Point, NY: Combating Terrorism Center, 2010).

23 See Abbottabad Documents, Combating Terrorism Center at West Point, SOCOM-2012-0000005, 3 May 2012; and Ayman al-Zawahiri, 'Zawahiri Reportedly Settles Dispute Between ISI, al-Nusra Front', Site Intelligence Unit, 9 June 2013.

24 Jason Burke, 'Why Bin Laden Is Losing His War on Terror', *Observer*, 11 June 2006.

25 Barak Mendelsohn, *The al-Qaeda Franchise: The Expansion of al-Qaeda and Its Consequences* (New York: Oxford University Press, 2016), pp. 25–36.

26 *Ibid.*, pp. 61–83.

27 Ayman al-Zawahiri, 'Letter from al-Zawahiri to al-Zarqawi, 9 July 2005', https://ctc.usma.edu/app/uploads/2013/10/Zawahiris-Letter-to-Zarqawi-Translation.pdf.

28 Mendelsohn, *The al-Qaeda Franchise*, pp. 116–26, 168–93.

29 Mendelsohn, *Combating Jihadism*, pp. 63–88.

30 *Ibid.*, pp. 45–62.

31 Ayman al-Zawahiri, 'General Guidelines for Jihad', 13 September 2013, https://azelin.files.wordpress.com/2013/09/dr-ayman-al-e1ba93aw-c481hirc4ab-22general-guidelines-for-the-work-of-a-jihc481dc4ab22-en.pdf.

32 David Armstrong, *Revolution and World Order: The Revolutionary State in International Society* (New York: Oxford University Press, 1993).

33 Barak Mendelsohn, 'God vs. Westphalia: Radical Islamist Movements and the Battle for Organising the World', *Review of International Studies*, vol. 38, no. 3, 2012, pp. 589–613.

34 Ian Lustick, 'Hegemony and the Riddle of Nationalism', in Leonard Binder (ed.), *Ethnic Conflict and International Politics in the Middle East* (Gainesville, FL: University Press of Florida, 1999), pp. 332–59.

35 Marc Lynch, 'Islam Divided Between Jihad and the Muslim Brotherhood', in Assaf Moghadam and Brian Fishman (eds), *Fault Lines in Global Jihad: Organizational, Strategic, and Ideological Fissures* (New York: Routledge, 2011), p. 167.

36 See, for example, 'Give the Tribes More Than They Can Handle', and 'The America Speech', Bin Laden's Bookshelf, Office of the Director of National Intelligence, https://www.dni.gov/index.php/features/bin-laden-s-bookshelf.

37 Lynch, 'Islam Divided Between Jihad and the Muslim Brotherhood', p. 162.

38 David Commins, 'Hasan al-Banna (1906–1949)', in Ali Rahnema (ed.), *Pioneers of Islamic Revival* (New York: Zed Books, 2005), pp. 135–7.

39 Alison Pargeter, *The Muslim Brotherhood: From Opposition to Power* (London: Saqi, 2013), p. 106.

40 Hazem Kandil, *Inside the Brotherhood* (Cambridge, MA: Polity Press, 2015), pp. 146–7.

41 Shmuel Bar, *The Muslim Brotherhood in Jordan* (Tel Aviv: The Moshe Dayan Center for Middle Eastern and African Studies, 1998), p. 8.

42 Barry Rubin, 'Comparing Three Muslim Brotherhoods', in Barry Rubin (ed.), *The Muslim Brotherhood: The Organization and Policies of a Global Islamist Movement* (New York: Palgrave Macmillan, 2010), p. 9.

43 Nathan Brown, 'The Irrelevance of the International Muslim Brotherhood', *Foreign Policy*, 21 September 2010. Notably, at times of crises in the Middle East, the instrumental relationship that some branches developed with foreign Arab regimes inevitably led to friction between branches. For example, Iraqi support for the Palestinians led the Brotherhood's Jordanian branch to defend Saddam Hussein after Iraq invaded Kuwait, thus enraging the Kuwaiti branch. See Pargeter, *The Muslim Brotherhood*, pp. 122–5.

44 Lorenzo Vidino, 'The European Organization of the Muslim Brotherhood: Myth or Reality?', in Roel Meijer and Edwin Bakker (eds), *The Muslim Brotherhood in Europe* (New York: Columbia University Press, 2012), pp. 51–5.

45 Bar, *The Muslim Brotherhood in Jordan*, pp. 9–16.

46 Roel Meijer, 'The Muslim Brotherhood and the Political: An Exercise in Ambiguity', in Meijer and Bakker (eds), *The Muslim Brotherhood in Europe*, pp. 295–320.

47 The Egyptian example reveals variation across time in the relations between a state and the local MB chapter.

48 Carrie Rosefsky Wickham, *The Muslim Brotherhood: Evolution of an Islamist Movement* (Princeton, NJ: Princeton University Press, 2013), pp. 197–201.

49 Pargeter, *The Muslim Brotherhood*, pp. 120–35.

50 The most notable example is the rift within the Egyptian MB concerning the response to Nasser's repressive tactics, which pitted the general guide of the MB against Sayyid Qutb.

51 Brown, 'The Irrelevance of the International Muslim Brotherhood'.

52 Pargeter, *The Muslim Brotherhood*, pp. 113–15.

53 *Ibid.*, p. 114.

54 Bar, *The Muslim Brotherhood in Jordan*, p. 22.

55 Steven Brooke, 'The Muslim Brotherhood in Europe and the Middle East: The Evolution of a Relationship', in Meijer and Bakker (eds), *The Muslim Brotherhood in Europe*, p. 31.

56 Nawaf Obaid, *The Muslim Brotherhood: A Failure in Political Evolution* (Cambridge, MA: Belfer Center for Science and International Affairs, 2017), pp. 37–40.

57 Pargeter, *The Muslim Brotherhood*, pp. 111–17.

58 *Ibid.*, pp. 113–14. Notably, the title of all other branch heads is general supervisor.

59 Of the 130 members of the Shura Council, which elects the leader of the IOMB, 90 are from Egypt. The international guidance bureau consists of 13 members, eight of them Egyptians. 'Statements by Muslim Brotherhood Leaders on Succession to "Murshid General"', *Al-Quds al-Arabi*, 8 April 2009.

60 Pargeter, *The Muslim Brotherhood*, pp. 116–17.

61 Robert Leiken and Steven Brooke, 'The Moderate Muslim Brotherhood',

Foreign Affairs, vol. 86, no. 2, 2007.

62 Brown, 'The Irrelevance of the International Muslim Brotherhood'.

63 *Ibid.*

64 Lorenzo Vidino, 'The Muslim Brotherhood in Europe', in Rubin (ed.), *The Muslim Brotherhood*, p. 111.

65 See Obaid, *The Muslim Brotherhood*, p. 73; and Pargeter, *The Muslim Brotherhood*, pp. 130–2.

66 'The International MB Is Clinically Dead', *Fanack Chronical of the Middle East and North Africa*, 12 June 2017.

67 Rubin, 'Comparing Three Muslim Brotherhoods', in Rubin (ed.), *The Muslim Brotherhood*, pp. 9–10.

68 Pargeter, *The Muslim Brotherhood*, p. 105.

69 Brown, 'The Irrelevance of the International Muslim Brotherhood'.

70 Brooke, 'The Muslim Brotherhood in Europe and the Middle East', p. 27.

71 Vidino, 'The European Organization of the Muslim Brotherhood', pp. 54–5.

72 'Islamic State Video Promotes Destruction of Iraq–Syria Border Crossing', Site Intelligence Group, 29 June 2014.

73 Mark Zacher, 'The Territorial Integrity Norm: International Boundaries and the Use of Force', *International Organization*, vol. 55, no. 2, 2001, pp. 215–50.

74 Ian Lustick, 'The Absence of Middle Eastern Great Powers: Political "Backwardness" in Historical Perspective', *International Organization*, vol. 51, no. 4, 1997, pp. 653–83.

75 Abbotabad Papers, Combating Terrorism Center at West Point, SOCOM-2012-0000019 and SOCOM-2012-0000005, 3 May 2012.

76 See 'Al-Qaida Paper: The Yemen Letters', Associated Press, 9 August 2013; and Rukmini Callimachi, 'Yemen Terror Boss Left Blueprint for Waging Jihad', Associated Press, 9 August 2013.

77 See Cole Bunzel, 'Abandoning al-Qaida: Tharir al-Sham and the Concerns of Sami al-'Uraydi', *Jihadica*, 12 May 2017; and Charles Lister, 'Al-Qaeda's Turning Against Its Syria Affiliate', *Middle East Institute*, 18 May 2017.

Sanctions After Brexit

Erica Moret and Fabrice Pothier

As the UK and EU enter the second phase of Brexit negotiations, during which their future relationship should be defined, questions over UK–EU cooperation in the security field are becoming more salient. Indeed, the UK and EU are reportedly seeking to fast-track a security and defence deal to allow a move to a new relationship straight after the UK's departure from the union.[1] EU security cooperation takes many forms, including joint action on illegal immigration and terrorism, and policies on sanctions and defence. Whereas most security areas will be governed by new or existing frameworks, such as NATO and various bilateral arrangements, the future of joint work on sanctions faces substantial risk.

Sanctions occupy a unique position in the EU's foreign-policy toolbox. They allow the union to make use of economic and legal tools to pressure, debilitate or punish troublemaking foreign regimes (such as Iran, North Korea, Syria and Russia) or groups (such as those engaging in terrorism). As such, they have become the weapon of choice for European member states seeking to deal collectively with common threats and crises.

As a leading political, economic and soft-power actor, and home to one of the world's premier financial centres (the City of London), the UK has

Erica Moret is Senior Researcher at the Global Governance Centre at the Graduate Institute of International and Development Studies and chair of the Geneva International Sanctions Network. **Fabrice Pothier** is senior consulting fellow at IISS, Chief Strategy Officer at Rasmussen Global, and was from 2010 to 2016 head of policy planning for the NATO secretary-general.

Survival | vol. 60 no. 2 | April–May 2018 | pp. 179–200   DOI 10.1080/00396338.2018.1448585

traditionally played a central role in shaping EU sanctions, contributing to their design and implementation, and participating in intelligence-sharing and consensus-building among member states. It is unlikely, however, that the UK will continue to do so once it withdraws from the EU. This would be to the detriment of both the UK and EU. British cooperation helps to make EU sanctions credible and effective. In turn, EU sanctions give weight to the UK's influence abroad.

The risk of divergence on sanctions between the EU and a post-Brexit UK should not be underestimated. Assurances by some senior British officials that London will remain aligned with EU sanctions cannot be taken at face value.[2] This is especially the case given the view prevalent among the upper echelons of the British government and the Conservative backbench that a more divergent approach to sanctions will signal that the UK has successfully reclaimed its sovereignty in foreign policy.[3] Such a stance is regarded by proponents as crucial at a time when the UK seeks to deepen its economic ties to key non-European economies and to find a new competitive edge. Nevertheless, the temptation for the UK government to engage in 'sanctions dumping', or the seeking of commercial advantage through non-alignment, would pose a significant risk to the EU's own policies. With Brexit likely to cause some economic stress, it is worth asking what might prevent the UK from diverging from the EU's most important sanctions when facing the difficult choice between political solidarity with former EU allies and national economic interests.

An ideal scenario would be for the UK to occupy a role between that of the US (as a global leader on sanctions) and non-EU European powers such as Norway and Switzerland (as closely aligned followers). But given the complex nature of designing and implementing sanctions, this cannot be achieved through a mere declaration of intent. Some institutional grounding will also be crucial. Any high-level British contribution will be limited if London is not involved in the design of new measures, which happens at lower levels in the EU. The question, therefore, is whether some institutional arrangement can be found that accommodates the UK's post-Brexit status while allowing it to remain aligned with EU sanctions policy.

The role of sanctions in EU external policy

EU sanctions policy is an area in which member states have been working together with mounting efficiency. Autonomous EU sanctions (employed in addition to, or in the absence of, UN measures) against targets such as Syria, Iran and Russia have been agreed at the European Council with unprecedented speed and unanimity in recent years. Unity has been preserved on even the most politically contentious sanctions, such as those on Russia, despite widely diverging interests across Europe. Sanctions have been used in the service of human rights, democracy, the rule of law and good governance; nuclear non-proliferation; conflict and post-conflict management; and counter-terrorism. Most recently, they were deployed in response to the violation of Ukraine's territorial integrity. They have also been adapted to cover emerging security threats, such as in mid-2017, when the European Council agreed to build a sanctions framework in response to cyber security, making the EU, alongside the US, one of the first world powers to do so.[4]

EU sanctions have displayed increasing sophistication as well, with more recent measures encompassing fund-transfer controls and complex restrictions on certain types of products.[5] Those against Iran and Russia have been particularly refined.

The EU's ability to implement autonomous sanctions has been growing in importance given mounting difficulties within the United Nations Security Council in agreeing appropriate responses to a range of pressing global security challenges. The EU has served as an alternative and powerful forum for sanctions-policy formation, given that EU members share a closer outlook on foreign and security policy than do the permanent members of the Security Council. Of the 35 sanctions regimes currently backed by the EU, 17% were enacted by the UN alone, 25% were enacted by the UN but supplemented by additional measures through the EU and 51% were enacted by the EU alone.[6]

A political and institutional process

EU sanctions regimes are the product of a sophisticated, complicated and time-consuming process that governs how member states arrive at legally binding decisions. The Treaty on European Union (TEU) cites 'restrictive measures' (sanctions) as one of a number of possible instruments that can be used in pursuit of Common Foreign and Security Policy (CFSP) goals, as outlined in Article 21 and governed by Article 30 of the TEU. UN sanctions are automatically converted into EU law. In the UK, UN sanctions are transformed into domestic law from EU law, something that will have to change given that the current procedure relies on the European Communities Act 1972 and falls under the jurisdiction of the European Court of Justice.

The imposition of an autonomous EU sanctions regime requires a CFSP Decision, which is drafted by the European External Action Service (EEAS) and adopted by the European Council. This sets out the specific measures that the council wants to adopt in relation to a given country or situation.[7] The European Council, in which unanimous decision-making is required, has ultimate authority over sanctions imposition, though little negotiating is done in this forum. The process is typically initiated through a political discussion, for example in the Foreign Affairs Council. Talks also take place within the geographical expert groupings of the EEAS (chaired by the EEAS with representatives from all members states)[8] and the Political and Security Committee (the committee of ambassadors that supports the Foreign Affairs Council).

After various levels of talks, a mandate is typically given to those with technical expertise to develop a set of options.[9] The EEAS is then usually responsible for drafting the legal acts that give effect to the council decision, representing the political commitment to implement sanctions. The draft produced by the EEAS is only finalised after amendments are made following negotiations with member states. According to Matthew Findlay, the deputy head of the International Organisations Department within the UK's Foreign and Commonwealth Office (FCO), the Service for Foreign Policy Instruments (the part of the EU that is responsible for operational expenditure in relation to EU external action) 'holds the pen and leads the co-ordination and control for the Commission at the working level for the preparation of sanctions measures'.[10] Other directorates-general and services – particularly those dealing with topics such as energy, financial and legal services, and the international market – also play an important role, both formal and informal, in the creation of new sanctions regimes via an inter-service consultation. They will also comment on drafts. If elements of disagreement arise that prevent unanimity at the working-group level, another round of talks may be held by the Committee of Permanent Representatives.[11]

Council regulations directly bind EU citizens and businesses. They are adopted through a joint proposal from the EU's High Representative for Foreign Affairs and Security Policy and the European Commission. They detail the precise scope of sanctions agreed at the European Council and how they will be implemented under the CFSP. The Commission plays a role in preparing regulations needed for those sanctions that fall under EU competences. In terms of timings, the Commission's drafting of a regulation and the EEAS's drafting of a CFSP decision increasingly happen around the same time (rather than in sequence) to ensure a quick turnaround and to avoid risks such as asset flight.[12]

EU sanctions are divided into EU and member-state competences. EU competences refer to trade and financial sanctions, which are implemented through an EU regulation. Member-state competences refer to the remaining measures, including arms embargoes and travel bans, which must be implemented on a national basis. Enforcement is carried out at the member-state level by each country's competent authority. In the UK, this is the Office of Financial Sanctions Implementation, a financial-sanctions agency overseen by HM Treasury which in the past year has seen its formal powers strengthened.[13] Competent authorities tend to work closely together, both within the EU and outside it, in order to address common challenges, and to collaborate on matters of compliance, enforcement and licence-issuing.[14]

The UK's role

In the past, the UK, France and Germany have often come to an informal decision on sanctions before seeking the agreement of other EU member states. The three countries' alignment on Iran, for example, did much to bring together the rest of the EU. While the confidential nature of the sanctions process makes it impossible to be certain about which proposals have been put forward or supported by each EU member state, one study estimates that the UK has been able to gain support for almost 80% of its proposals within the EU.[15] Certainly, the country is widely recognised as a leading force in EU sanctions policy, having been described as among the most proactive and committed member states in the cases of Iran,[16] Syria,[17] North Korea and Russia,[18] as well as in relation to various other conflicts in the EU's wider neighbourhood. This contribution has taken a number of forms.

Firstly, the UK plays an important political function in encouraging other member states to support new sanctions (and to renew existing ones) at the European Council. Achieving the required unanimity among member states has often depended on strong support from the UK. This is particularly important in light of the EU's 'sunset clause', which requires sanctions to be renewed every 12 months, or every six in the case of Russia. The UK's departure from the EU could lead to more difficulties in attaining unanimity at the European Council, particularly in cases involving competing political, commercial, ideological or historical links to the targeted country among member states, such as with Russia.[19] A compromise can sometimes be reached if the costs of sanctions are seen to be spread as evenly as possible across a given alliance of countries, but this prospect could potentially be diminished by Brexit.

Close coordination is key to successful implementation

Close coordination and alignment between major economic and political powers is widely recognised as key to the successful implementation of sanctions, particularly to avoid creating gaps that could be exploited by third parties for evasion or trade diversion. Moreover, because sanctions never operate in isolation, their effectiveness frequently relies on the ways in which they are combined with other foreign- and security-policy tools, such as dialogue, mediation, peacekeeping, conflict prevention and crisis management. The twin-track approach employed in response to the Iran nuclear programme – sanctions, combined with dialogue and negotiations – is a case in point. Working within the EU framework has allowed the UK and its EU partners to employ a wider range of instruments than the UK could have done by itself.[20]

The EU tends to follow Washington's lead in pursuing sanctions, while also seeking to shape them – and in some cases tone them down –

in accordance with its own interests. In recent years, however, the EU has increasingly taken a leadership role, as in the case of transatlantic sanctions against Russia. US sanctions, while valuable in keeping the more reluctant European member states aligned, had a more limited economic impact because of the small trade balance between the US and Russia.[21] The UK's role as a conduit to Washington, along with its expertise in coordinating transatlantic sanctions, has proven critical for the effectiveness of wider EU sanctions regimes.[22]

The UK has also played an important role in bolstering the EU's institutional capacity on sanctions, particularly through the sending of highly valued seconded national experts to the EU. The loss of this resource is likely to be strongly felt once the UK leaves the EU, given that most member states have little relevant experience and only small sanctions units of their own. Furthermore, the UK has assumed a leading role in framing sanctions and identifying the targets of specific measures.[23] The senior legal adviser to the European Council recently highlighted the UK's key role in the listing of new targets in a 2017 House of Lords' report on the legality of sanctions,[24] while another sanctions expert has described the UK as responsible for 'the majority of designation decisions in the EU'.[25] The British government has also been responsible for promoting enhanced standards intended to bolster the credibility of due process and the evidential foundations for the listing of new targets among EU member states.[26]

Indeed, the British government has been a key player in the development of specific areas of sanctions policy more generally, including asset freezes and financial sanctions. This is due to a combination of factors, including the UK's role as a global financial centre, its advanced intelligence capabilities and strong national legislation, and its effective business-enforcement mechanisms. EU sanctions scholar Mikael Eriksson has argued that 'the EU will need the UK's support on financial sanctions' if these are to remain effective instruments.[27] British involvement in designing specific sanctions measures is also in the country's own economic interest. By helping to delineate the sectors and individuals that should be targeted, London can prevent the implementation of measures that could hurt its businesses.

Building an independent UK sanctions policy

While the scope of the future security- and foreign-policy relationship between the UK and the EU is far from agreed, one thing is clear: the UK will lose its seat at the EU decision-making table. The remaining 27 EU member states will make decisions on new sanctions, or renew those already agreed, regardless of British interests. Yet many of those decisions will affect, either directly or indirectly, the UK's economy, firms and foreign-policy orientations. The UK faces a choice between continued alignment and ongoing influence over EU decisions on the one hand, or divergence on the other. In both cases, however, the British government will need to build an independent sanctions policy.

To begin with, the UK will need to forge an entirely new legal basis for imposing sanctions. According to Maya Lester, a specialist in EU and British public law, a 'robust, flexible legal framework' is required that 'permits rapid and flexible decision-making' on which areas of EU sanctions to implement but that 'also enshrines sufficient practical and effective safeguards for people and entities whose fundamental rights are infringed by the imposition of sanctions'.[28] A new 'Sanctions and Anti-money Laundering Bill' had its third reading in the House of Lords on 24 January 2018 before being passed to the House of Commons, where it has undergone a number of readings. The bill will allow the UK to keep enforcing UN measures, and also to use sanctions to 'meet national security and foreign policy objectives' and to 'enable anti-money laundering and counter-terrorist financing measures to be kept up to date'.[29] UK Finance, an organisation representing some 300 leading British financial and banking firms, argues that the bill is necessary to ensure that the British government is 'equipped to implement its foreign policy and national security priorities following Brexit' and that, 'as sanctions practices develop and evolve … EU–UK foreign policy cohesion [remains] a central priority'.[30]

Thought will also need to be given to the implications for EU nationals employed by British financial institutions (and vice versa) if only one side adopts a set of measures, given the potential for conflicting obligations. The role of EU courts post-Brexit remains uncertain, and it is unclear whether 'reasonable grounds to suspect' should be interpreted in line with the notion of 'sufficiently solid factual basis' as provided by the European Court of Justice.[31] The UK must also be prepared to deal with an increase in legal challenges in British courts once the EU General Court in Luxembourg stops hearing such cases on the UK's behalf.

A post-Brexit UK will need to bolster its capacity in other areas too. For instance, it will need to develop its ability to monitor compliance, as this is currently done mainly by the EU. To some extent this is already happening: the UK is creating an autonomous sanctions unit within the FCO, and is increasing the resources allocated to key fields such as trade.[32] Yet questions remain as to whether the UK will set up new channels of communication with regimes affected by sanctions, or whether it will depend on those already used by the EU and others.

The British government has given repeated assurances to its European partners that it intends to remain aligned with EU sanctions policy. Yet some pro-leave Conservative MPs, including cabinet members, are reported to hold a different view.[33] They see a non-aligned British sanctions policy as helping the UK to reclaim what they perceive as the country's lost sovereignty. A flexible and autonomous policy on sanctions, which could imply a level of divergence from the EU, is also seen as holding the potential to provide the UK with a competitive edge in the global economy. It could give the British government an advantage when negotiating new trade deals and seeking to attract foreign investment.

Such a policy would raise the risk of the UK engaging in sanctions dumping, particularly if the country suffers an economic downturn or the City of London is disadvantaged by Brexit. The UK might seek to derive unfair economic advantage in cases where EU businesses have withdrawn from a targeted country in response to EU sanctions. According to two former senior US officials:

> Without a need to create balance in sanctions measures, one could easily imagine the UK adopting sanctions on a future adversary that include industries of little value while maintaining ties in industries of significance. The EU may have the same impulse, especially since it will have to manage consensus politics in a way that the UK will not.[34]

A non-aligned approach would also carry some significant risks for the UK itself, however. The first and most obvious would be a backlash from EU member states, who would see any significant divergence as an attempt to gain an unfair competitive advantage. Mounting warnings from EU capitals and institutions about the potential consequences of British divergence from EU regulations and norms, including in environmental standards and state subsidies, can be seen as indicative of the tensions that could result from deviation on sanctions.[35] Such a scenario would further undermine the UK government's claim that it will remain a closely aligned European power even after leaving the EU.

A second risk is the possibility that the British government will become more vulnerable to counter-sanctions, which are easier to apply against a single country than the entire EU, as well as more susceptible to business lobbying once its own sanctions regime is in place. Moreover, businesses, non-governmental organisations (NGOs) and individuals face greater risks if future sanctions are not closely aligned, given an increase in compliance costs and the difficulties of interpreting multiple regimes. Market distortions may also result if one sanctions regime is more permissive than another. UK Finance has underlined the risk of foreign business withdrawing from the UK due to legal uncertainty around sanctions measures.[36]

Avoiding a divergent sanctions policy

The EU will be reassured, however, by the expectation that most Western companies, including those in a post-Brexit UK, will over-comply with the strictest global sanctions regime in place, particularly that of the US. Furthermore, it is likely that the UK will continue to respect the so-called 'duty of co-operation' established by EU treaties with regard to the behaviour of EU member states on foreign policy.[37] Certainly, this would be in line with the actions of most non-EU European companies, which opt to align with EU sanctions measures on a voluntary basis. To take but a few examples, the Swiss government ensures that it does not reap economic advantages from sanctions imposed by its main trading partners,[38] and the Norwegian government cites the importance of alignment in contributing to a 'level-playing field for European businesses'.[39]

If the UK wants its sanctions to carry weight in the future, it will most likely need to combine forces with at least two of the three major economic world powers: the EU, the US and China. While closer cooperation with China is occurring on some levels, it is unlikely to become the norm. Equally, the UK should exercise caution in aligning more closely with the US on its sanctions policy at the expense of ongoing close coordination with the EU, not least in light of the unpredictable and fractious presidency of Donald Trump. US sanctions tend to be far more hardline than those imposed by the EU, often combining extra-territorial reach (secondary sanctions) with more aggressive and visible enforcement mechanisms – something that is made possible by the unmatched resources and staffing numbers of American institutions. The US government also tends to play the role of 'bad cop' in key diplomatic forums, while its European counterparts tend to adopt the 'good cop' role, as in the case of Iran. These roles are often reflected in the sanctions policies adopted by each party.

Given the highly bureaucratic and complex processes required to design sanctions, clarifying the mechanisms through which the UK and the EU will continue to cooperate will be critical for the effectiveness and credibility of any mutual efforts. Most third countries currently align themselves with EU sanctions in one of two main ways: the US way, or that of Norway, Switzerland and other allies, which can also include non-EU European neighbours; other major world powers (particularly Japan, Australia and Canada); and regional groupings, such as the Arab League, the African Union and the Economic Community of West African States.

The US is responsible for the vast majority of autonomous sanctions regimes, with the EU typically aligning itself with most US measures, albeit with some differences, and often with a time lag. A formal EU–US coordination effort involves regular meetings and ongoing communication, which enables the sharing of best practice and mutual updates on processes, approaches and operational details. Both the EEAS and EU member states, especially the UK, liaise with the US on specific aspects of new and existing sanctions regimes on a regular basis.[40]

As for non-EU European partners, once a decision has been made on a new sanctions regime by the EU, neighbouring countries are invited to implement similar measures. Little to no consultation with these countries takes place, and they are not accorded a decision-making role. Whether they align themselves with EU measures is a domestic political decision, and there is no legal obligation for them to do so.

Switzerland, for example, is not involved in the political process underlying EU sanctions elaboration, but coordinates on implementation and enforcement with the EU through diplomatic channels linking Bern with the EEAS and the European Commission. It also communicates with other countries, including the US and other allies, as well as with targeted countries. Under the Swiss Embargo Act of 2002, Switzerland can opt to participate in sanctions imposed by the UN, the OSCE or its key trading partners. The act grants autonomy to the Federal Council to make decisions on the extent to which Switzerland might adhere to any third-party regime.[41] The country is not permitted by Swiss law to unilaterally impose its own measures, however. It has opted to align with most EU sanctions, including those against Syria, Myanmar, Libya and Belarus, but less so with regard to those against Iran and Russia, given Swiss concerns over its diplomatic role representing US consular and diplomatic interests in Iran as a 'protecting power' of the US in that country, and as a mediator in the early days of the Russia–Ukraine crisis, given its role as chair of the OSCE.

If Norway decides to align itself with EU sanctions, it typically translates the EU's Council Regulation into domestic regulation, along with certain modifications. A similar process is employed for UN sanctions. These regulations remain in place until repealed. Norway does not have any formal or routine consultation process with the EU on sanctions. It does engage in dialogue, particularly with the EEAS, on sanctions-related matters – though not always before EU measures are put in place.[42]

It is highly unlikely that the UK will be able to influence the design of EU sanctions in anything but a passive way once it withdraws from the EU, unless new institutional arrangements can be established to enable more active participation. The ideal scenario would be for the UK to occupy a role that sits somewhere between that of the US and non-EU European powers, given its experience, global role and expertise.

A new formula for UK–EU cooperation?

EU sanctions formation is already marked by (mainly informal) cooperation in other political groupings. Regular dialogue and intelligence-sharing takes place at the bilateral level between major EU powers, and in settings such as the G7 and the Financial Action Task Force, which establishes global standards for counter-terrorism financing and anti-money-laundering, and carries out assessments of compliance measures and sanctions implementation. Nevertheless, a range of Western sanctioning powers acknowledge the need for closer coordination on a number of autonomous sanctions regimes to ensure they become more effective, while also reducing the bureaucratic burden imposed by compliance requirements.[43]

A recent paper published by the UK government on foreign policy, defence and security cooperation argues for a broad-ranging and deep security partnership with the EU.[44] According to Caroline Wilson, Director Europe at the FCO, London would like to establish 'specific forms of dialogue and consultations with the option of agreeing joint positions, as well as specific co-operation on crises, consular assistance [and] development'.[45] In a similar vein, Alan Duncan, minister for Europe and the Americas, has stated, 'We will look for a tailored arrangement to work with the EU … in a way that invariably will replicate and work alongside EU sanctions'.[46] Likewise, Richard Nephew, former principal deputy coordinator for sanctions policy at the US State Department, and David Mortlock, former director for international economic affairs at the White House National Security Council, have argued for the creation of 'like-minded' coalitions on particular sanctions regimes, adding:

> Even if both the UK and EU retain [a] separate decision-making apparatus for sanctions enforcement, having some kind of formal role for one another in advising the creation of sanctions rules would help to preserve at least some of the benefits that existed prior to [Brexit], particularly harmonization … Like-minded collectives existed to deal with Iran and North Korea, and a scaled-up approach could involve annual gatherings of European, British, East Asian, and other interested governments to discuss a range of sanctions topics.[47]

What concrete options exist, then? It seems highly unlikely that the UK will retain a formal position (such as that of permanent observer) in the CFSP, or have any ongoing involvement in the EU's Political and Security Committee, after it leaves the union. Some observers, such as Maya Lester, have highlighted the merits of creating a network similar to the 'successful European Competition Network by which national competent authorities of EU member states cooperate with each other and exchange experience and best practice on a wide range of competition issues'.[48] Others, such as John Sawers, the former chief of Britain's Secret Intelligence Service (MI6), have suggested the creation of a smaller compact of major powers including France, Germany, the UK and the US, along with Russia and China when necessary.[49] Other possibilities are outlined in a recent parliamentary report on the future of UK diplomacy in Europe, including a special partnership complemented by an Enhanced Framework Participation Agreement.[50]

Indeed, sanctions coordination among a small collection of countries and regional groupings on pressing global challenges is already commonplace, as in other areas of foreign policy and defence. In the case of Russia sanctions, for example, the US, the EU, Canada and Japan joined in an informal group that came to be known as the G7+, in which Norway also participated.[51] Australia was invited to take part in a similar grouping on North Korea. The Iran nuclear talks, which culminated in the Joint Comprehensive Plan of Action (JCPOA), demonstrated the effectiveness of multiple 'minilateral' alliances on sanctions working alongside (and at times driving) the wider multilateral process, as well as seeming to facilitate eventual agreement at the UN level. E3/EU+3 negotiations with Tehran were mostly conducted outside the UN framework, but the deal was swiftly approved by the UN Security Council once agreement was reached.[52] The future use of similar minilateral groupings to bring together the EU and the UK on sanctions would chime with Theresa May's February 2018 call in Munich for more bilateral and ad hoc groupings on security post-Brexit.[53] It is worth stressing, however, that any future British involvement in sanctions decision-making at a head-of-state or ministerial level in some kind of minilateral or contact-group setting would not necessarily be as successful in the future as it is now. This is because, as noted, a large proportion of any policy's details is worked out at lower institutional levels.

Arrangements to share sensitive data on targets is another area in which greater coordination and collaboration is already needed, but one which could become more challenging after Brexit. The UK will need to forge a clear agreement with the EU and other sanctioning partners on how shared data will be handled and protected in legal terms, a question that goes far beyond the world of sanctions. In the past it was not possible to use intelligence findings in European Courts, and while a mechanism was created in 2015 to allow for this, the UK was not happy with its safeguards, and it has yet to be actually used. Moreover, information-sharing with EU allies depends on mutual trust, which could be at risk if Brexit negotiations do not progress smoothly.

One way forward would be to consider a more flexible and innovative institutional formula. NATO and its close cooperation with Sweden and Finland, two non-NATO members, offers a noteworthy model. Since the Russian aggression in Ukraine, NATO has deepened its ties with Sweden and Finland under a so-called 28+2 format, in which they not only meet on a more regular basis, but also increasingly share intelligence on the regional situation, discuss common issues – starting with Russian activities and posture – and jointly plan and conduct large-scale exercises. Formally, Sweden and Finland do not fall under the collective-defence clause of the Washington Treaty (Article V), but in practice, the cooperation they enjoy with the Alliance makes them very close to full members.

A similar formula could be developed for the UK's association with the EU's sanctions regime. While the integrity of decisions made by the EU member states will need to be maintained in line with TEU obligations, the UK could be included in the decision chain as early and as thoroughly as possible. Like at NATO, this could be called 'joint decision-shaping', which in diplomatic language sits just below decision-making, which must remain the purview of EU members.

*   *   *

It is no exaggeration to say that Brexit poses the greatest challenge to the UK since the end of the British Empire. The country must extract itself from more than 40 years of regulation and institutional anchoring within continental Europe, while defining a new global role for itself. At the same time, it must face the challenges confronting all medium-sized powers, including terrorism, cyber crime, increased competition and threats from revisionist powers such as Russia and China. It would be easy under the circumstances to see the question of sanctions policy as secondary. Yet it is clear that sanctions sit at the interface between economic power and foreign policy, the two principal components of the Conservatives' vision of a 'Global Britain'. As such, whether the UK remains aligned with its European partners on sanctions policy, or diverges from them, will be an important decision.

Should alignment be the preferred option, some institutional arrangements should be defined to avoid uncertainty, unexpected costs or, in the worst-case scenario, a degree of sanctions dumping, which would undermine the UK–EU relationship. Creative thinking that looks beyond existing frameworks and structures will be essential for both sides of the Brexit negotiations. The risk that the EU's weapon of choice will be partially disarmed, and the UK's credibility as a global player further damaged, is too great for the issue to be neglected. A new institutional formula of EU27+1 in shaping and co-implementing sanctions is one way forward. Such an approach would be a win–win for both the EU and the UK. It would also allow the EU to assert its role as a sanctions power by preserving the possibility of inviting other relevant partners to the decision table.

Notes

1   Alex Barker, 'EU and UK Seek Speedy Brexit Deal on Defence and Security', *Financial Times*, 4 February 2018.

2   See, for example, the speech given by UK Prime Minister Theresa May at the Munich Security Conference on 17 February 2018, in which she said the UK 'will want to continue to work closely' with the EU on sanctions and 'will look to carry over all EU sanctions at the time of our departure' (https://www.gov.uk/government/speeches/pm-speech-at-munich-security-conference-17-february-2018). Similarly, in a speech on 14 February 2018, UK Foreign Secretary Boris Johnson said that after Brexit 'it would be illogical not to discuss such mat-

ters as sanctions together, bearing in mind that UK expertise provides more than half of all EU sanctions listings' (https://www.youtube.com/watch?v=V-LEkBnyn5A).

3 This is according to a senior British official.

4 Erica Mort and Patryk Pawlak, 'The EU Cyber Diplomacy Toolbox: Towards a Cyber Sanctions Regime', European Union Institute for Strategic Studies (EUISS), Brief No. 24, 12 July 2017, https://www.iss.europa.eu/sites/default/files/EUISSFiles/Brief_24_Cyber_sanctions.pdf.

5 Ross Denton, Partner, Baker and McKenzie LP, corrected oral evidence, Select Committee on the European Union, External Affairs Sub-Committee, 'Brexit: Sanctions Policy', Evidence Session No. 1, 20 July 2017, http://data.parliament.uk/written-evidence/committeeevidence.svc/evidencedocument/eu-external-affairs-subcommittee/brexit-sanctions-policy/oral/69306.html.

6 The EU currently implements some 15 UN-approved sanctions regimes, covering around 200 countries. Six of these are solely UN measures (including Mali), and nine are UN measures complemented by additional autonomous EU sanctions (as in the cases of North Korea and Iran). Eighteen autonomous EU sanctions regimes have been imposed in the absence of UN sanctions, which only have effect in EU member states. These regimes mainly involve asset freezes, travel bans, arms restrictions and some wider sectoral sanctions, for example on finance or specific areas of trade, and include the sanctions placed on

Syria and Russia. Such regimes are typically matched by the US and other allies. The UK currently has autonomous powers to freeze terrorist assets (which are restricted to some 20 individuals and entities) and to enact sanctions in certain cases of nuclear non-proliferation and weapons of mass destruction. The UK also implements arms embargoes linked to Armenia and Azerbaijan through the OSCE.

7 Roger Matthews, Dechert Senior Director, corrected oral evidence, Select Committee on the European Union, External Affairs Sub-Committee, 'Brexit: Sanctions Policy', Evidence Session No. 4, 12 October 2017, http://data.parliament.uk/writtenevidence/committeeevidence.svc/evidencedocument/eu-external-affairs-subcommittee/brexit-sanctions-policy/oral/71365.html.

8 *Ibid.*

9 Matthew Findlay, Deputy Head of International Organisations Department, FCO, corrected oral evidence, Select Committee on the European Union, External Affairs Sub-Committee, 'Brexit: Sanctions Policy', Evidence Session No. 3, 14 September 2017, http://data.parliament.uk/writtenevidence/committeeevidence.svc/evidencedocument/eu-external-affairs-subcommittee/brexit-sanctions-policy/oral/70460.html.

10 Matthews, corrected oral evidence.

11 *Ibid.*

12 *Ibid.*

13 *Ibid.*

14 Rena Lalgie, Head of the Office of Financial Sanctions Implementation, corrected oral evidence, Select

Committee on the European Union, External Affairs Sub-Committee, 'Brexit: Sanctions Policy', Evidence Session No. 3, 14 September 2017, http://data.parliament.uk/written-evidence/committeeevidence.svc/evidencedocument/eu-external-affairs-subcommittee/brexit-sanctions-policy/oral/70460.html.

15 Seth Jones, *The Rise of European Security Cooperation* (Cambridge: Cambridge University Press, 2007), cited in Clara Portela, written evidence, Select Committee on the European Union, External Affairs Sub-Committee, 'Brexit: Sanctions Policy', 24 July 2017, http://data.parliament.uk/writtenevidence/committeeevidence.svc/evidencedocument/eu-external-affairs-subcommittee/brexit-sanctions-policy/written/69280.pd.

16 The UK has played a direct role in talks with Iran since 2003, along with France and Germany, through the E3 process. While initially reluctant, it became a strong advocate for the use of sanctions against Iran beginning in 2005. The three European powers then joined forces with the US, Russia and China (E3+3 or P5+1, and later the E3/EU+3).

17 The UK successfully pressured the EU to alter its sanctions regime in the case of Syria in relation to its arms embargo that was allowing one side of the conflict to continue accessing weapons. Francesco Giumelli, corrected oral evidence, Select Committee on the European Union, External Affairs Sub-Committee, 'Brexit: Sanctions Policy', Evidence Session No. 2, 20 July 2017, http://data.parliament.uk/written-evidence/committeeevidence.svc/evidencedocument/eu-external-affairs-subcommittee/brexit-sanctions-policy/oral/69307.html.

18 Erica Moret, 'What Would Brexit Mean for EU Sanctions Policy?', European Council on Foreign Relations, 23 March 2016, http://www.ecfr.eu/article/commentary_what_would_brexit_mean_for_eu_sanctions_policy6046?src=ilaw.

19 Erica Moret and Shagina Maria, 'The Impact of EU–Russia Tensions on the Economy of the EU', in Lukasz, Kulesa, Ivan Timofeev and Joseph Dobbs (eds), *Damage Assessment: EU–Russia Relations in Crisis* (London: European Leadership Network, 2017), pp. 17–24, https://www.european-leadershipnetwork.org/wp-content/uploads/2017/10/170615-ELN-RIAC-Damage-Assessment-EU-Russia-Relations-in-Crisis.pdf.

20 Erica Moret, written evidence, Select Committee on the European Union, External Affairs Sub-Committee, 'Brexit: Sanctions Policy', http://data.parliament.uk/written-evidence/committeeevidence.svc/evidencedocument/eu-external-affairs-subcommittee/brexit-sanctions-policy/written/70456.pdf July 2017.

21 Erica Moret, Francesco Giumelli and Dawid Bastiat-Jarosz, 'Sanctions on Russia: Impacts and Economic Costs on the United States', Programme for the Study of International Governance, Graduate Institute of International and Development Studies, Geneva, 20 March 2017, http://graduateinstitute.ch/files/live/sites/iheid/files/sites/internationalgovernance/shared/

Russian-Sanctions-Report.pdf.

22 Erica Moret et al., , 'The New Deterrent? International Sanctions Against Russia Over the Ukraine Crisis: Impacts, Costs and Further Action', Programme for the Study of International Governance, Graduate Institute, Geneva, 12 October 2016, http://graduateinstitute.ch/files/live/sites/iheid/files/sites/international-governance/shared/The%20New%20Deterrent%20International%20Sanctions%20Against%20Russia%20Over%20the%20Ukraine%20Crisis%20-%20Impacts%2c%20Costs%20and%20Further%20Action.pdf.

23 Matthews, corrected oral evidence.

24 House of Lords, European Union Committee, 'The Legality of EU Sanctions', HL Paper 102, 2 February 2017, https://publications.parliament.uk/pa/ld201617/ldselect/ldeu-com/102/102.pdf.

25 Maya Lester QC, Barrister, Brick Court Chambers, corrected oral evidence, Select Committee on the European Union, External Affairs Sub-Committee, 'Brexit: Sanctions Policy', Evidence Session No. 1, 20 July 2017, http://data.parliament.uk/written-evidence/committeeevidence.svc/evidencedocument/eu-external-affairs-subcommittee/brexit-sanctions-policy/oral/69306.html.

26 Maya Lester QC, written evidence, Select Committee on the European Union, External Affairs Sub-Committee, 'Brexit: Sanctions Policy', 26 July 2017, http://data.parliament.uk/writtenevidence/committeeevidence.svc/evidencedocument/eu-external-affairs-subcommittee/brexit-sanctions-policy/written/69281.pdf.

27 Mikael Eriksson, Researcher, Swedish Defence Research Agency, written evidence, Select Committee on the European Union, External Affairs Sub-Committee, 'Brexit: Sanctions Policy', 26 July 2017, http://data.parliament.uk/writtenevidence/committeeevidence.svc/evidencedocument/eu-external-affairs-subcommittee/brexit-sanctions-policy/written/69282.pdf.

28 Lester, written evidence.

29 House of Lords, 'Sanctions and Anti-Money Laundering Bill [HL]: Explanatory Notes', 24 January 2018, https://publications.parliament.uk/pa/bills/cbill/2017-2019/0157/en/18157en.pdf.

30 UK Finance, 'Impact of Brexit on the Future Application of UK Sanctions', Parliamentary Briefing, 16 November 2017.

31 Question raised by UK Finance in its written evidence to Select Committee on the European Union, External Affairs Sub-Committee, 'Brexit: Sanctions Policy', 19 September 2017, http://data.parliament.uk/written-evidence/committeeevidence.svc/evidencedocument/eu-external-affairs-subcommittee/brexit-sanctions-policy/written/70455.pdf.

32 Paul Williams, Director Multilateral Policy, FCO, corrected oral evidence, Select Committee on the European Union, External Affairs Sub-Committee, 'Brexit: Sanctions Policy', Evidence Session No. 3, 14 September 2017, http://data.parliament.uk/written-evidence/committeeevidence.svc/evidencedocument/eu-external-affairs-subcommittee/brexit-sanctions-policy/oral/70460.html.

33 Authors' conversations with senior British officials.

34 Richard Nephew and David Mortlock, *Brexit's Implications for UK and European Sanctions Policy* (New York: Columbia University, Center on Global Energy Policy, October 2016).

35 Authors' conversations with EU member-state officials.

36 UK Finance, written evidence.

37 Findlay, corrected oral evidence.

38 Embassy of Switzerland in the United Kingdom, written evidence, Select Committee on the European Union, External Affairs Sub-Committee, 'Brexit: Sanctions Policy', 19 September 2017, http://data.parliament.uk/written-evidence/committeeevidence.svc/evidencedocument/eu-external-affairs-subcommittee/brexit-sanctions-policy/written/70458.pdf.

39 Royal Norwegian Embassy, written evidence, Select Committee on the European Union, External Affairs Sub-Committee, 'Brexit: Sanctions Policy', 12 October 2017, http://data.parliament.uk/written-evidence/committeeevidence.svc/evidencedocument/eu-external-affairs-subcommittee/brexit-sanctions-policy/written/71045.pdf.

40 Matthews, corrected oral evidence.

41 Embassy of Switzerland in the United Kingdom, written evidence.

42 Royal Norwegian Embassy, written evidence.

43 Based on interviews held in 2015–17 with EU, US and third-country officials working on sanctions implementation.

44 Department for Exiting the European Union, 'Foreign Policy, Defence and Development: A Future Partnership Paper', 12 September 2017, https://www.gov.uk/government/uploads/system/uploads/attachment_data/file/643924/Foreign_policy__defence_and_development_paper.pdf.

45 Caroline Wilson CMG, Director Europe, Foreign and Commonwealth Office, corrected oral evidence, Select Committee on the European Union, External Affairs Sub-Committee, 'Brexit: Sanctions Policy', Evidence Session No. 6, 26 October 2017, http://data.parliament.uk/written-evidence/committeeevidence.svc/evidencedocument/eu-external-affairs-subcommittee/brexit-sanctions-policy/oral/72304.html.

46 Sir Alan Duncan MP, Minister for Europe and the Americas, Foreign and Commonwealth Office, corrected oral evidence, Select Committee on the European Union, External Affairs Sub-Committee, 'Brexit: Sanctions Policy', Evidence Session No. 6, 26 October 2017, http://data.parliament.uk/written-evidence/committeeevidence.svc/evidencedocument/eu-external-affairs-subcommittee/brexit-sanctions-policy/oral/72304.html.

47 Nephew and Mortlock, *Brexit's Implications for UK and European Sanctions Policy*, p. 3.

48 Lester, written evidence.

49 Sir John Sawers GCMG, former chief of the Secret Intelligence Service (MI6), corrected oral evidence, Select Committee on the European Union, External Affairs Sub-Committee, 'Brexit: Sanctions Policy', Evidence Session No. 5, 19 October 2017, p. 14, http://data.parliament.uk/written-evidence/committeeevidence.svc/

evidencedocument/eu-external-affairs-subcommittee/brexit-sanctions-policy/oral/71916.html.

50 House of Commons Foreign Affairs Committee, 'The Future of UK Diplomacy in Europe', Second Report of Session 2017–19, 30 January 2018, https://publications.parliament.uk/pa/cm201719/cmselect/cmfaff/514/514.pdf.

51 Findlay, corrected oral evidence.

52 Erica Moret, 'Effective Minilateralism for the EU: What, When and How', European Union Institute for Security Studies Brief, No. 17, 3 June 2016, https://www.iss.europa.eu/sites/default/files/EUISSFiles/Brief_17_Minilateralism.pdf.

53 Theresa May, 'PM Speech at Munich Security Conference: 17 February 2018', https://www.gov.uk/government/speeches/pm-speech-at-munich-security-conference-17-february-2018.

Review Essay

Democracies Don't Die, They Are Killed

Erik Jones

How Democracies Die
Steven Levitsky and Daniel Ziblatt. New York: Crown, 2018.
$26.00. 299 pp.

The death of American democracy is a whodunnit, even if the crime is still in progress and the outcome is uncertain. There are many suspects, each of whom has motive, means and opportunity. Donald Trump, his allies and his enablers are at the top of the list. But populists like Trump have been around a long time, so it is also worth asking who fell asleep on the watch. There, perhaps, we should point a finger at political parties – democracy's gatekeepers. Somehow the Republican Party seems to have lost that critical function. As we look more closely at who did what and when, we uncover a gallery of rogues stretching back to the Nixon administration (if not earlier) who conspired to bend political institutions to their own designs. If Republicans let a few populists like Trump in through the back door, that was more by self-distraction than intent.

Look closer still and even the 'good' guys in the Democratic Party have backstories that are less than pleasant, to put it mildly. They may be on the side of the angels now, but they were terrible villains back in the day. Consider the shameful role played by Democrats in the disenfranchisement

Erik Jones is Professor of European Studies and Director of European and Eurasian Studies at the Paul H. Nitze School of Advanced International Studies (SAIS), Johns Hopkins University; Senior Research Fellow at Nuffield College, Oxford; and a Contributing Editor to *Survival*.

Survival | vol. 60 no. 2 | April–May 2018 | pp. 201–210   DOI 10.1080/00396338.2018.1448588

of former slaves in the South during the post-Reconstruction period. Even in their efforts to make good on past misdeeds, the Democrats broke tacit agreements across the political spectrum and so unleashed the whirlwind. If Nixon made appeals to white nationalism, that was only possible because the Democrats failed to sell their civil-rights agenda to their own core constituencies. Everyone is complicit in this investigation. The wonder is not that democracy is dying but that it ever lived. Only enormous collective effort can save it.

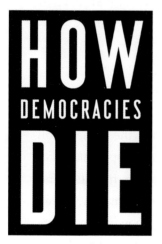

Steven Levitsky and Daniel Ziblatt offer one of the best forensic accounts available of the crimes against democracy in America. The first two paragraphs of this essay only summarise the highlights. Moreover, Levitsky and Ziblatt build their argument by tackling America's greatest weakness head-on. Their book is a powerful indictment of the myth of American exceptionalism and the religion that has grown up around the US constitution as a founding document.

The United States is exceptional in many ways, not the least of which is the depth of American commitment to democracy and the rule of law. The people of other countries would have overturned their political systems or allowed those systems to be subverted under similar strains and stresses – and have, repeatedly, in other eras or parts of the world. So far, the United States has remained resilient. The constitution played an important role in that resilience by providing a framework for Americans to support their commitment to democracy and to check the power of government.

Nevertheless, it is important for Americans to realise that they can learn a lot from the experience of other countries. That experience suggests we should not take American commitment to democracy and the rule of law for granted. Indeed, if Americans could peer over their rose-tinted glasses, they would also realise that the constitution needs constant care and attention. Even the best political arrangements can be broken if the people who control the institutions of government do not want them to function.[1] The norms that define how Americans act outside the formal requirements of the constitution are arguably even more important than what the framers wrote or intended. Indeed, and whether or not they recognise it today, Americans have learned the hard way over the last two centuries and more that they must tolerate disagreement, accept that opposition is not enmity and exercise power with self-restraint, if they are not to transform the constitution into a mockery of democracy.

Levitsky and Ziblatt do a great service by helping us understand who is responsible for the political problems Americans face, why they played the roles they did and what the implications are for the United States if Americans do not take remedial action. In their forward-looking scenarios, they paint a stark future of polarisation and dysfunction in which the great resilience of American institutions and even American commitment to democracy and the rule of law will be tested. This argument should be read alongside excellent recent work by Edward Luce on the crisis of Western liberalism, and Ivan Krastev on the travails of democracy in Europe.[2]

However, where Levitsky and Ziblatt try to point the way out of the current mess, although the strength of their diagnosis is overwhelming, the remedies they offer are unconvincing. Democrats, they argue, should resist the temptation to join in the polarising tactics developed by members of the Republican Party; instead, they should work to build a broad-based coalition in defence of American democracy. Along the way, Republicans should abandon appeals to white nationalism while the Democrats recast themselves as the supporters of an inclusive, multi-racial, European-style universalistic welfare state. It is hard to disagree with these recommendations in principle, particularly for anyone whose political instincts tend toward the centre-left. Nevertheless, if the experience of other democracies under stress is any guide, that formula is not going to work and any efforts to implement these remedies may prove counterproductive.

Political parties, gatekeepers and populists

Political parties make terrible gatekeepers, particularly when the enemy is 'populism'.[3] The reason is simple: political parties do not exist to keep populists out; they exist to mobilise voters, train and socialise elites, contest elections and gain power. When political parties are good at these core tasks, they tend to monopolise the democratic process by raising barriers to entry for newcomers. It does not matter whether these newcomers are rude and ill-mannered, or elegant and charming. Any office-seeker that does not belong to the party is a threat that the party will try either to co-opt or to keep away from political power. If this notion of political parties sounds exclusive and at least potentially undemocratic, that is because it is. That is also why James Madison wanted to design the US constitution to avoid the politics of 'faction', which is eighteenth-century jargon for political parties.[4]

Alas, individuals have a hard time beating institutionalised groups at mobilising voters, training and socialising elites, contesting elections and gaining power. Political parties may not be democratic, but they are good at working the democratic process. Moreover, the advantages of having an institutionalised group to compete in a democracy tend to grow disproportionately as the electorate increases in size. It is not surprising, therefore, that the heyday of political parties coincided with the rapid expansion of democratic electorates. Popular political entrepreneurs such as Charles Lindbergh, Oswald Mosley and Pierre Poujade may have tried to seize power by moving outside the existing party system or creating their own political movements, but the political parties operating in the United States, Britain and France were strong enough to hold them at bay.

If anything, political parties were too successful at dominating the democratic process and, by monopolising positions of power for themselves, they prevented new groups or interests in society from finding expression. This is true particularly in those countries such as Belgium, the Netherlands and Italy where elites across the whole party system conspired, more or less openly, to prevent anyone else from gaining access to political power. They even had a name for this elite condominium: 'consociational democracy' in Belgium and the Netherlands, and 'partitocrazia' in Italy. The result in all three cases was to exclude ever larger numbers of individuals and groups from the political process, and so to create ever more favourable conditions for political entrepreneurs to mobilise voters against the system.[5]

The new groups that emerged in Belgium, the Netherlands and Italy in response to traditional party elites ran the spectrum from language nationalists such as the Flemish Block to regional separatists such as the

Northern League, and from post-materialist, pro-democracy groups such as Democrats '66 (now called D66) to post-democratic, pro-materialist groups such as Silvio Berlusconi's Forza Italia. Probably the most eclectic of the lot was the Dutch firebrand Pim Fortuyn. Fortuyn gained notoriety for his stand against immigration, but he gained followers for his stand against consociationalism. The Dutch politicians who have sought to capitalise on Fortuyn's inheritance include the socialist Jan Marijnissen on the left as well as Geert Wilders on the right.

These stories about the revolt against party dominance matter because they shed light on how voters are likely to respond when confronted by grand coalitions. Voters who go to the polls to choose between left and right only to find themselves confronted with a post-electoral coalition of the two alternatives have good cause to feel disillusioned. When the explicit purpose of that post-electoral coalition is to preclude new voices from gaining access to power, then the disillusionment is only enhanced. This is the lesson from Austria's long experience with broad centrist coalitions; it is something that German political parties are also learning.[6] The more political parties emphasise their role as gatekeepers, the more they create the conditions for what we might think of in very broad terms as 'populism', or a mobilisation against those in power. That is why almost all European democracies with proportional electoral systems have party systems that are increasingly volatile and fragmented.

First-past-the-post electoral systems do not defend hegemonic political parties indefinitely. Where new voices cannot find expression through the creation of new political movements, they will seek to penetrate and, they hope, dominate one of the mainstream political parties instead. This is what happened in the United Kingdom. The divisions now evident in the Conservative Party and the Labour Party are an evolved reaction to the cross-party consensus that prevailed in Great Britain from the end of the Second World War through the early to mid-1970s. Of course, Britain's two great parties did not agree on everything; but they did agree on economic policymaking and on European integration. Those who disagreed on these issues were shut out – and subsequently found a way to make themselves heard.[7]

Levitsky and Ziblatt tell a similar story about the United States. In their account, however, the focus for exclusion does not centre on economics or on Europe but on race. The cross-party consensus depended in many ways on preventing African Americans from exercising their democratic rights. The civil-rights movement emerged as a long-overdue reaction to this all-white monopolisation of democratic institutions. And the unintended consequence of the success of that movement was to break the cross-party consensus and sow the seeds for polarisation instead. The first-past-the-post electoral system not only failed to insulate America's more moderate political establishment but, through the expansion of political primaries within the two main political parties, it exacerbated the polarisation.

Multiculturalism, identity politics and the welfare state

The politics of race in the United States is unique in many ways because of the country's long association with a racialised form of slavery. Nevertheless, it would be a mistake to believe that the US experience has no parallels in other countries. The basic building blocks exist wherever established political parties hold readily identifiable groups away from the institutions of power, and the trigger for conflict arises wherever one or more of those established parties decides to open itself up to the group that is excluded. This is the paradox of multicultural democracy. Each time political elites extend access to some new group, those who previously enjoyed a monopoly of representation either retreat into a reactionary crouch or rebel against the system.

The instabilities of multiculturalism stem again from the nature of political parties. The focus is on 'mobilise' and 'compete', and the insight is simple: no expansion of the electorate is perfectly symmetrical, so any party that seeks to benefit by making itself attractive to newcomers will find itself facing an opposition that positions itself as the defence of the old regime. This pattern is as old as Labour and Conservative (or left and right), and it explains why Levitsky and Ziblatt have such success finding useful parallels between moments of democratic polarisation in the past and the polarisation we face in the present. From this perspective, the question is not why democratic systems tip into conflict but, rather, how they find accommodation. Levitsky and Ziblatt stress the role of informal rules and attitudes in making that transition. Parties have to stop seeing one another as enemies, tolerate disagreement and show self-restraint in their use of political institutions. These are the norms that protect the constitution from abuse.

What Levitsky and Ziblatt do not explore enough, perhaps, is the role of identity and culture in underpinning those norms. Tolerance and forbearance help to foster cross-party consensus and cooperation, on a good day, or cartelisation and collusion, on a bad day. In other words, they are part and parcel of the learned relationship that evolves among established political parties and politicians. Deep down, they rest on a mutual recognition of membership in the group and hence a fundamental acceptance of the need for equality of opportunity among those who participate in the political process. This is the domain of culture and of identity politics. The politicians who embrace these norms not only share the same values but are 'the same' in important respects. Hence, when political parties make their appeals to the electorate, they never put these values into play.

By contrast, when politicians make appeals to cultural distinctiveness and engage in divisive forms of identity-based political mobilisation, they implicitly also challenge the norms of tolerance and forbearance. This is the logic of difference as opposed to sameness. That logic becomes all the more compelling when what is at stake is access to economic resources and public services. This is a fundamental insight that Cas Mudde revealed in some of his earliest work on what were then called 'new radical right' parties in Europe. Such parties were only anti-immigrant insofar as immigrants were an obvious source of difference to use in underscoring the 'sameness' of the political groups these parties promised to represent. Moreover, the new radical-right parties were uninterested in traditional right-wing economic objectives. Instead they promised to restrict access to public services so that they could preserve the welfare state for their core constituency. And the more other parties tried to liberalise access to public services, the more strongly the new radical-right parties would emphasise welfare chauvinism as part of their electoral mobilisation.[8]

This is not an argument for restricting access to public services pre-emptively. It is just an observation about the difficulties involved for any political party that embraces a multicultural and universalistic welfare state. The same argument also explains why any effort to extend equality of opportunity to previously excluded groups depends so heavily on active state intervention to succeed. The protection of civil rights in America is not simply a matter of legislation. Given the many opportunities for groups to mobilise around restricting access to public services and political institutions, the state must play a prominent role in ensuring that newly enfranchised groups receive what they have been promised.[9] Moreover, such active state involvement must continue so long as political parties rely on the politics of identity for their mobilisation strategies. The problem, of course, is that active state promotion of multiculturalism and civil rights is fuel to the fire of identity-based political mobilisation.

No obvious solution

The challenge is to neutralise this reinforcing spiral of polarisation and discrimination before one group or another captures the democratic process and then re-engineers it to ensure there is no further alternation. Levitsky and Ziblatt highlight the plight of North Carolina, where the national Republican Party is sheltering authoritarian behaviour at the state level. They could just as easily have pointed to the relationship between the European People's Party and Hungary.[10] Unfortunately, it is hard to imagine how this challenge can be successfully faced.

Traditional political parties seem unable to arrest the death of democracy; indeed, wherever they band together to hold on to power they seem to make matters worse. Efforts to promote greater inclusiveness and to widen access to public services – no matter how well-intentioned – also seem self-defeating if the goal is to prevent political polarisation from going from bad to worse. Here just think of Tony Blair's decision not to restrict freedom of movement for workers from Central and Eastern Europe, or Angela Merkel's decision to suspend the Dublin regulations for the treatment of asylum seekers. These were bold, progressive gestures with profound unintended consequences.

The only way to save democracy is to start by building or rebuilding a sense of shared democratic community. There is no easy formula for achieving that objective. I find myself – like Levitsky and Ziblatt, I suspect – out of my depth. The diagnosis is compelling, and their book is essential, even compulsive, reading. Now we just need to figure out a solution to the problem they have articulated.

Notes

1 See also Erik Jones and Matthias Matthijs, 'Democracy without Solidarity: Political Dysfunction in Hard Times', *Government and Opposition*, vol. 52, no. 2, 2017, pp. 185–210.

2 See Edward Luce, *The Retreat of Western Liberalism* (New York: Atlantic Monthly Press, 2017); and Ivan Krastev, *After Europe* (Philadelphia, PA: University of Pennsylvania Press, 2017).

3 I want to be careful how I use the term 'populism' here. There is an important body of literature mapped out by writers such as Cas Mudde that has made great strides in helping us to understand what 'populism' is. I do not need to engage with that literature to make my argument, but I do not want to deny their important accomplishments either. See, for example, Cas Mudde, *On Extremism and Democracy in Europe* (Abingdon: Routledge Focus, 2016).

4 James Madison, 'The Same Subject Continued: The Union as a Safeguard Against Domestic Faction and Insurrection', *Federalist Papers*, no. 10, 1787.

5 Erik Jones, 'The Decline and Fall of Three Hegemonic Parties in Europe', *SAIS Review*, vol. 37, no. 1S, supplement 2017, pp. S71–S87.

6 Wade Jacoby, 'Grand Coalitions and Democratic Dysfunction: Two Warnings from Central and Eastern Europe', *Government and Opposition*, vol. 52, no. 2, 2017, pp. 329–55.

7 See, for example, Matthias Matthijs, *Ideas and Economic Crises in Britain from Attlee to Blair* (Abingdon: Routledge, 2011).

8 See, for example, Cas Mudde, 'The Single-Issue Party Thesis: Extreme Right Parties and the Immigration Issue', *West European Politics*, vol. 22, no. 3, 1999, pp. 182–97.

9 Desmond King, 'Forceful Federalism against American Racial Inequality', *Government and Opposition*, vol. 52, no. 2, 2017, pp. 356–82.

10 R. Daniel Kelemen, 'Europe's Other Democratic Deficit: National Authoritarianism in Europe's Democratic Union', *Government and Opposition*, vol. 52, no. 2, 2017, pp. 211–38.

Book Reviews

United States

David C. Unger

What Happened
Hillary Rodham Clinton. New York: Simon & Schuster, 2017.
£20.00/$30.00. 492 pp.

This is a frustrating and sometimes infuriating book. What happened is that Hillary Clinton lost an election she was universally expected to win against a widely disliked and minimally qualified opponent. Though she won the nation-wide popular vote by more than three million votes, she fell short in those states that the built-in anti-democratic bias of the American electoral system makes pivotal. By now, most Americans know all too well what happened, and many, if not most, have seen the grave political, economic and social consequences. What people still seek to understand is *why* this happened. Clinton does not really tell us in this book, despite being an articulate, well-placed eyewitness.

That is not because she is unwilling to admit to her own mistakes. She does so repeatedly, although she also, with varying degrees of justification, blames others too – chiefly former FBI director James Comey for his repeated, untimely public announcements; Russian President Vladimir Putin for his aggressive, state-sponsored internet-propaganda campaign and alleged orchestration of Russian cyber attacks; and Donald Trump, her Republican opponent, for his serial distortions of both her record and his own. She also, less persuasively, blames mainstream press coverage of her emails, Bernie Sanders's primary campaign, the shortfalls of Barack Obama's presidency and even the Clinton-favouring Democratic National Committee.

In such a close election, everything counts. But with so many villains, deliberate and accidental, there is a danger of losing focus on the most important question

Survival | vol. 60 no. 2 | April–May 2018 | pp. 211–230   DOI 10.1080/00396338.2018.1448591

of all, namely why the contest was so close that Russian-bought Facebook ads, Comey's announcements and a media-led narrative of 'false equivalence' were able to swing the election in the key battleground states – Michigan, Pennsylvania and Wisconsin – to give Trump his Electoral College victory.

To her credit, Clinton asks this all-important question, but disappointingly, she provides no satisfactory answers. She seems to think that if rust-belt voters in key states had only seen more newspaper and TV stories about her wonkish position papers and fewer about her personal email server and the Clinton Foundation, she would now be living in the White House again, rather than back home in Chappaqua. Well, maybe. Then again, maybe she was just the wrong candidate, running in the wrong election year. After 24 years in public life, Clinton was always going to have difficulty convincing hurting and angry voters – who had a fairly clear idea of what they thought of her after so many years in the spotlight – that she was not part of the political establishment that so many now felt let down, and even betrayed, by. And after 24 years at the centre of America's viscerally nasty political battles, she should not have been surprised that some of her opponents said viscerally nasty things about her on the campaign trail, or that Donald Trump behaved like Donald Trump, or that a Russian autocrat whom she had repeatedly and publicly portrayed as America's public enemy number one tried to thwart her election as American president. Did not four years as secretary of state prepare her to expect such behaviour from Putin?

The most interesting part of Clinton's extended discussion of her overblown email trouble is her linking of it to the real problem of over-classification in foreign policy and the differing classification standards used by the State Department and intelligence agencies for the same information. Those differences, in particular the tendency of intelligence agencies to over-classify information that others had (probably correctly) judged unclassified, may have contributed to a public impression that Clinton's own characterisations of certain information were slippery when, in fact, they were not. I hope that this agonising experience will turn Clinton into a sturdy champion of classification reform.

American politics is often ugly, but the 2016 presidential campaign was uglier than most. Clinton was constantly lied about and unfairly subjected to a plainly sexist double standard. She won more popular votes than any candidate of either party in American history except for Barack Obama. And yet Donald Trump is president of the United States.

The key problem now for the Democrats is winning back at least some of the white-working-class and rural voters they have been losing over the past 50 years. That steady exodus cannot be entirely explained by unreconstructed racism, or blamed on 'deplorables', losers or Luddites. Some of these formerly Democratic voters feel that the Democratic candidates they once put their faith in and helped elect, such as Jimmy Carter, Bill Clinton and Barack Obama, did not deliver the rising living standards, social mobility and sense of 'fighting for us' that earlier generations of Democratic candidates did. For the Democrats' core 'rainbow coalition' of urban career women, racial and religious minorities, immigrants and LGBT voters, the rights revolution that the Democrats delivered and then defended against Republican attacks offsets this to a large degree. That helped Obama win twice, but it was not quite enough for Hillary Clinton. That's what happened.

Safeguarding Democratic Capitalism: U.S. Foreign Policy and National Security, 1920–2015
Melvyn P. Leffler. Princeton, NJ: Princeton University Press, 2017. £32.95/$39.95. 348 pp.

This richly rewarding collection of essays spans the career of Melvyn P. Leffler, professor of American History at the University of Virginia, and one of today's most insightful writers on US foreign policy and national security. It showcases the development of Leffler's thinking about the economic, cultural and intellectual wellsprings of American foreign policy and grand strategy.

The book opens with a fascinating extended intellectual autobiography, in which Leffler explains how his scholarship evolved through his research and his interactions with other thinkers, and with the evolution of American foreign policy itself. While all of these factors were important, Leffler's greatest strength is his deep mastery of the relevant archives: his research often involved perspicaciously tracking down the connections and interrelations between business history, diplomatic history and military history. These recollections are followed by 11 essays written between 1972 and 2016 on subjects as varied as American policies on First World War debt; Russia's and America's respective records on honouring their agreements with each other; the way that policy struggles over Pentagon budgets and force structure, and not obsessions with the Soviet threat, helped push the first US defense secretary James Forrestal's anxieties and paranoia to the suicidal breaking point; and the way that fiscal austerity had the positive effect of disciplining foreign-policy decision-making. Nuggets of original and provocative thinking abound throughout. Leffler has always insisted on thorough research, and has been prepared to let the findings of that research drive (and modify) his theories, rather than the reverse.

Leffler's early work, like that of many of his contemporaries, was shaped by the path-breaking formulations and challenges to orthodoxy of William

Appleman Williams. Leffler's own writings have in turn served to influence the work of succeeding scholars. In this book's first three essays, all written in the early 1970s, Leffler comes across as a challenger, recognisably in the Williams tradition, of the then-conventional wisdom about supposed Republican inter-war isolationism. Subsequent essays showcase his emergence in the 1980s and 1990s as an influential re-interpreter of the early Cold War. The volume's concluding essays draw on Leffler's recent efforts to incorporate post-Cold War foreign policy, especially George W. Bush's 'war on terror', into the analytical frames he has been developing over the past four decades. The closing (and most recent) essay proposes a national-security analytical paradigm built around the interaction of changing and subjective threat perceptions with the relatively stable core values of American policymakers.

It is clear from this collection that Leffler has been developing this kind of analytical tool all along. This has allowed him to demonstrate essential continuities in American strategy from Woodrow Wilson to his so-called isolationist successors, and from the liberal internationalist policies of the Truman administration to the pre-emptive and preventive war doctrines of George W. Bush. It will be interesting to see if he detects similar continuities in the supposedly discontinuous and disruptive policies of Donald Trump.

The Crisis of the Middle-Class Constitution: Why Economic Inequality Threatens Our Republic
Ganesh Sitaraman. New York: Alfred A. Knopf, 2017.
£22.50/$28.00. 423 pp.

This is an ambitious, revisionist account of American constitutional theory and history. Ganesh Sitaraman argues that the true intellectual foundations of the American republic can be found not so much in the theories of Locke and Montesquieu, but in those of their fellow Enlightenment philosopher James Harrington, and his influential seventeenth-century treatise, *The Commonwealth of Oceana*. Harrington's main concern was not institutional checks and balances or social-contract theory, but rather avoiding, or taxing away, severe inequalities in landed property, which he thought could make republican government impossible.

In the eyes of the contemporary observers cited by Sitaraman, the original 13 American states started out with significantly less property inequality than was common elsewhere in the late-eighteenth-century Atlantic world, at least among the white males who alone were politically enfranchised in the original US constitution. This happy circumstance allowed the framers to design what Sitaraman calls a 'middle-class constitution', as opposed to the more typical design he calls a 'class-struggle constitution'. (The latter aims to balance the political effects of economic inequality rather than trying to prevent it.) In truth, eighteenth-century America was far from egalitarian when indentured servants and the propertyless men who hired out their labour were factored in, let alone the majority of the population who were not white males. As the once predominantly agrarian United States developed into a commercial and industrial society in the course of the nineteenth century, the dangers of economically powerful citizens coming to dominate American politics as well became evident, along with the likelihood of their using American political institutions to foster even greater inequalities. Sitaraman argues, as did worried contemporaries, that this threatened the functioning of America's Harringtonian, middle-class constitution.

As Sitaraman tells it, abuses of power during the Gilded Age led to Progressive Era reforms, and ultimately to Franklin Roosevelt's New Deal. These, along with the 'great compression' of incomes that followed the Second World War, restored some of the balance. This seems to suggest that America's middle-class constitution can, with help, be self-correcting. Yet domestic and global developments since the 1970s have seen inequality soar once again.

Sitaraman, a law professor at Vanderbilt University and a former adviser to Senator Elizabeth Warren, devotes the last quarter of his book to potential remedies, including tax and regulatory reform, campaign-finance reform and a revitalised labour movement. Most of these mesh closely with positions taken by Senator Warren or Bernie Sanders, but also include some original twists.

Sitaraman's historical perspective allows us to see the ways in which the new taxation system ushered in by the constitution, which shifted more of the burden to richer merchants engaged in international commerce, initially reduced economic inequality. It also leads him to uncover some progressive social and economic intentions behind McKinley-era Republican protectionism. Less successful are the author's attempts to apply his Harringtonian critique to current judicial doctrines, and his excessive resort to social-science theories which assume that political leadership can only come from elites, with grass-roots movements confined to mobilising outside pressure for change.

The Impossible Presidency: The Rise and Fall of America's Highest Office
Jeremi Suri. New York: Basic Books, 2017. $32.00. 343 pp.

As recently as the 1960s, it was common for American historians to argue that US constitutional democracy functioned best when strong-minded presidents expanded the powers of the office to achieve ambitious social, economic and national-security goals. That view of the presidency earned George Washington, Thomas Jefferson, Abraham Lincoln and Theodore Roosevelt their places on Mount Rushmore; Franklin Roosevelt would likely have been immortalised there too if his presidency had unfolded before rather than after the mountain-carving began.

Since the Vietnam War, however, historians have rightly shown greater scepticism toward what became known, unflatteringly, as the 'imperial presidency'. Now Jeremi Suri, who teaches history and global affairs at the University of Texas, harks back to that earlier view by arguing in *The Impossible Presidency* that effective presidents are essential to a well-functioning American democracy, and that the diminished stature of recent incumbents is a problem that needs attention and remedy. This diminution has occurred precisely because the most successful past presidents, culminating in Franklin Roosevelt, incrementally enlarged the powers of the office past the point at which any mere human, no matter how talented (here he cites Clinton and Obama as recent examples), could manage them.

It is a provocative argument – and demonstrably true, at least in part. Yet like many grand theories, it runs the risk of overshadowing other important reasons for recent disappointing presidencies. For example, it surely must be taken into account that a changed fiscal and political environment has turned recent presidents into managers of budgetary austerity, not dispensers of governmental largesse. Also, the increasingly technocratic features of governing modern and complex societies have marginalised, demoralised and alienated large numbers of citizens. Meanwhile, the incremental and cumulative excesses of liberal Wilsonian internationalism have increasingly pushed the United States toward the thankless role of world policeman, while reducing the public visibility and accountability of national-security debates to a degree that is less than healthy for a vibrant American democracy. Some of these additional factors can be partly traced to expanded presidential ambitions. But they also reflect changes in the global economic and security context in which today's presidents must operate.

In successive chapters on Washington, Jackson, Lincoln, Theodore and Franklin Roosevelt, Suri explains how each of these presidencies expanded the reach of presidential power into new areas. He then turns to the frustrations of Kennedy, Johnson, Reagan, Clinton and Obama to show how it has become impossible to have a successful presidency, although he does credit Reagan for being an effective visionary for peace, while still hemmed in in other areas by the impossible presidency.

Suri offers some bold, but perhaps not very realistic, ideas for making the presidency viable again by limiting or dividing its powers. If today's American presidency has become 'impossible', this is not just because of the aggrandise-ments of past presidents. The problem is also a function of growing American power in an increasingly complex world.

Presidents' Secrets: The Use and Abuse of Hidden Power
Mary Graham. New Haven, CT: Yale University Press, 2017.
£25.00/$30.00. 258 pp.

This is a timely, readable account of the management, and more often mis-management, of secrecy by US presidents from Washington to Obama. Mary Graham, co-director of the Transparency Policy Project at Harvard's Kennedy School of Government (and long-time spouse of former *Washington Post* pub-lisher Donald Graham), brings passion, first-hand knowledge and a sense of history to the subject, though this regrettably fails to save her from several minor factual glitches – CIA director Robert Gates never was a general, for example, while NSA leaker Edward Snowden had already fled to Hong Kong when he turned much of his data trove over to selected journalists.

Graham gives particular, and appropriate, emphasis to the twentieth and twenty-first centuries, a period during which the American presidency took on vast new powers and increasingly operated in secret. The framers of the US Constitution, for all their concern with accountability, checks and balances and transparency, well understood the importance of keeping some things secret, such as the operational details of military campaigns and the content of diplo-matic negotiations. Yet they spelled out no clear exceptions to the general rule of open government, leaving it to future presidents, congresses, judges and, ultimately, voters to work out the precise boundaries of permissible secrecy.

An admirably scrupulous George Washington got things off to a reason-ably positive start, though he stumbled over the politically and regionally contested Jay Treaty with Britain. But as Graham clearly demonstrates, many of Washington's twentieth- and twenty-first-century successors knowingly or unknowingly abused executive powers of secrecy to the long-term detriment of American democracy. One particularly interesting chapter spells out in some detail how Woodrow Wilson used repression, secrecy and government propa-ganda operations to strip away constitutional liberties during and after the First World War. After suffering a massive, disabling stroke in October 1919, Wilson again abused secrecy to hide his true condition from the nation for 18 months. Another chapter describes how Harry Truman created America's first peace-time national-security state by greatly expanding the amount of government business hidden from public view behind proliferating systems of security clas-sification and agencies whose very existence was kept secret. A third chapter shows how Lyndon Johnson deliberately and successfully thwarted the new Freedom of Information Act before and after its passage in 1966. Graham's historical overview ends with Barack Obama defeating his own pledges of greater transparency and isolating himself politically in the process. One can only wonder what mixed legacy of indiscreet, late-night tweets combined with covert policies the current administration will leave.

As these and other examples show, presidential powers of secrecy can be severely abused, undermining the rule of law itself, as happened under Wilson and Johnson. Or they can backfire at high political cost, as the Wilson and Obama presidencies demonstrate. Striking the right balance in real time can be exceedingly difficult. But doing so is essential to preserving an accountable constitutional democracy. Graham remains optimistic about the long-term resilience of the system and its ability to mend itself over time.

Politics and International Relations
Gilles Andréani

Faces of Moderation: The Art of Balance in an Age of Extremes
Aurelian Craiutu. Philadelphia, PA: University of Pennsylvania
Press, 2017. £50.00/$59.95. 295 pp.

The virtue of moderation is not readily defended: it is often associated with shyness and a lack of character, a petty-bourgeois attitude practised by the risk-averse and the middle-of-the-road. Furthermore, many of those in the public eye who display it never explicitly characterise it as a wilful choice. As a result, moderation tends to be either disparaged as a flaw, or practised in silence. It does not stand as a recognised school of thought.

Aurelian Craiutu sees moderation differently. A professor at Indiana University, he defends it as a distinct political and intellectual virtue requiring clarity, character and courage. As he puts it, it is a 'fighting virtue' (p. 19), indispensable to the functioning of open societies. He attempts to give shape to moderation, if not as a doctrine, then at least as a recognisable attitude. *Faces of Moderation* extends Craiutu's previous research, which resulted in important publications on French liberalism, most notably on Alexis de Tocqueville, and on the Doctrinaires (that is, the centrist liberals who sought to balance the principles of the French Revolution with a concern for order and stability in post-Napoleonic France).

The result is a nuanced, elegant and remarkable book. It explores the various facets of moderation through five intellectual and moral figures, each associated with a specific aspect of moderation: Raymond Aron, Isaiah Berlin, Norberto Bobbio, Michael Oakeshott and Adam Michnik. Chapters describing the contribution made by each man to the political debates of his time are in themselves extremely good short monographs on their subjects, who are placed in historical perspective.

With Bobbio on the left, Oakeshott on the right, Aron and Berlin in the middle, and Michnik a proponent of 'radical moderation' and hence not easily located, Craiutu is able to take the reader across a wide political spectrum in a captivating journey inside what he calls 'the archipelago' (p. 228) of moderation, in search of this 'human, ordinary, and humble virtue' (p. 234).

At the end of this journey, Craiutu undertakes to define moderation in a final chapter which lives up to the opening challenge of the book: to recognise in moderation a distinct school of thought. In Craiutu's view, moderation is not merely a negative refusal of fanaticism, extremism and zealotry, but an attitude which consists in starting from the facts, valuing dialogue and pluralism, and acknowledging that there are inherent tensions between various values and interests among which any balance is bound to remain transitory and imperfect.

Craiutu's definition of moderation is neither dogmatic nor fixed. Rather, it encompasses a set of qualities, both personal and political, which may combine in many different ways. Moderation is not a virtue for all people and all seasons, and appears in many different shapes and forms, but it is one without which political life would be impossible to imagine. In the final analysis, it is inextricably political, intellectual and moral.

As a result, *Faces of Moderation* is not only an intellectual quest, but a plea – appropriately enough, a moderate, though still energetic, one – in favour of moderation at a time when immoderate speech and doctrines abound, and the fanaticism of self-righteousness is indulged in by all sorts of characters, including some at the helm of liberal democracies.

The Fate of the West: The Battle to Save the World's Most Successful Political Idea
Bill Emmott. London: Profile Books, 2017. £20.00. 257 pp.

The subject matter of *The Fate of the West* is not, as the title might suggest, the struggle between the geopolitical entity familiarly known as 'the West' and its enemies abroad, but rather the corruption and disease which its enemies within are causing by subverting its core values, such as openness, equality of rights and opportunities, and fair competition.

In this brilliant and persuasive book, Emmott is clear about who these enemies are, and what they are bringing about:

> The most recognizable enemies to have built political power by democratic means in order to create privileges that damage the wider public interest are – perhaps you have guessed – the banks and other financial service firms. Taken as a whole, bankers and other financiers have in the past decade been the single cause of rising inequality, distortion of public policy, and generation of collective economic pain and anger at 'the system'. (p. 54)

Other enemies include business federations and monopolies; pensioners; and 'the tyrannous majorities of employees in countries such as Japan, France and Italy' (p. 54), all of which have worked to defend their privileges against competitors such as other firms, young people and anyone seeking to find their own place within rigged markets.

The crash of 2008, of which the banking system and its ability to influence the political system were the main culprits, further aggravated already rising inequalities, estranged the most vulnerable parts of society from politics, and eventually resulted in the election of Donald Trump in the US and the 2016 Brexit vote in the UK.

Bill Emmott, who was a journalist with *The Economist* for 25 years, and its editor-in-chief from 1993 to 2006, is the chairman of the Wake Up Foundation, a charity aimed at spreading awareness of the risks facing Western societies and promoting reforms to address them. *The Fate of the West* is in substance a manifesto in defence of the truest values of liberal-democratic societies based on openness and competition, but is in style a careful analysis served by a remarkable wealth of knowledge and information. The book draws on two of the most respectable British intellectual traditions: liberal thought and its instinctive abhorrence for rent and other forms of unjustifiable inequality, and high-quality economic journalism as represented by, among others, *The Economist*.

Emmott's analysis of what has gone wrong in the affluent democratic societies of the West is not, however, the main part of the book. He goes on to show that there are ways to redress the problems of these societies, and to bring them into closer conformity with their foundational principles. Western societies still have unparalleled strengths and energy, which proper reforms will unshackle, provided they are just, and foster equality and openness.

The Fate of the West addresses the issue of reform in two distinct sets of chapters: country-specific ones, which deal with the United States, Britain, the European Union's inner core, Japan, Sweden and Switzerland; and those that deal with issues common to all countries, of which the two most salient address the rising inequality of the Western world, and the challenge of ageing. The book concludes by enunciating a series of guiding principles for the West as a whole. While these might seem general in nature, they tie in neatly with Emmott's views of fairness, openness and equality as not only politically desirable in liberal democracies, but the principles upon which the survival of Western market economies depends.

Age of Anger: A History of the Present
Pankaj Mishra. London: Allen Lane, 2017. £20.00. 405 pp.

It would be very difficult to conceive of two books more different than *The Fate of the West* and *Age of Anger*. The first of these looks at the world from a Western perspective, while the second offers a non-Western one; the first defends the case that Western societies, if managed according to their best principles, still can thrive, while the second describes these societies as the object of anger, both from the non-Western world and from those who find themselves disenfranchised within increasingly unequal Western societies. As a result, it is difficult to like both books, something this reviewer will not pretend to do.

On the surface, *The Fate of the West* may suffer from a certain lack of passion, even if it contains an undercurrent of indignation directed at the privileged insiders who brought about the disaster of 2008. Pankaj Mishra not only tells a story of anger, but seems himself to partake of that anger, to the point where his book at times seems more sentiment than analysis, at the expense of its undeniable qualities.

There is no disputing that anger is a phenomenon of our time: the rise of social inequality and the collision of traditional values with the rapid changes brought about by globalisation have caused enormous dissatisfaction, resentment and even violent revolt. Trump's most ardent supporters in the United States and the militant supporters of Hindutva in India, along with suicidal jihadists and nationalist hackers everywhere, all share a sense of humiliation from which populist and extremist movements have prospered.

Mishra is right to draw our attention to this global wave of resentment (he prefers the French term 'ressentiment'), and his subject is certainly timely and legitimate. He brings to it a remarkable wealth of knowledge and erudition, tracing contemporary ressentiment back to Rousseau, whom he contrasts with the bourgeois and cosmopolitan Voltaire, in whom he sees a precursor of today's globalised elite. For Rousseau, commerce in its broadest sense – the global interaction of goods, ideas and people – could not help but foster envy and the corruption of manners, and was thus fundamentally incompatible with democracy.

Mishra goes on to explore the schools of thought which, following in Rousseau's footsteps, built on feelings of popular ressentiment to advocate solutions – often violent in nature – ranging from nineteenth-century ethnolinguistic German nationalism, to Russian nihilism, to Italian fascism, to the transnational wave of anarchist terrorist attacks at the outset of the twentieth century, in which Mishra sees the most direct precursor of today's global jihadists. In so doing, the author effectively makes two interesting points. The first is that today's violent subversive movements, and especially jihadist terrorism, are modern political phenomena, rather than the expression of traditional world views challenged by modernity. The second is that the Western inspiration of anti-Western movements is not new, and that, from their outset, Middle Eastern and Asian nationalisms have been intertwined with Western revolutionary and extremist movements belonging to a genealogy that Mishra brilliantly describes (discussing, for example, Giuseppe Mazzini's influence in India and China).

Still, Mishra ultimately goes too far. Anger is not the same in all places and at all times, and the author's analysis is not well served by a concept which lumps together Trump's followers and 9/11 terrorists. By the same token, Mishra exaggerates the importance of the anarchist wave of terror in the early 1900s, and the reaction against it. Theodore Roosevelt did not launch an 'international crusade against terrorism' (p. 316), and the impact of the anarchist scare remained fairly limited in most countries. Nor can it be said that in today's advanced democracies 'an everyday culture of cruelty and heartlessness' is in evidence (p. 328).

All in all, this otherwise erudite and captivating book is undermined by a certain imbalance between reason and emotion, which weakens even the author's attempt to trace the corrosive impact of globalisation back to Rousseau. For even though Rousseau believed that modern society would estrange man from his true self, he equally believed that if reason were given a chance, man and nature, freedom and society could ultimately be reconciled. In other words, Rousseau – a perennially angry man – knew that one had to look beyond anger.

Post-Truth: The New War on Truth and How to Fight Back
Matthew d'Ancona. London: Ebury Press, 2017. £6.99. 167 pp.

At the outset of this short book, author Matthew d'Ancona, a British journalist and writer, quotes George Orwell, who, in response to the success of fascist propaganda during the Spanish Civil War, gave voice to his fear that 'the very concept of objective truth is fading out of the world … So, for all practical purposes, the lie will have become the truth' (p. 24). A similar sense of helplessness and despair in response to the contemporary advance of non-truth is the focus of this excellent and timely book.

In 2016, the *Oxford English Dictionary* added an entry for 'post-truth', declaring it 'word of the year'. That same year, Donald Trump displayed a certain creativity with the truth that culminated in early 2017 with the now-proverbial assertion by Kellyanne Conway, one of his advisers, that the administration possessed 'alternative facts'. This was in defence of the new president's fanciful assertion that the crowd at his inauguration had been the largest ever.

D'Ancona makes clear that 'post-truth' preceded the Trump campaign, asserting that Trump represents 'more symptom than cause' (p. 20). He explores the mechanisms which make the dissemination of falsehood so pervasive (and so difficult to fight), citing information technology and networks; the prevalence of the internet and social media; the erosion of traditional channels of information; and the loss of respect for social and political authorities. D'Ancona also explores the intellectual foundations of post-truth, including the relativism and ideological contempt for truth displayed by the post-modern philosophers of the 1960s.

One of the most troubling – and interesting – aspects of d'Ancona's investigation lies in his analysis of the diminished resistance of the public to lies. According to the author, the current era of post-truth is distinguished not only by the internet and social media, but by the receptivity of the public to falsehood, its lack of trust in science and other traditional sources of authority, and its readiness to believe in conspiracy theories, which result not only in weak resistance to falsehood, but in a positive desire for it. 'Outrage gives way to indifference, and finally to collusion', says d'Ancona (p. 26).

The final part of the book explores ways of resisting post-truth and fighting back. The author makes an appeal for imagination, civic sense and statesmanship, all of which are clearly needed, but the advent of which is far less clear.

Churchill and Orwell: The Fight for Freedom
Thomas E. Ricks. New York: Penguin Press, 2017. $28.00. 339 pp.

At first glance, it is difficult to see what George Orwell and Winston Churchill had in common to warrant a book such as this. The two men never met. Orwell occasionally expressed views on Churchill, but there is no trace of Churchill's views on Orwell, if he had any. The social backgrounds, ideas, careers and characters of the two men could not have been more different.

Be that as it may, Thomas E. Ricks, a journalist and writer who specialises in military affairs (he is the author, among other books, of *Fiasco*, a brilliant account of the 2003 war in Iraq), manages to make a substantial and inspiring comparison between Churchill and Orwell. The literary genre of parallel biographies is as old as Plutarch. Ricks revives it here, providing convincing and vivid accounts of these two outsized personalities.

He does so by using freedom as the common thread uniting his two heroes, suggesting that both men's concern for their own liberty took them to the borders of eccentricity, and occasionally beyond. They both displayed moral and physical courage, and an awareness that liberty was not a given, but something that needed to be fought for, which they certainly did.

A crucial period in the lives of both men was the 1930s, a time when each was lucid enough to discern the rising perils to liberty, and when each distanced himself from erstwhile political allies. Churchill stood isolated in his opposition to Munich. Orwell, who fought in the Spanish Civil War on the Republican side, witnessed how the Stalinists crushed the Trotskyites and Anarchists who were fighting Franco, causing him to radically change his mind on communism.

Thus, both Churchill and Orwell, whose initial political instincts had been, respectively, anti-communism and anti-fascism, came to embody – albeit in very different ways – the spirit of resistance to totalitarianism. Ricks ultimately concludes that both men shared a respect for facts, a sense of faith in their own judgement and a determination to live up to their convictions. He is certainly correct to suggest that, in the absence of such qualities, there can be no genuine, lasting freedom.

Middle East
Ray Takeyh

Revolution Without Revolutionaries: Making Sense of the Arab Spring
Asef Bayat. Stanford, CA: Stanford University Press, 2017.
£19.99/$24.95. 294 pp.

Asef Bayat's impressive *Revolution Without Revolutionaries* tries to explain why nearly all the exhilarating uprisings in the Middle East eventually failed. Even when some of the autocrats were displaced, existing elites and their governing systems largely survived. A closer look at Tunisia, for example, which has been touted as one of the few successes of the Arab uprisings, reveals more continuity than not with the past. Bayat is not the first scholar to tackle this issue, the field of Middle East studies having offered up its share of autopsies, but his lucid and readable account does provide the most plausible explanation. In the end, revolutions cannot succeed without leaders who have spent decades in oppositional politics honing their ideology and sharpening their strategy. There is a difference between mass mobilisation and a successful revolutionary takeover.

Bayat's assessment begins with a look back at the twentieth-century revolutions, particularly those in Iran and Nicaragua, that managed not just to mobilise the masses and decapitate the old elite, but to successfully impose a new order. For decades, these nations seemed to have revolutionaries but no sign of a revolution. The dissidents were given time to consider their stratagems and prepare for the day when the masses would finally embrace their postulations. When popular protests finally broke out, a cadre was ready to lead the charge, articulate a new vision of state power and dispose with the old order – root and branch. It turns out that oddballs who spend years engaging in quixotic dissent are actually essential for the success of any uprising.

The author's most intriguing passages detail how the politics and even the urban topography of the Middle East changed in the 1990s in a manner that made existing ideologies of dissent, such as Islamism, largely irrelevant. Under the banner of what Bayat calls 'neoliberal' policies, many Middle Eastern countries sought to reform their economies along the lines mandated by the World Bank and the IMF. This was the era of privatisation, which led to crony capitalism and the dismantling of many social safety nets. The welfare state took a hit, but a more productive economy did not follow in its wake. This was also a decade during which the university-educated population grew and social-media access became more widespread. In Bayat's view, this led to the creation of a new class, which he calls the 'middle-class poor'. This cohort was middle class in terms of its educational attainment and social-media footprint, yet poor because of its lack of jobs and residence in impoverished neighbourhoods. Islamists could not speak to their needs because they sought employment, not salvation. Marxists could not come to their rescue because history had rendered their prescriptions unworkable. This class produced revolutions, but no revolutionaries that could guide them to success.

Still, Bayat fails to consider that Middle Eastern countries had little choice in the 1990s but to implement privatisation measures, however ham-fisted. His notion that they could have followed the model of unrepentant socialist states such as Venezuela and Bolivia seems far-fetched. Yet this is a minor quibble with an otherwise important book that judiciously examines one of the central dilemmas of the Middle East today.

Kings and Presidents: Saudi Arabia and the United States since FDR
Bruce Riedel. Washington DC: Brookings Institution Press, 2018. $25.99. 251 pp.

Nearly two years ago, Saudi Arabian Crown Prince Mohammed bin Salman announced his intention to make sweeping changes to the Kingdom's traditional ways. For the preceding century, the national compact that had guided the monarchy had offered its subjects economic rewards in exchange for political passivity. The Kingdom survived many challenges to its rule by relying on an expansive welfare state, religious orthodoxy and unity among the princely class. Now, a young prince is seemingly upending this arrangement as unworkable in an age of austerity, having apparently decided that the Saudis will have to work and pay taxes, that the religious police needs to yield to new freedoms, and that those princes and businessmen who stand in the way should be summarily exiled. In this context, Bruce Riedel's timely and incisive book tackles the troubled history of US–Saudi relations, and sheds much light on key episodes of this contested relationship.

From the moment Franklin Roosevelt met the founder of the Saudi monarchy, King Abdul Aziz ibn Abdul Rahman al Saud, in 1945, their nascent alliance was an unusual one. A democracy built on the will of the people and a desert autocracy relying on tribal bonds and militant Islam seemed an odd pairing. And yet, the two sides had oil and their opposition to Soviet communism to bring them together. Saudi oil fuelled the European and Asian recovery after the Second World War, and allowed the industrial West to revive. Through much of the Cold War, the Saudis proved an essential ally, challenging radical Arab republics allied with the Soviet Union in the 1960s, an Islamist Iran in the 1980s and finally Saddam Hussein's Iraq after its invasion of Kuwait in the 1990s. Along the way, the Saudis' overproduction of oil may have crippled the Soviet economy, while the Kingdom's support for rebels in Afghanistan drained the Soviet army.

In the aftermath of the Cold War, the relationship was bound to suffer from diverging interests. So long as Saddam stood by menacingly and the Iranian mullahs fulminated against America, the two sides could still blur their lines of contention. The tragic attacks of 9/11 exposed the monarchy's insidious ties to militant Islamists, and how its Wahhabi proselytising had radicalised the region's political culture. And yet, the two sides patched up the relationship, improbably allowing the bonds between them to survive. The Americans politely lectured the Saudis, who politely pretended to listen.

Riedel's deft narrative moves from administration to administration, as he uses archival evidence and secondary literature to advance his case. Given his vast experience in US government, this book is not a mere exercise in academic speculation, but a reasoned tome from someone who observed the relationship from his perch within the CIA, and who managed it while in the White House. *Kings and Presidents* is thus an indispensable book coming just as the Kingdom is entering one of its most crucial turning points.

A Life in Middle East Studies
Roger Owen. Washington DC: Tadween Publishing, 2017.
$18.99. 194 pp.

Roger Owen, a former professor at Harvard and Oxford, has written a delightful and discursive memoir that illuminates both an academic specialty and a Middle East that no longer really exist. Owen seems to have entered the field of Middle East studies through his military service, during which a stint as a draftee in Cyprus led to curiosity about the Arab world. The Oxford of the early 1960s seems to have offered little in the way of formal study of the region's politics and history, leading to much improvisation by the enterprising Owen. His first few chapters discuss his many stays and travels in the region, and a graduate lifestyle that involved as much archival work as parties with locals and expats. To his credit, Owen did not limit himself to Arab states, spending some time in Israel as well. There is a refreshing lack of anti-Israel bias in this book, which differentiates it from many others in its field. The polarising effect of the Arab–Israeli wars seems to have left little room for reasoned assessments of the origins of the conflict.

Owen soon gained notoriety as one of the few Middle East scholars to study the region's economic history. Like most members of his generation, he concentrated on Egypt and the centrality of cotton in its finances. Egypt was then the epicentre of Arab politics: what mattered in the Middle East first mattered in Cairo. Yet the suffocating Nasserist dictatorship and its stagnant socialism make few appearances in this book. Owen would turn his attention to the nature of the Arab regimes with his much-cited textbook, *State, Power and Politics in the Making of the Modern Middle East*. The Arab order was said to be manned by governments whose repressive apparatuses could contain any popular insurrection. The Arab Spring put a momentary end to this familiar theory. The experts got the Arab revolutions wrong, and have yet to find their footing.

In many ways, the region that Owen spent his life studying no longer exists. The Middle East of sturdy dictatorships has yielded to a region littered with failed and failing states. The Arab Cold War that once pitted conservative monarchies against radical republics has been beset by a sectarian conflict fuelled by the Wahhabi Saudi monarchy and a Persian Shia theocracy. Meanwhile, the great powers that so often intervened in the region's politics are growing indifferent to its predicament as its oil matters less and less to their economies. The professoriate has also changed, as the founders of the field, such as Albert Hourani and Bernard Lewis, with their mastery of languages, have been displaced by a new cadre of instructors more at home with paradigms then narrative history.

Roger Owen became a professor when he failed his entrance exams to the Foreign Office. Reading this book, one is left with the impression that he was always going to be happier in the academy than in the bureaucracy.

A Social Revolution: Politics and the Welfare State in Iran
Kevan Harris. Oakland, CA: University of California Press, 2017.
£24.95/$29.95. 316 pp.

Nearly four decades after its founding, the Islamic Republic continues to divide its chroniclers. For some, it is a much-maligned experiment in Third World liberation. For others, it is a cruel regime draping itself in sanctimonious rhetoric while drowning in corruption. Kevan Harris has stepped forward with a reasoned and well-researched presentation of the theocracy as a traditional welfare state. Statistics and polling data leap off nearly every page, but Harris's essential argument is that the regime has gone a long way toward providing healthcare, education and retirement benefits for its growing constituency. A government that continuously evokes God may thus actually rest its legitimacy on the distribution of wealth. Sort of a New Deal, mullah-style.

To some degree, there are continuities between the monarchy and the theocracy that displaced it. The shah also tried to expand educational opportunities, distributed land to the peasants, offered free healthcare for the indigent and affordable housing for the urban poor. Those efforts were often hamstrung by poor management, misjudgement and corruption – the curse of all developing nations, but especially glaring in Iran. Uneven economic growth and dashed expectations eventually provoked a popular revolt that the shah was unable to contain.

The Islamists took up the monarch's mantle of development under more harrowing circumstances of their own making. Iraq may have invaded Iran in 1980, but the clerics were the ones who unwisely prolonged the war. The revolution needed enemies, and America too often served as a convenient but self-defeating foe. Iran's enmities toward America and Israel, and its penchant for supporting unsavoury terrorist actors, invited sanctions that further derailed its economic plans. Given its many destructive policies, the Islamic Republic almost had no choice but to offer its preferred constituency, the urban poor, a helping hand. The regime's propaganda extolled the lower classes while its programmes provided them access to healthcare and education. There were improvements as literacy rates and life expectancy went up. Ironically, Harris spends little time on Mahmoud Ahmadinejad's presidency, Iran's most disastrous experiment in populist government. And too often, the burden of subsidies and the sheer scale of graft go unnoticed in a book rich in quantitative analysis.

In December 2017, the urban poor that traditionally constituted the backbone of the regime took to the streets, with slogans that must have unnerved the clerical rulers. Instead of offering their appreciation for meagre subsidies, they complained about corruption and class cleavages. This was no reform movement, as the protesters called for the overthrow of the regime and the deaths of its leaders. In the end, all the clinics and schools that Harris discusses seemed to have failed to tether this class to the regime. As with the shah, the mullahs are now recognising the limits of the welfare state as a source of political power.

Montazeri: The Life and Thought of Iran's Revolutionary Ayatollah
Sussan Siavoshi. Cambridge: Cambridge University Press, 2017. £23.99/$29.99. 318 pp.

In this compact and important book, Sussan Siavoshi offers a nuanced, if not sympathetic, assessment of one of the Islamic Republic's founding fathers. Hussein Ali Montazeri was one of Ayatollah Ruhollah Khomeini's early disciples, serving as his student and later as his representative when he was exiled. He was not as cunning as other Khomeini aides such as Hashemi Rafsanjani, nor as erudite as Morteza Motahhari. His simple speech and down-to-earth manner were at times wrongly seen as a lack of intelligence. Montazeri would spend the monarchical years often imprisoned or in internal exile. The improbable success of Iran's revolution catapulted the little-known cleric to a position of privilege that he was never fully at ease with.

Montazeri's tenure in power coincided with the most radical phase of Iran's revolution. The 1980s was a decade in which the revolutionaries devised an intolerant regime, mercilessly purged their erstwhile allies and waged war against Iran's neighbours, if not the wider world. Montazeri was one of the instigators of all these radical enterprises. He was the head of a commission that revised Iran's constitution, creating the office of the supreme leader and all of its unaccountable prerogatives. He was a key figure behind Iran's support for so-called liberation fronts that often meant aiding terrorist organisations. He was an early supporter of Iran's war with Iraq, and insisted on prolonging the war long after Iraq was evicted from Iranian territory. And yet, Montazeri was also the only Iranian leader to object to the mistreatment of prisoners, risking his career by opposing the mass execution of political prisoners in 1988. The following year he gave a speech on the tenth anniversary of the revolution in which he chronicled its many failures and injustices. This act of courage led to his dismissal as Khomeini's chosen successor.

Siavoshi delves into these contradictions with care, shedding light on the decade's many controversies. It is today difficult to recall just how contentious Iran's internal disagreements were, and how often the Islamic Republic was divided against itself. Once purged from power, Montazeri seemed to find his voice as a dissident. Not even house arrest could diminish his zeal to confront the republic that he did so much to create, and he often spoke out against the regime's excesses. He would eventually become a reliable supporter of the reform movement, and later the Green Revolution. It is regrettable that he did not discover the virtues of such liberalising movements when he was in power. Still, he did lend important support to those struggling against the regime's many acts of cruelty.

The author organises the book in an unusual manner by devoting the first half to Montazeri's life, followed by a section exploring his ideas on issues such as human rights. A more seamless narrative would have made the book a livelier read.

Closing Argument

Iran Disillusioned

Anonymous

I

For an Iranian living abroad, the experience of homecoming starts the moment one boards the plane. For some reason, my most recent seatmates have all been businessmen. They are a caustic bunch. Exhorting me to expand my tour of European universities as long as I could, one of them asked me: 'do you think things will get better with *Barjam?*' (He was using the Persian acronym for the nuclear deal – in English, the Joint Comprehensive Plan of Action, or JCPOA.) My reply met with his approval: I could not understand why political commentators were predicting significant change.

On a more recent flight, I had been excited to rediscover my country after nearly two years of absence. My spreadsheet-modeller of a neighbour soon brought me down to earth. Answering, with some exasperation, my question of how he found the experience of trading in his country of birth, he ended on a note of self-Orientalism: 'Not even the grandchildren of your children will see an Iran to be proud of.'

Iran is by no means back in business. In a recent University of Maryland poll, 58% of Iranians felt that economic conditions were deteriorating. Only 12% of them believed that the United States would live up to its obligations under the JCPOA.[1] Donald Trump's election has dashed any hope of achieving rapprochement and smoothing Iran's path towards normality.

The **author** is an Iranian national living in Europe.

Survival | vol. 60 no. 2 | April–May 2018 | pp. 231–236   DOI 10.1080/00396338.2018.1448598

In spite of my natural scepticism, I had experienced the negotiation of the JCPOA as a national tale of resistance and rebirth, admiring the Palais Coburg in Vienna as if I was staring at the building where world peace would be saved. For many other Iranians, too, the negotiations were worthy of the myths of the *Shahnameh*, the eleventh-century Persian epic. National heroes such as Mohammad Javad Zarif battled countless diplomats representing the world's major powers, and secured Iran's status on the global stage.

Two full years after the climax of these exploits, the surreal magic of the moment is a distant memory. First-tier (and, for that matter, second-tier) financial institutions still avoid Iran, fearing American fines and ignoring European inducements. 73% of Iranians believe that multinationals are dragging their feet,[2] and many unsuspecting Iranians abroad have seen their bank accounts closed due to stricter regulations.

As the national mood surrounding the JCPOA sours, myths are taking root. The majority of sampled Iranians now believe that the United States has not lifted all the secondary sanctions it promised to withdraw.[3] This is false – yet it is true that most of my compatriots do not see any benefit from the much-hyped JCPOA. On the one hand, economic results are far from being catastrophic: macroeconomic indicators, such as growth and inflation, are relatively positive, thanks to President Hassan Rouhani's attempts to bring much-needed structural reforms to Iran's economy. On the other hand, unemployment – especially among the young – is increasing, and the state of the exchange market is disastrous, the result of dollar shortages and Trump's vitriolic rhetoric.

II

The problem is not just that the economy is struggling, but that expectations had been greatly raised.[4] Having beaten the drum too strongly for the advent of a new Iran after the JCPOA, Rouhani is guilty of having ginned up hopes without taking into account the many political, social and economic obstacles in his way. Ministers' public requests for hundreds of billions of dollars from foreign investors relied on the unrealistic assumption that foreign money would flood into Iran as soon as secondary sanctions were lifted.

Despite the signature of a dozen Memoranda of Understanding (MoU) with European companies, Iran's traditional ally China is still confident that it can maintain, and even increase, its market share by once again replacing Europeans in the case of sanctions' snapback. Although this might compensate for the potential loss of European investments, as CNPC's guarantee of taking over Total's substantial agreement on Iran's gas industry suggests, the general feeling among Iranians remains that Chinese goods are of an inferior quality, their ubiquity in the country a sign of its inability to diversify trade partners.

The public mood is therefore mixed. People are no longer dying in hospital for lack of medication. Fresh foreign faces are more and more visible in big cities – and yes, big brands have opened flagship stores in the capital. But, while 49% of sampled Iranians believe that their children will be better off than them, 43% think the reverse.[5] This divide, between the middle and lower classes in Iran, was palpable during the protests of late 2017. While empathising with the grievances of poorer Iranians, the middle classes remained passive, clinging to their belief that Rouhani is on their side.

This position will become increasingly difficult to sustain, however. Now that crippling sanctions are withdrawn, it is much harder for the government to divert people's attention away from social restrictions and the chronic mismanagement of public resources. 63% think that domestic economic mismanagement and corruption are the primary cause of concern; 96% believe that the government should do more to fight financial and bureaucratic corruption.[6] Episodes such as the awful collapse of publicly funded buildings following earthquakes, repetitive failures of unregulated financial intermediaries and the bombastic behaviour of political personalities' offspring have all exacerbated the rift between the people and their elected officials. When Hamid Reza Aref, son of prominent reformist politician Mohammad Reza Aref, praised 'good genes' as shorthand for his parents' good fortune and the supposed roots of his own success, he became a symbol of the arrogance and nepotism of some government officials.[7]

Many young Iranians, like their European counterparts, do not identify with traditional political factions. In Iran, too, the traditional political spectrum – hardliners, moderates and reformists – has been greatly disrupted. From somber clerics posing with frivolous rappers to the Supreme Leader asking the Revolutionary Guard to let go of their control over the economy, a strange atmosphere has developed. Politicians frequently leave their ideological comfort zone, widening existing fractures. Implicitly comparing current officials' detachment from the people to the era of the shah, and calling for the use of referendums to solve disagreements, Rouhani has been at the forefront of this political disruption. A report based on a study from Rouhani's first year in office, and surprisingly released, showed that at least 49% of surveyed Iranians reject a central pillar of the Islamic Republic: the compulsory veil.[8] The release came after Iranians launched the #GirlofEnghelabStreet movement, which saw courageous women defy the rules by appearing in public without a hijab. Overall, Rouhani has reinforced his pro-youth rhetoric since his 2017 campaign and moved further away from the traditional consensual politics of the Islamic Republic.

III

In the age of Trump, Rouhani is set to fail. However painful and 'neoliberal' his proposed policies, they were a necessary step towards long-term growth and a long-sought step out of isolation. But the most audacious parts of his 1397[9] budget have now been shoved aside in order to satisfy the large majority of Iranians who, understandably, wish to keep gasoline and other subsidies in place.[10] In the meantime, the main change that I see whenever I return to Tehran is the proliferation of shopping malls, especially in the northern district of Shemiran, where overtaxed and unaffordable luxury goods are sold to make fortunes for importers and real estate developers. The southern regions of Iran still suffocate in a blend of pollution and sand, while the majority of Iranians care more about any potential economic push the government can provide them than about sparking fundamental change through another bloody revolution. To believe otherwise is a Washington think-tank delusion. Will Trump withdraw from the JCPOA in April? I could not care less. He has already mutilated a fragile deal, and asked for the impossible by exhorting Iran to abdicate its sovereign right to defend itself with home-made missiles.

In US–Iranian relations since the Islamic Revolution there have been cycles of hope and disappointment. The Khatami–Clinton rapprochement continued into the George W. Bush administration, with real cooperation in Afghanistan after 9/11 and an Iranian initiative for a 'grand bargain'. This opportunity was destroyed when Bush included Iran in his Axis of Evil speech. Another cycle of hope culminated under Rouhani and Obama in the JCPOA, and a relationship between US secretary of state John Kerry and his counterpart Mohammad Javad Zarif, who had each other's phone numbers on speed dial. That promising diplomacy has been destroyed by the current US president.

I will fly back to Iran for *Norooz*, this time uninterested in hearing about my flight mates' dashed hopes. I am already convinced that a cosmic misalignment will continue to set Iran and the US apart, and that Iran is bracing itself for another period of great hardship.

Notes

1 Esfandyar Batmanghelidj, 'In First Survey Since Iran Protests, Expressions of Solidarity as Economic Outlook Darkens', *Bourse and Bazaar*, 2 February 2018, https://www.bourseandbazaar.com/articles/2018/1/31/in-first-major-survey-since-iran-protests-expressions-of-solidarity-as-economic-outlook-darkens.

2 *Ibid*.

3 Barbara Slavin, 'Latest Iran Poll Suggests Trump Rhetoric Benefits Hardliners', *Al-Monitor*, 2 February 2018, http://www.atlanticcouncil.org/news/in-the-news/slavin-in-al-monitor-latest-iran-poll-suggests-trump-rhetoric-benefits-hard-liners.

4 Mohammad Ali Shabani, 'Protests in Iran Unlikely to Bring About Change', *Al-Monitor*, 29 December 2017, https://www.al-monitor.

com/pulse/originals/2017/12/iran-protests-change-unlikely-mash-had-inflation-high-prices.html.

5 Batmanghelidj, 'In First Survey Since Iran Protests, Expressions of Solidarity as Economic Outlook Darkens'.

6 *Ibid*.

7 Shabnam Von Hein, 'Iranian Elite Cite "Good Genes" in Nepotism Controversy', Deutsche Welle, 30 August 2017, http://www.dw.com/en/iranian-elite-cite-good-genes-in-nepotism-controversy/a-40303398.

8 Eliza MacKintosh, 'Iran Publishes Report Saying 49% of Iranians Against Compulsory Veil', CNN, 6 February 2018, https://edition.cnn.com/2018/02/05/middleeast/iran-hijab-law-report-intl/index.html.

9 Or 2018–19.

10 Slavin, 'Latest Iran Poll Suggests Trump Rhetoric Benefits Hardliners'.